# Designing and Developing
# BUSINESS COMMUNICATIONS PROGRAMS THAT WORK

## More Training Books from Scott, Foresman

**CONTEMPORARY ORGANIZATION DEVELOPMENT:** Current Thinking and Applications
*D. D. Warrick, Editor*
**THE INTERACTIVE JOB INSTRUCTION WORKSHOP**
*Dugan Laird and Ruth House*
**LISTENING YOUR WAY TO MANAGEMENT SUCCESS**
*Herbert R. Adams and Allan A. Glatthorn*
**THE TRAINER'S CLASSROOM INSTRUCTION WORKSHOP**
*Dugan Laird and Ruth House*
**WRITING FOR SUCCESS**
*Allan A. Glatthorn*

**THE SCOTT, FORESMAN PROCOM SERIES:**
**BETTER WRITING FOR PROFESSIONALS:** A Concise Guide
*Carol Gelderman*
**BETWEEN YOU AND ME:** The Professional's Guide to Interpersonal Communication
*Robert Hopper, with Lillian Davis*
**COMMUNICATION STRATEGIES FOR TRIAL ATTORNEYS**
*K. Phillip Taylor, Raymond W. Buchanan, and David U. Strawn*
**THE CORPORATE MANAGER'S GUIDE TO BETTER COMMUNICATION**
*W. Charles Redding, with Michael Z. Sincoff*
**THE ENGINEER'S GUIDE TO BETTER COMMUNICATION**
*Richard Arthur, with Volkmar Reichert*
**GETTING THE JOB DONE:** A Guide to Better Communication for Office Staff
*Bonnie M. Johnson, with Geri Sherman*
**THE GUIDE TO BETTER COMMUNICATION IN GOVERNMENT SERVICE**
*Raymond L. Falcione, with James G. Dalton*
**THE MILITARY OFFICER'S GUIDE TO BETTER COMMUNICATION**
*L. Brooks Hill, with Major Michael Gallagher*
**THE NURSE'S GUIDE TO BETTER COMMUNICATION**
*Robert E. Carlson, with Margaret Kidwell Udin and Mary Carlson*
**THE PHYSICIAN'S GUIDE TO BETTER COMMUNICATION**
*Barbara F. Sharf, with Dr. Joseph A. Flaherty*
**THE POLICE OFFICER'S GUIDE TO BETTER COMMUNICATION**
*T. Richard Cheatham and Keith V. Erickson, with Frank Dyson*
**PROFESSIONALLY SPEAKING:** A Concise Guide
*Robert J. Doolittle, with Thomas Towers*

**For further information, write to**
Professional Publishing Group
Scott, Foresman and Company
1900 East Lake Avenue
Glenview, IL 60025

# Designing and Developing
# BUSINESS COMMUNICATIONS PROGRAMS THAT WORK

**Judson Smith**
Executive Director – Training Program Development
Multi-Media, Inc.
Minneapolis, Minnesota

**Janice Orr**
Instructor – Inver Hills College
Inver Grove Heights, Minnesota

Poynter Institute for Media Studies
Library

**Scott, Foresman and Company**
Glenview, Illinois          London

ISBN 0-673-15943-4

Copyright © 1985 Scott, Foresman and Company.
All Rights Reserved.
Printed in the United States of America.

**Library of Congress Cataloging in Publication Data**
Smith, Judson, 1944–
  Designing and developing business communications programs that work.
  Includes index.
  1. Communication in management.  2. Communication in management—Data processing.  3. Communication in management—Audio-visual aids.  I. Orr, Janice, 1951–   . II. Title.
HF5718.S58    1985        658.4′5       84-16302
ISBN 0-673-15943-4


1 2 3 4 5 6 7 – RRC – 89 88 87 86 85 84

# Preface

What's the one common denominator that will be found in every type of business, regardless of what that business produces? Communications. It's the single most important factor in any type of business. As the world of business becomes more and more sophisticated, it's not surprising that the need for effective business communications is becoming greater.

This book reflects the need for more sophistication and diversity in modern business communications. It deals with a wide range of media and an even wider range of methods to put those media to effective use.

This book also anticipates the major trend facing business today—rapid change. Although common media and media-production techniques are covered in depth, the focus of the book is on the underlying concepts behind effective business communications—concepts that will remain constant in the face of change.

For instance, the computer is rapidly becoming a business communications tool that can help business communicators shape meaningful and memorable messages. But the computer of today is not the computer of yesterday . . . or of tomorrow. So this book discusses the basics behind using computers for word-processing and as part of interactive communications systems. It provides the foundation required to use any of today's computers effectively for communication . . . and to be ready for tomorrow.

This book is written to help with business communications today and tomorrow. What will tomorrow bring? Clearly, the trend is toward more need for communication. When changes occur as rapidly as they do in our modern business world, rapid and concise communication is the only way to make certain that everyone receives the new information. The words "rapid" and "concise," incidentally, are equally important. It's vital that communication occur rapidly, but it's just as vital that the communication be concise. We live in an age of information overload, where people must pick and choose the communication they wish to acknowledge and accept.

This book will help business communicators shape messages rapidly . . . and well. It will help them make certain that they understand their audiences and will offer techniques to ensure that the message is shaped to fit that audience.

This book also deals with the technical aspects of producing business communications. It describes cost-effective ways of working with audio, with video and with various photographic media. But it does not neglect the printed word. An entire chapter is devoted to working with the common print media used for business communication.

A major objective of this book is to help nonprofessionals learn two things: how to work with professional communications producers and how to handle some parts of the job without professional help. Developing effective business communications is not a job reserved only for the experts.

Most people have the ability to make good common-sense judgments concerning what works and what doesn't. So a second major objective of this book is providing both background and examples to reinforce common-sense judgment.

Finally, a third major idea within this book is that the options available to business communicators are enormous. That includes both job opportunities and choices of media and media techniques. As more and more organizations recognize how important business communications is, more and more business communicators—both full-time professionals and part-time professionals for whom communication is just part of the job description—will find that com-

## PREFACE

munications skills are vital . . . and valued . . . throughout the business world.

This book is designed to acquaint you with those skills . . . and to arm you with the knowledge and techniques required to design and develop effective business communications programs.

# Contents

**Part One: PREPRODUCTION
           CONSIDERATIONS** ———————————  **1**

    Analysis and Organization      1

**1  THE BUSINESS COMMUNICATIONS
    PROCESS** ——————————————  **3**

    Introduction      3
    What Are Business Communications Programs?      3
    The Business Communications Process      4
    The Elements of a Good Business Communications
        Program      6
    The Importance of Long-Term Program Planning      13
    Conclusion      19

**2  FRONT-END ANALYSIS** ——————————  **21**

    Introduction      21
    Time Spent Now Is Time Saved Later      22
    Components of Front-End Analysis      22
    Briefings      23
    Interviews and Discussions      24

|   |   |
|---|---|
| Readings and Research | 26 |
| Defining Objectives | 27 |
| Statement of Purpose | 28 |
| Creative Concept | 29 |
| Treatment Sheet or Proposal | 31 |
| Conclusion | 36 |

## 3 CHOOSING THE CORRECT MEDIUM — 39

|   |   |
|---|---|
| Introduction | 39 |
| The Medium Is Not the Message | 40 |
| Audiovisual Media | 40 |
| A Guide to Audiovisual Media | 47 |
| Audio | 52 |
| Print | 53 |
| A Guide to Print Material | 56 |
| Electronic Books and Videotext | 58 |
| Conclusion | 60 |

## 4 SOME BUSINESS WRITING CONCEPTS — 63

|   |   |
|---|---|
| Not the First Step, but a Big One | 63 |
| What Makes Good Writing? | 64 |
| Some Basic Writing Concepts | 64 |
| Some Differences Between Print and AV Script Writing | 72 |
| The Computer as a Business Communications Tool | 76 |
| Conclusion | 86 |

## Part Two: PRODUCTION TECHNIQUES — 87

|   |   |
|---|---|
| The Role of the Business Producer | 87 |
| Components of a Production | 88 |
| The Evolution of a Program | 89 |
| Do-It-Yourselfer or General Contractor? | 90 |

## 5 DEVELOPING PRINT PROGRAMS — 93

|   |   |
|---|---|
| Something Old, Something New | 93 |
| Program Design | 94 |
| Some Basic Layout Ideas | 94 |
| Standard Design Elements | 99 |

| | | |
|---|---|---|
| | The Rough Draft or Thumbnail Sketch | 102 |
| | Working with Type | 103 |
| | Dealing with Photographs and Other Graphic Elements | 111 |
| | Pagination and Folding | 117 |
| | Creative Considerations | 119 |
| | Conclusion | 122 |

## 6  SOUNDTRACKS: THE RIGHT SIDE OF THE SCRIPT — 125

| | | |
|---|---|---|
| | Introduction | 125 |
| | Audio Plus Visual | 126 |
| | Where Do You Begin? | 127 |
| | Script Format and Directions | 128 |
| | Components of a Soundtrack | 130 |
| | Motivation | 136 |
| | Intelligibility | 138 |
| | Some Creative Considerations | 145 |
| | Difference Between Motion and Still Media | 148 |
| | Putting It All Together | 149 |
| | Conclusion | 159 |

## 7  VISUALS: THE LEFT SIDE OF THE SCRIPT — 161

| | | |
|---|---|---|
| | Static Versus Dynamic Visuals | 161 |
| | How to Visualize a Script | 163 |
| | Graphics, Text Slides, and Other Visual Choices | 166 |
| | Program Design | 169 |
| | Visual Style | 170 |
| | Visual Clarity | 173 |
| | Scenes and Sequences | 175 |
| | How People Perceive Visuals | 177 |
| | Fluidity | 180 |
| | When to Change Shots | 182 |
| | Assembling Visuals | 183 |
| | Presenting Visual Programs | 185 |
| | Conclusion | 187 |

## 8 INTERACTIVE AND COMPUTER-AIDED PROGRAMS — 189

| | |
|---|---|
| Introduction | 189 |
| What Makes a Program Interactive? | 190 |
| The Wisdom of Socrates and the Patience of Job | 193 |
| How a System Interacts | 196 |
| How to Create an Interactive Program | 197 |
| Types of Interactive Media | 200 |
| Selecting Specific Media for Interactive Programming | 203 |
| Conclusion | 204 |

## Part Three: CASE STUDIES AND POSTPRODUCTION CONSIDERATIONS — 205

| | |
|---|---|
| Situation and Needs Analysis | 205 |
| Needs Analysis to Define an Objective | 206 |
| Situation Analysis to Develop a Plan | 207 |
| Execution Analysis to Ensure Effectiveness | 208 |
| Why Do Good People Produce Bad Programs? | 209 |

## 9 CASE STUDIES — 213

| | |
|---|---|
| Introduction | 213 |
| Quality Improvement Motivation and Training | 214 |
| Productivity Improvement Program | 219 |
| Multinational Promotion Program | 223 |
| A Sales Training Program | 230 |
| A Theft-Reduction Program | 237 |
| A Televised Panel Discussion | 241 |
| Conclusion | 245 |

## 10 PRODUCING SPECIFIC TYPES OF PROGRAMS — 247

| | |
|---|---|
| Be a Successful Imitator | 247 |
| Public and Press Relations | 248 |
| Advertising and Sales Promotion | 253 |

## 11 PACKAGING, STORAGE, DISTRIBUTION, AND PRESENTATION — 259

From the Abstract to the Concrete — 259
Packaging — 259
Storage — 264
Filing: Finding What You've Stored — 268
Distribution — 270
Presentation — 273
Environmental Conditioners — 279
Conclusion — 282

## INDEX — 285

# PART ONE
# Preproduction Considerations

## ANALYSIS AND ORGANIZATION

Analysis and organization are critical considerations in any business communications program. The communicator must analyze the need and the audience, and then find the best way to meet that need for that audience. In addition, the communicator must organize available people and money to accomplish the job most productively and effectively.

Within the first section of this book, we devote several chapters to this analysis and organization function. In the first chapter, we take a broad look at the basics of business communications, analyzing the process of persuasion and the communications model. In the second chapter, we discuss the importance of front-end analysis to determine several critical factors that will affect the medium and the approach chosen for the program. In chapter 3 we offer some suggestions about the advantages and disadvantages of various media. Note that it isn't until the fourth chapter—last in this section—that we talk about writing. This may seem unusual to those who think that a business communications program begins when a communicator puts words down on paper as a script or as print copy. But experience has taught us that it is better to fill your mind with information about a topic and an audience than it is to fill your wastebasket with false starts. This is why we spend so much time discussing all the things that must be considered before actual production begins on a business communications program.

Part of organizing and analyzing effective business communications programs is knowing about technical and creative production skills. Most business communicators have neither the time nor the access to equipment required to gain and maintain a state-of-the-art knowledge of the technical aspects of production. Many may not have the talent or inclination to become experts in the creative aspects of production. Therefore, it's far more important that they know how to direct others who have those skills and talents and know how to develop and produce programs that communicate effectively.

For that reason, this book—and especially this first section—emphasizes the underlying concepts behind business communications programs, including production and direction elements more than the technical elements. That is, this book deals more with "how-to-think-about" a production element than "how-to-do" the technical parts of a production element. Frankly, the equipment available for business communications programs is changing at lightning speed. By the time this book is published, current equipment may well be old hat. But one thing doesn't change—the need for business communicators to understand the best way to use creative and technical skills to solve business communications problems.

The first section of this book is designed to help accomplish that task through effective analysis and organization. This is the first, and most important, step to designing and developing business communications programs that work.

# 1

# The Business Communications Process

## INTRODUCTION

Within this chapter, we'll provide an overview of the business communications process. The purpose of this overview is to define business communications, to explain the process of business communications, and to formally identify elements common to all business communications programs. In addition, we'll discuss the importance of long-term organization and planning to ensure that a communications program meets its objectives.

After reading this chapter, you should be able to look at your own communications programs and those of others and identify the major parts of the communications process as they relate to a specific program. Further, you should be able to isolate problem areas, parts of the program where the communications process is flawed.

## WHAT ARE BUSINESS COMMUNICATIONS PROGRAMS?

In its broadest definition, business communication is any means people use to transmit business messages. But many of these com-

3

munications don't really involve programs; that is, they don't involve an organized and substantial effort to communicate a message through some medium or combination of media. Instead, they are impromptu meetings, brief notes or formal business letters, a telephone call, or an in-person dialogue.

This book deals with the other type of business communication: the program. "Program" is any sort of planned and produced communications vehicle, ranging from a photocopied bulletin to an industrial television or film presentation. In some cases, the information presented about business communications programs applies to personal communications, to journalism, to advertising, or to informal communication between business people. The major thrust of this book, however, is on one topic—producing memorable and meaningful messages through any type of planned and produced communication vehicle designed specifically to meet business objectives.

## THE BUSINESS COMMUNICATIONS PROCESS

Although the business communications process often requires special techniques to create meaningful and memorable messages, the way in which we communicate is always based on a well-known theoretical model. Understanding that model will help you understand what is involved in communications and what can make business communications programs succeed or fail.

The communications process starts when a "sender" transmits a "message" through a "medium" to a "receiver." In some cases, "feedback" from the receiver is also transmitted through a medium to the sender.

This model works equally well for all forms of communication; it describes the communication between two neighbors waving hello and the communication between a corporation and the audiences who view a film about that corporation. It also shows all the places communication can fail.

## How Business Communications Can Fail

An analysis of the communications model shows a disturbing fact: If any part of the process is faulty, the message is faulty; a message can be communicated effectively only when every part of the process works perfectly. What makes an understanding of this model especially important for business communicators is that many forms of business communications involve no feedback... no way for the receiver to tell the sender that the message failed.

For instance, a business communicator could develop an exceptional training manual that explained precisely how to repair a specific device. That communicator could correctly identify the audience and transmit the message to the audience, yet that message can fail to be communicated. Why?

One simple reason would be that the audience did not or could not read the manual. The message was right, but the medium was wrong or the motivation for the audience to read the message was wrong, so the message was not communicated.

Or a business communicator could produce a superb audio-visual presentation outlining all the benefits of a new product. That communicator could identify the correct audience and transmit the message directly to the audience, perhaps at a trade show. Yet the message could fail to be communicated. Why?

One reason might be that trade show environments are often so noisy and confusing that no one could pay attention to the program. The message may be right, the medium may be right, but the receiver's environment might be wrong.

But perhaps the medium and the environment are both right. How could a message then fail to be communicated?

It could be the wrong message or the wrong audience. Or the receiver just simply may not like the sender. For example, what if the owner of a small business receives a brochure about an extraordinarily expensive computer system designed for multinational corporations? The message and medium could be right, but the receiver would be wrong... and the message would fail.

You can see that there are many different ways a memorable and meaningful message can fail to be communicated. When that happens, the results are lost time, lost money, sometimes even lost jobs. That's why one of the first considerations for every business communications program is analysis to make certain that the medium, the message, the sender, and the receiver are right for the program objectives. Without such an analysis, it's often just pure luck when a program succeeds.

### How Business Communications Succeed

Business communications can consistently succeed only if all parts of the communications system are correct. The sender must shape a message that is memorable and meaningful. That message must be transmitted through a medium that will reach the receiver in the correct environment for communication. And the receiver must understand the message and be receptive to it.

This obviously complex task involves both technical and creative considerations. It also involves a knowledge of the three elements necessary for effective communication: motivation, information, and action. Business communicators try to motivate someone to pay attention to some information and to take action. Typically, if a program does not include at least a modicum of each element, it will not be successful. If the program is successful it will be due to luck or some other unplannable factor.

### Business Communication Is Selling

Most business communicators don't think of what they do as selling, but it is. It's selling someone a new idea or a new product or a new understanding of a product or idea that already exists. It's selling people on the need for training or motivating them to greater business efforts. In short, any time you want people to listen to what you have to say, first you have to sell them on the idea that it is worth their time and attention. You must persuade; you must sell.

## THE ELEMENTS OF A GOOD BUSINESS COMMUNICATIONS PROGRAM

Most business communications programs will typically have some similar elements. These elements are also similar to those within a typical sales presentation. When a good salesperson makes a presentation, he or she will follow a plan something like this:

1. Gain favorable attention.
2. Provide a reason to listen.
3. Provide an overview of the topic.
4. Present information and reasons to buy.
5. Answer questions and handle objections.
6. Review main benefits.
7. Close the sale.
8. Follow up.

These elements may have different names for successful business communications programs, but the approach and content would be similar to the sales presentation. There may be different weights given to different parts of the program, but a good business communications program will usually involve all these elements. A bad program may well lack one or more of these elements. By using this "generic" plan, therefore, business communicators can follow a proven formula to make sure they have developed a persuasive program.

### Gain Favorable Attention

Many sales representatives believe that a sale can't be made based on a good first impression, but that a sale can be lost through a bad first impression. In the same way, a good business communications program can help make a good first impression to help you gain favorable attention as soon as possible.

Part of gaining favorable attention is packaging. You might begin with a catchy musical score or some superb visuals. You might invest extra production dollars in high quality paper and printing. Or you might set up a special presentation environment. However it is done, the business communicator must make certain that the audience immediately develops a favorable impression, just as a sales representative is carefully groomed and dressed to make certain that the prospect receives a favorable impression before the first word is spoken.

Another part of gaining favorable attention is the content of the opening message, the first words read in print communication or the first words heard in audiovisual communication. Just as a skilled sales representative spends some time at the start of the sales presentation discussing positive and pleasant generalities, so do effective business communications programs typically begin with some words that set a positive tone for the rest of the communication yet don't immediately hit the heart of the message.

## Provide a Reason to Listen

One of the best ways to provide a reason to listen, both for business communications programs and for sales presentations, is by enticing the audience with "WIIFM," or What's In It For Me? It's the WIIFM that motivates an audience member to participate and to take whatever action the message suggests. More important, the WIIFM provides the audience with a reason to pay attention to the rest of the program.

Isolating the WIIFM that will appeal to each audience member is a basic part of planning any communications program. Understanding which benefits will entice the audience facilitates the design of an effective and persuasive communications program.

For example, a certain training program may feature computer-assisted learning methods. The benefit of that feature is that learners can set their own pace and tailor their own sequence of instruction.

The crucial consideration at this stage in any business communications program is holding the attention gained, and increasing that attention. Although a benefit approach is usually effective, other creative approaches can be used. For instance, the program could start with an example or case history, creating interest through storytelling. Humor or mystery could also be used. This part of the communication process can occur in several places.

The reason to continue paying attention, by the way, can be either a positive reason or a negative reason. A positive reason, "the carrot," might be some new opportunity to advance or to make a job easier and more productive. A negative reason, "the stick," might be a statement that without the development of a new skill or more productive work habits, the job may disappear. In most cases, the carrot is more effective than the stick. But some programs, and some program objectives, can only be met if negative motivation is used.

When negative motivation must be used, it's often most effectively used in a way that removes the threat as far as possible from the audience. For instance, a filmstrip about employee theft could begin with a positive motivator—that honesty is the best policy. But a negative motivator—that crime will be punished—might be stronger and more effective. However, it would be better to use an anecdote or example from a different company or a different industry, rather than from the audience's own company or industry. And it would also probably be smart to preface the program with a statement that acknowledges that most employees are honest.

## Provide an Overview of the Topic

As in the case of some sales presentations, some business communications programs need no overview. But many programs benefit from a brief introduction that outlines what will be discussed in the rest of the program. This overview occurs early in the presentation, after the audience's attention has been gained and it has been given a reason to continue paying attention. The crucial factor is that the overview happens early enough to give each audience member a framework for the rest of the communications program.

This is true for both audiovisual and print communications programs. A book or training manual, for instance, may start with a contents page, while a videotape or audiovisual program may start with an introductory sentence or two that outlines what the rest of the program will discuss.

The overview indicates what will be discussed, but does not go into detail. Then the details will be presented in such a way that they lead to a logical and positive conclusion.

## Present Information and Reasons to Buy

The bulk of most sales presentations, and most business communications programs, is information; this information provides reasons to buy, reasons to take a certain action, or reasons to adopt a certain attitude or concept.

In business communications programs, the information element can range from a few words to a few million words. For instance, some communications programs do very little more than generate enthusiasm for a simple concept or idea, such as the slogan,

"Work Smarter, Not Harder." Most of the program is devoted to motivating the audience to put that slogan into practice. But other programs provide detailed information to help the audience understand a major body of knowledge.

Most successful programs actually combine both types of information. They generate enthusiasm for a concept or idea, then provide detailed information to help the audience put that enthusiasm to good use. Further, some business communications programs follow a building process in which each new concept or idea is introduced by a key phrase or slogan; then that concept is developed through more detailed information.

For example, a productivity improvement program may begin with an audiovisual program to generate interest, perhaps through a discussion of how the audience members can benefit from increased productivity (the WIIFM). And that WIIFM could very well be that productivity improvement will allow everyone to work smarter, not harder. Then the emphasis might shift to developing a large body of knowledge, perhaps through a series of training manuals aimed at specific productivity improvement concepts. Each of those manuals may also begin with a WIIFM and a slogan. Finally, the communications program might end with another motivational audiovisual program that reviews all those WIIFMs and slogans and shows how the information gained in the program can benefit everyone.

## Answer Questions and Handle Objections

In a sales presentation, there is usually a simple, straightforward objective—to get the prospect to become a customer. To reach that objective, some sales people "accentuate the positive and eliminate the negative"; that is, they focus the entire presentation on those elements that will be perceived by the prospect as good reasons to buy.

For most sales presentations, this works well because the prospect has an opportunity to ask questions or raise objections. And most good sales representatives encourage the prospect to ask questions immediately, even if it means breaking the flow of the presentation. In that way, the representative can make certain that the prospect's attention is not on the question rather than the presentation.

Few business communications programs allow that immediate feedback. As a result, it's crucial to anticipate questions and objections, and to answer them as soon as possible within the program. Because the audience can't interrupt the flow of the program, in most cases, the business communicator must include answers in the program. In that way, the audience does not lose other important information while thinking about a specific question or objection.

Lack of feedback is a crucial factor in most business communications programs. It creates several problems, but the most important problem is that the business communicator must know the audience so well that he or she can anticipate questions and objections. Even more important, at least for those programs where feedback isn't possible and the audience is diverse, the business communicator must include answers to all questions and objections, because it's not possible to anticipate just which ones will be raised by a specific audience or audience member.

### Review Main Benefits

Both sales representatives and business communicators must walk a fine line between providing enough information and providing too much information. Make sure that the audience understands and recalls what's been presented, but do not repeat things so often that familiarity breeds contempt.

In many cases, the best way to handle a review is through a "summary conclusion" to the program, that lists the main topics covered within the program. Many business communicators will follow the same psychological ploy used by sales representatives during the review; they will use the review as a time to get agreement, to get the prospect to begin saying "yes."

For instance, a film on a company's manufacturing capabilities may describe several innovations and concepts that make that firm's products less expensive and more effective than the competition's. During the conclusion of the film, it would be effective to recall each of those innovations and concepts and rhetorically ask the audience each time if they agree that this element is important. In theory, at least, if the audience agrees that each element is important and gets comfortable with the idea of agreeing, the audience will be much more receptive to the next step—taking action.

## Close the Sale

In a sales presentation, the action step is closing the sale, getting the prospect to become a customer. In a business communications program, there can be several different action steps. But the same concepts are important in both closing situations.

For example, one key to a successful close is a positive attitude, assuming that the prospect will buy. Then the next step is simply suggesting an action step to follow that will lead to the purchase. In the same way, a business communicator could end a program by assuming that the audience members agree with everything that's been explained in the program, then suggest the next step to take based on that agreement.

Two things usually should be done during the closing part of a sale or of a business communications program: First, avoid any negative statements. Second, provide some logical direction, some way for the audience to take action based on the information that has just been communicated to them.

However, there are also two ways of making the close less effective: First, closing too soon, attempting to suggest an action before you've convinced the audience that the action is worthwhile. Second, suggesting the wrong action, persuading the audience to do something far different than the objective you set for the program.

In business communications programs, one of the best ways to avoid both problems is to not expect any one program to do everything. Instead, take small chunks out of a business problem, or small steps toward developing new ideas and concepts. So it's crucial that business communicators understand the way in which people absorb information—the learning curve.

## The Learning Curve and Follow-Up

When a sales presentation is completed and the prospect has become a customer, the sales representative's task is essentially done. Some follow-up is necessary, of course, to ensure customer satisfaction and pave the way for future sales. But the sales representative's major objective is met when the sale is made.

In a business communications program the objective is usually to create a memorable and meaningful message. Both parts of that objective frequently require follow-up and the element of time. Many meaningful communication messages require time for full understanding. And follow-up, reinforcing the message over time, is often required to make a message meaningful.

This corresponds to a generalized pattern of adult learning sometimes shown as a "learning curve." Such a curve plots retention against time, and clearly indicates that the longer the learning process, the greater the amount of information retained. Another learning curve plotting retention against repetition indicates that the more times something is repeated, the greater the retention is.

There are limits, of course, to the amount of time that should be spent learning something or to the number of repetitions. But the general idea is that most people will retain more if they have more time to think about it and have a few reinforcements of the message over that time period.

## THE IMPORTANCE OF LONG-TERM PROGRAM PLANNING

One reason some communications programs fail is that they try to do too much too fast. The communicator, or the communicator's bosses, want an instant solution, a quick fix. Unfortunately, a quick fix is usually just as quickly forgotten. Behavior change—and that's usually a basic objective of most communications programs—comes over time, through repetition and reinforcement. This is especially true when the behavior change must involve modifying a concept that is high in the hierarchy of opinions, attitudes, and beliefs.

### Opinions, Attitudes, and Beliefs

The time involved in changing behavior depends upon how the communications objectives relate to the hierarchy of thought. Some objectives low in the hierarchy can be met rapidly. Others, involving objectives high in the hierarchy, require a long-term effort continuing over months or years.

Opinions are the lowest level of the hierarchy of thought. Most opinions are based on hearsay, general experiences, a few facts, and the audience member's environment or life-style.

Attitudes are the second echelon in the hierarchy. They are

often based on an audience member's relationship to others, plus long-term experience, environment, and life-style.

Beliefs are the top of the hierarchy of thought. They are strongly held feelings, often based on the experiences of a lifetime.

The way you attempt to persuade an audience member to change an opinion, attitude, or belief depends upon many factors. But a good rule of thumb is this: You can change opinions with new facts; you can change attitudes with facts plus experience over time; but changing beliefs requires major long-term and continuous effort. Often the only way to change a person's belief is through a "Eureka Moment" of great magnitude.

For centuries, everyone thought the world was flat. Columbus changed that opinion with a fact. For even longer, some people felt that women should work only at home. Women changed that attitude with facts, experiences, new environments, and new business relationships with men. Some people believe the world was created in seven days, while others believe just as strongly that creation took eons. People on either side of this issue rarely change their beliefs.

Business communicators are often frustrated when they bring all their persuasive powers to bear on an issue, only to find no change in the audience's behavior. But change will occur, in some cases, if enough time is spent on the process and if the business communicator follows a logical process to create that change.

## A Logical Process for Behavior Change

Most communications programs should follow a logical progression. In some cases, every step in that progression can take place in one program. But in most cases, spreading the progression over time is better. This takes advantage of the learning curve and of the fact that sometimes people must gather examples from their own lives to back up what they've been told in a communications program.

The logical progression for communications programs will normally follow these four steps:

1. Awareness.
2. Involvement.
3. Commitment.
4. Action.

In some ways these steps correspond to the sales process. The difference is that the final objective of this plan is not just a simple action step—a purchase—but, rather, the retention of a meaningful and memorable message. Because retention improves with repetition and with time, this four-step process involves both a span of time and some repetition of the message. However, the span of time may be no more than a few minutes, and the repetition may be no more than once. This would be true, for instance, if the objective of the communication is simply to change an opinion about some simple concept low in the hierarchy of thought.

However, as the objective involves ideas higher in this hierarchy, more time and effort will be involved. To see how this works, assume that our objective is to create a behavior change relating to on-the-job safety while handling chemicals. Within that framework, we'll define and describe the four-step process.

### Awareness

The first step in behavior change is awareness. People cannot change anything unless they are aware that something might need changing. In many industries, for example, the health danger from handling certain chemicals became apparent only after many years. Although some union groups and industry organizations suggested that certain precautions be taken, little happened until people became ill and the cause was traced to chemicals with which they had worked.

Many programs fail at this stage in the communications process. Unless the business communicator spends some time explaining that a problem exists, creating an awareness, the audience will not pay attention to the program that follows.

In essence, this step corresponds to the first step in the sales process, gaining favorable attention. This is the way a business communicator tells his or her audience that the information to follow will be of some importance to them.

In a program to teach employees to handle chemicals more carefully, the awareness stage might involve some print or audiovisual communication explaining that many chemicals can be dangerous—perhaps citing statistics and examples to show that there is a direct link between these chemicals and the health problems of those who handled them.

## Involvement

Awareness is important, but not everyone who is aware of a situation is willing to do anything about it. The next step in changing behavior is to create involvement. This obviously corresponds to the WIIFM step in the sales process, giving people a reason why they should buy or why they should pay attention to a message relating to them.

Involvement often depends upon harmony; that is, the communications program must be in harmony with the opinions, attitudes, and beliefs of the audience. Think of the entire persuasion process as a building process, similar to the way nature builds a coral reef. Coral has to build on something; there must be some foundation materials that are harmonious with the growth of coral. The more facets on the foundation materials, the more places coral can grow, creating shape and substance. Finally, millions of tiny corals join together to create a massive reef.

In the same way, involvement builds when people can add the new information they have received onto a foundation of existing knowledge and opinions, attitudes and beliefs. In this way, people can bring their experience and education into the picture, helping to fill in the gaps.

If, on the other hand, the new information you are presenting to the audience is not compatible with the experience and education they already hold, they will reject involvement. That's why it is crucial to shape this portion of the communication so it does not conflict with the hierarchy of thought. You want the audience to begin thinking of a potential WIIFM and of the issue or idea as one with which they should be involved.

You can use the same communications techniques for involvement that you used for awareness, but you should shape the message differently. For example, you might begin telling the audience about the specific health problems caused by some specific chemicals with which they have worked. And you might begin pointing out small signs and symptoms with which the audience might be familiar.

The involvement stage should not demand participation nor lay blame for the problem on any audience member. Rather, it should be another gradual revelation of an issue or an idea. As in most persuasion elements, the most effective way to get involvement is through "self-selling," letting the audience discover the need for their involvement rather than demanding that they become involved.

## Commitment

Involvement should naturally lead to commitment, but this is not always the case. People can be involved with an issue without being committed to do anything about it. Involvement, in a sense, is the start-up step, like turning the key and starting up an automobile. Until you put the car in gear and begin controlling speed and direction, you're just standing still.

Commitment implies investment. The audience must be prepared to invest some time and effort in making a change. Commitment also implies participation, but participation toward a goal. For instance, audience members may now be aware of the health problems caused by the chemicals with which they work and involved in learning more about the specific problems, but they still must take one more step—the commitment step—to begin participating in the solution of the problem.

Two elements that help persuade people to commit themselves to something are peer pressure and opinion leader affirmation. People look to one another for support and reinforcement; they look to certain individuals whom they hold in high regard for affirmation that they are following the correct path or holding the right views. A good way to gain commitment from all audience members is to develop commitment from a few leaders.

This happens frequently in politics. When rank-and-file union members, for instance, learn that their leaders have endorsed a specific candidate, it is far easier for them to commit their votes to that candidate. On the other hand, when a candidate fails to get the endorsement of opinion leaders, he or she will have great difficulty gaining commitment from followers.

In business communications programs, sometimes it seems more economical to produce just one presentation for management, supervisors, and employees, and then to present the program to everyone at the same time. However, this can backfire, especially if the topic is at all controversial.

For example, suppose a firm presented a program on chemical safety to everyone in a plant at the same time. As part of that program, perhaps the company will suggest a procedure for handling chemicals that might involve more time spent by supervisors in "unproductive" safety techniques. Unless the supervisors are committed to the importance of safety, some supervisors might consciously or subconsciously sabotage the program by commenting to their employees that it seems like a time-waster.

If the supervisor is respected, it would not take much for that one individual to ruin the effectiveness of the entire program for his or her employees. And this might happen simply because the supervisor had a knee-jerk opinion immediately after participating in a program. With time, that opinion might change, but the damage would be done.

For this reason, many effective business communications programs involve opinion leaders early. For instance, supervisors in various chemical plants might be asked to be advisors during the production of this safety program. In that way, the opinion leaders have an opportunity to become committed to the program prior to its presentation to all employees . . . and the opinion leaders then will be more willing to exert effort to get everyone committed to the program.

## Action

The goal of all business communications programs is an action step of one sort or another. Surprisingly, some communications programs don't suggest a logical and reasonable action step. Rather, they present all the information, but never tell the audience what to do with that information.

On the other hand, some programs suggest an action step which does not relate to the program, perhaps one that is far too complex or difficult to attain. When this happens, the problem can often be traced back to the beginning stages of program development, when the objectives for the program are set.

Those familiar with management by objectives (MBO) know that objectives should be realistic, attainable, and measurable. The same thing holds true for the action step in a business communications program. For example, the objective of a program on chemical safety might be to reduce in-plant hazards by 10 percent through the implementation of two new safety procedures. The action step suggested at the end of the program might list those two new safety procedures and tell audience members how to put them to use. This would probably be a realistic and attainable action step, and the success of the step could perhaps be measured by observing how well those safety procedures were put to use.

By making certain that the action steps suggested by a program are measurable, realistic, and attainable, the business communicator is following a proven path—promoting behavior change in small increments rather than trying to make massive changes at one time. Further, the business communicator is working with the assistance of time and repetition, rather than fighting against these elements.

## CONCLUSION

Much of the information presented within this chapter is just common sense... and so is much of the information required to produce effective business communications programs. The challenge facing the business communicator is adapting and adjusting the things he or she knows about persuading people to the specific audience, medium, and objective for a program.

What should be clear after reading this chapter and observing how successful—and unsuccessful—business communications programs use the persuasion process and the four-step process of communication, is that our original definition of business communications programs holds especially true for successful programs. In this era of communications overload, it's important that messages be meaningful and memorable. And the best way to create meaningful and memorable messages is through a planned and produced program or series of programs that follows a logical path to an objective that is realistic and attainable.

# 2

# Front-End Analysis

## INTRODUCTION

Front-end analysis is the first step in the development of most business communications programs. Through this process the business communicator determines the shape of the program by considering all parts of the communication process, including the audience, the medium, the message, and the objectives of the program. Front-end analysis is done through research, interviews, briefings, and introspection. Front-end analysis results in a direction, an approach, that can be followed to develop the program so it contains memorable and meaningful messages.

Within this chapter, we will discuss the importance of front-end analysis and offer some techniques for conducting that analysis. The purpose of this discussion is to begin laying a groundwork for the creative and technical aspects involved in developing programs in a variety of media. Front-end analysis, however, is useful for all media and for every type of communication program.

After reading this chapter, as a business communicator you should understand the value of spending enough time prior to beginning the actual development of a program to make sure that the program is developed along logical lines. In addition, you should have the tools required to conduct an effective front-end analysis for any type of business communications program.

## TIME SPENT NOW IS TIME SAVED LATER

Most business communicators are action-oriented, not data-oriented. We want to produce something, not think about producing it. The time spent in thinking about a program and analyzing it from every aspect is not wasted time. It's actually the most productive and effective way to save time while creating a quality product.

An important part of front-end analysis is determining what quality level will conform to the requirements of the communications objectives. Another part is determining which medium will be used to transmit what message, and which creative approach will work best for the specific audience.

Time spent in front-end analysis will result in fewer false starts, clearer focus, and less time spent on the production process. The time involved in front-end analysis will depend upon several factors, including how much you know about the audience and the objectives, and the length and complexity of the final product.

## COMPONENTS OF FRONT-END ANALYSIS

Although each step in front-end analysis has a definite and distinct purpose, the overall goal is to learn as much as possible about the audience and about the communications content. Then you can use that knowledge to focus your program design and approach to meet the program objectives in a meaningful and memorable manner. Sometimes this will involve more emphasis on one step than on another, but most programs will involve at least some consideration of all these factors:

Briefings—To set the scope of the project and identify objectives.

Interviews and discussions—To get basic information from content experts and audience members.

Readings and research—To learn facts and vocabulary about the content and the audience.

Defining objectives—To list measurable and attainable specific goals for the program.

Statement of purpose—To briefly describe what the communication is supposed to accomplish.

Creative concept—To succinctly state the program theme in an interesting and informative slogan or sentence.

Treatment sheet or proposal—To describe all of the program elements in summary form as a contract between yourself and the program instigator.

These steps are presented in chronological order, although sometimes several steps are conducted at the same time. However, most programs will begin with a briefing.

## BRIEFINGS

Briefings are actually interviews, distinguished by a special name since they are interviews with the person or persons in charge of the project. The briefer might be a senior official within an organization or a colleague with a special need for a communications program. In some cases, you may act as your own briefer on programs you are developing to meet a need you have perceived.

At the briefing, you will determine the scope of the project. You will discover perceived objectives and perceived audience demographics, the budget, the time available, and how this project is prioritized by the briefer.

Note the word "perceived." For most programs, you actually have two audiences: the briefer and the actual audience. The difference is sometimes significant. The briefer may be far removed from the audience in age, occupation, or philosophy. So part of your job during front-end analysis will be to determine how best to reach the actual audience, and then to convince the briefer that you are right.

The briefer may also perceive objectives as generalized ideals rather than specific and attainable goals. Again, part of your role is to shape realistic goals that are possible with the specific business communications program and audience.

Identify budget and time constraints immediately. Your budget will probably include two types of cost considerations: actual funds available and in-house services. In many major organizations, there's a "charge-back" system that accounts for the time and materials spent by personnel within the organization. Remember that these in-house services are not free. In addition, most in-house service providers have limited time. What may be high in your priorities might be low in theirs.

That's why you want to persuade the briefer to set a priority for the project, perhaps even to ask the briefer to call his or her counterparts within other departments to establish that priority with them. In this way you leverage your clout with the clout of the briefer, which can smooth the way for you.

If you're dealing with actual budget dollars, establish this amount as soon as you can. The total budget figure will help you determine not only what medium to choose, but also what quality level you should set for the project within that medium. For instance, a high-priority slide presentation with a very small budget will probably not be done to the level of perfection you might want, or that the briefer would prefer. At this point the briefer must either allocate more budget dollars or lower his or her expectations of the quality level. Determine this early, before you or the briefer are so invested in the project that you have overspent the budget.

The briefer should also give you some content, or at least help you identify some content experts who can tell you more about the specifics of the program. Get as detailed information as possible from the briefer about who can help provide content and about what sources are available for further reading and research. Don't be surprised if the briefer has very little specific knowledge of the subject area. Your job is to gain that knowledge, or to gain access to someone who has it.

Finally, and perhaps most important, you want the briefer to state the purpose of the program. You may also have to work with the briefer to modify that purpose, to create objectives that are measurable and attainable, and that fit the audience. During the rest of your front-end analysis, keep this briefing clearly in mind, especially the stated purpose of the program. You may find that you have to make some adjustments after you've analyzed other aspects of the proposed program.

## INTERVIEWS AND DISCUSSIONS

The best way to find out what the audience is thinking is by talking with audience members. But this obvious step is often neglected or ignored. Talking with the audience can also be difficult due to geography or logistics. However, it is worth the extra effort because you must talk *with* the audience to understand how to talk *to* the audience.

The same holds true for content experts. Even if the briefer has given you a great deal of written material, you should still seek out content experts, especially those who wrote the material. Interviews and discussions will provide a perspective not possible from background research and readings.

When talking to audience members, you're looking for several types of information:

> How much they already know about a subject.
> Their opinions, attitudes, and beliefs about the subject as well as about their business and personal lives.
> Areas of common interest that could be useful for analogies.
> Preconceived notions, including erroneous thinking about a topic.
> Taboo subjects and favorite "in" jokes.
> The vocabulary they use, listening for the general education level and for specific terms.

You'll probably never get that "laundry list" of information from one person, nor should you rely upon information gained from a single interview with one person. You should plan on conducting several interviews or conducting an interview with several people at the same time.

One effective interviewing technique is the "focus group." This is an interview with several people who are asked to focus upon a single topic. You act as the facilitator, keeping the conversation on that topic, but not inserting your own opinions into the discussion.

A successful focus group interview will generate a great deal of information. In fact, you should plan on audiotaping the discussion so you can recall all that is said and how it is said. In this way, these words and ideas can be used in the program, adding realism.

Interviews may seem time consuming, but they often lead to time saved. They can help you make the most of the program content because you can identify what the audience already knows about the subject.

For instance, one briefer suggested that a quality improvement program should begin with a discussion of the Japanese productivity experience, involving quality circles and similar participation groups. Focus groups with typical audience members, however, revealed that the audience was well aware of the Japanese experience; it came up almost immediately in the discussion. Based on this, the program could concentrate on more sophisticated material.

Conversely, other briefers have assumed too much knowledge on the part of their audiences. In these cases, focus groups on individual interviews and discussion can be used to develop the best way to present that information to the audience.

This is where some understanding of the opinions, attitudes, and beliefs of the audience is important, as is knowledge of their areas of common interest and preconceived notions or erroneous data. Find a way to present information that is in harmony with the audience's attitudes and beliefs, that presents facts to reverse incorrect opinions, and that will link new information to existing knowledge.

Interviews will also help you avoid a common problem—tunnel vision. It's easy to get locked into a certain way of thinking about a subject. If that way of thinking is wrong, it's hard to see that from inside our own tunnel. So it's helpful to gather as much data as possible before beginning to think about possible approaches.

One key to successful interviewing is the ability to listen more than you talk. Since this sometimes doesn't work with shy or retiring people, develop the ability to ask leading questions—those that can't be answered with "yes" or "no." By asking questions that require a lengthy explanation, you'll not only gain information, but you'll also begin to make the interview subject more comfortable . . . and more willing to give you the information you need to develop a worthwhile program.

## READINGS AND RESEARCH

The research and reading part of front-end analysis usually involves two distinct types of resources. One type is general background information. The other is specific information about the program topic. You want to build a broad understanding of the topic as well as to learn the vocabulary used to discuss that topic and gain specialized information important for an individual program.

In addition to the obvious resources, such as product literature or technical papers, seek out some other sources of information. Reading novels and nonfiction books relating in some way to the topic may seem like a rationalization for pleasure reading, but these books can actually be a way to gain in-depth understanding of a subject area and to understand how people within that subject area talk and think.

For the same reason, reading the trade publications that audience members read or the newsletters and other materials they receive will lead to an increased understanding of how the audience members presently receive information. If other communications programs have been produced in either print or audiovisual format for this audience, study them. And it will be especially helpful if you can interview members of the audience who have seen or read those other programs, to find out what they liked and didn't like about the presentation.

The research and reading stage is one of the most flexible stages in the front-end analysis. Sometimes this can be accomplished with a rapid scanning of materials, but it can also take many days and weeks of full-time work to understand all the necessary information about the topic or subject area. It may also take hands-on work, especially if you are called upon to describe a process or technique in detail.

## DEFINING OBJECTIVES

For most communications programs, you cannot accurately define objectives until you have analyzed the audience and the program content. You should, however, have some idea of the objectives as soon as you begin the front-end analysis. In that way, you can compare the objectives you think will be correct with the reality you uncover during the analysis.

You may also find that you have both overt and covert objectives. These words may have some negative meaning, such as covert activities by spies, but the meaning in this context is positive. Sometimes it just is not possible to overtly state every important objective within a business communications program . . . at other times it is not politically wise.

For instance, all sorts of government and societal regulations may make the mention of a dress code inappropriate as part of an orientation program. Yet most organizations do have a dress code. One way around the problem is to overtly say nothing about the dress code, but covertly show all the people within the program dressed according to the organization's code.

Of course, one reason there are covert objectives is that no one wants to talk about them. So you may have to do some digging in the briefing to find out what all the objectives are for a program. Once you have unearthed the overt and covert objectives, you can begin to define a set of realistic program objectives.

When defining objectives, a realistic approach is mandatory because most programs will be judged on how well they accomplish these objectives. If the objectives aren't realistic, they won't be accomplished and the program will be perceived as a failure.

Also, make sure the objectives are specific, not vague. By listing specific objectives, you help focus the program content as well as provide some means of measuring results. In addition, the act of refining objectives to make them more specific will help you begin to develop concrete, substantive purposes and approaches for the program.

## STATEMENT OF PURPOSE

The statement of purpose is a brief statement that tells what the program is to accomplish. Chances are, when you first talked with the briefer, he or she immediately stated a purpose for the project. But chances are just as good that your interviews and research show the need to modify that purpose in some way. Clarify this new statement as soon as possible, especially if it will involve a major change in the thrust of the program.

Defining the purpose of a program seems simple, but it is not. Just as it is often easier to write a full-page trade advertisement than it is to distill that message into billboard words read at freeway speed, so is it often easier to write a program than to write a concise statement of what that program should do.

But the statement of purpose is vital to the program's success. Without a clear understanding of the purpose, it's almost impossible to attain that purpose. More important, it's difficult to focus all your efforts so they relate to that purpose.

For instance, if your stated purpose is to help clerical support people improve their filing skills, any mention of typing or telephone techniques is out of place. In the same way, a program about typing improvement shouldn't involve a discussion of filing techniques—that clutters up the program, and defeats the purpose.

It is tempting, however, to kill several birds with the same stone—to get your money's worth out of a program by discussing several topics. This smorgasbord approach creates the same problem people face with too many choices on a menu. The variety is so distracting that it is hard to make any choice at all, or to put together a sensible and substantial meal.

The statement of purpose should be brief, usually less than one paragraph. But it should include a great deal of information. One way to organize that information is through an old journalistic mnemonic device—five *W*s and an *H*.

Make sure your statement of purpose includes *W*ho, *W*hat, *W*hy, *W*here, *W*hen, and *H*ow. Who is the audience? What should they do based on the program? Why is it important? When and Where will they receive this information? And How should the information be presented?

After writing the statement of purpose, don't just file it away somewhere. Refer to it as you work on the program. Often the process of creating something leads you off on several side roads that have little to do with your goal. Use the statement of purpose as your road map to a destination, and take the shortest route to that destination.

## CREATIVE CONCEPT

Often, the statement of purpose will include a phrase or sentence that encapsules the entire program theme. This is the "creative concept," the main message you want to impart.

You can think of the creative concept as a topic sentence or a slogan. Once the audience has that information, they will at least know the main concept of the program. And if the audience members have paid any attention, they should recall several main points about the program at any time they hear or see that topic sentence or slogan.

The creative concept gives you a framework, a stepping-off point. It allows you to organize your message around a central theme. For instance, your statement of purpose for a program might be:

> "We need to help the audience focus on the future because the future of our industry will involve new technologies, new competition, new challenges."

If so, your creative concept could well be "Focus on the Future." Using this creative concept for a program about productivity, you might begin with:

> "Focus on the future. That's more than a slogan. It's something that must become a way of life for all of us. If we don't focus on the future . . . focus on new and better ways of doing business . . . someone else will.
>
> "One major focus of our future will be on new technology . . ."

"Focus on the future" becomes a theme throughout the program, something you can return to again and again as you focus the audience's attention on each important element in their future. So the creative concept adds cohesiveness to the program as well as making the job of writing and designing the message easier.

Think of the statement of purpose as a synopsis—a concise description. Think of the creative concept as the title of that synopsis. The creative concept is the fast answer you would give if someone asked you what the program was all about; the statement of purpose is the lengthy explanation you would give to explain your fast answer.

The creative concept also helps you position the concept of the program in the minds of the audience. "Positioning" is a word used frequently in advertising to describe the place within the mind of a prospect where a specific product "lives," in terms of similar "neighboring" products. For instance, the Seven-Up Company chose to position their product as an "uncola," taking up a position in the minds of prospects that was opposite the position filled by cola drinks, like Coke and Pepsi.

In terms of most business communications programs, you have two choices concerning positioning. You can position this program as similar to something else, but perhaps "new" or "improved." Or you can position this program as unlike anything else, "the uncola." If you position a program as similar to another one, make certain the other program is appreciated by the audience. Then you can build on the positive feelings they have about the other program. If you position a program as new and different, make sure it is not only new and different, but also make certain the audience members understand why the new, different program is of value to them.

The idea, of course, is to give the audience members a reason to buy the concepts in the program, or at least to pay attention to the program a little longer so you can do some more persuasion.

## TREATMENT SHEET OR PROPOSAL

After you have completed the briefings, interviews, research and reading, and developed a statement of purpose and a creative concept, it's time to put that information into an organized plan for the communication program. For audiovisual programs, this plan is usually called a "treatment sheet," while print programs normally begin with a "proposal." Actually, both serve the same purpose: to feed back your plan to the briefer and to provide guidelines for production.

Think of the proposal or treatment sheet as a contract, your contract with the people involved in the project. You'll describe the project in brief and include information about the major elements. Most of all, you'll be saying, "Here's what I think I'm going to do. Is that right?"

The major elements involved in either a treatment sheet or proposal are the same. They are:

Introduction.
Objectives.
Audience Demographics.
Format.
Creative Approach.
Budget and Schedule.
Conclusion.

The length of the treatment sheet or proposal will vary based on the complexity of the project and the need of the people involved in the project for detailed information. In some cases, a paragraph about each element is more than enough. But in most cases, the treatment sheet or proposal will run one to two pages per element, with creative elements such as "Creative Approach" requiring a little more space than factual elements such as "Audience Demographics."

### Introduction

In the introduction, it's usually good to repeat your understanding of what the briefer said to you as an introduction to this project. This is a good way to let the briefer know that you understood what was said, and to give the briefer an opportunity to change or clarify what he or she said if it was not what was meant.

A typical introduction is an overview of what the project is, who it is for, and why it is being done. The introduction should be little more than that. Use the introduction to position the program, but not to provide detail.

### Objectives

Begin this section with the statement of purpose. Incorporate all the major objectives, then define each objective in measurable and attainable terms, such as: "Raise sales by 13 percent," or "Reduce misfiled documents by 30 percent." Define the objectives precisely, so that you know whether or not you have met them.

### Audience Demographics

Remember that you actually have two audiences—the briefer and the audience. You may have to negotiate a bit with the briefer to show that the audience requires a change in the statement of purpose or the creative concept. Do this by defining the audience effectively and by using detailed data and, if possible, actual quotes gleaned during audience interviews.

You'll probably want to include at least the following data about the audience:

Audience age range.
Percentage of male and female audience members.
Any taboos you've uncovered.
Important attitudes, opinions, and beliefs.
Favored media, hobbies, sports, and similar personal information.

### Format

The word "format" categorizes two different elements: the medium chosen and how that medium will be used. For instance, you may choose the format of a documentary film. This defines both the medium, film, and the format, a documentary approach using film.

When selecting a format, begin by considering the environment in which the audience will receive the message. If your program is a take-home design, you obviously need a format that will be easy to use away from the office. A training manual can go anywhere, but a six-screen computer-controlled multimedia program cannot.

Next, look at the way in which the audience generally receives information, and enjoys receiving it. Are they readers or viewers? Do they like computer games or hate them? Whichever medium is most familiar to the audience will probably be the one that the audience will most accept and understand.

### Creative Approach

Under "Format," you may have outlined a specific type of media approach, such as an on-location videotape. Under the heading of "Creative Approach," you would expand that information by offering a general description of the program and your reasons for choosing the format and program type. You'll also include your creative concept, and show how that creative concept fits the approach as well as meets the program objectives.

Under this heading, you'll typically be selling ideas. So build the creative approach step-by-step. For instance:

> "Because the audience shows an extraordinary interest in sports, a sports theme is appropriate. For this young, well-educated audience, especially because it includes many Euro-

pean and South American males, a favorite sport is soccer. Therefore, we recommend a creative concept of 'Kick It Around One More Time' for this program on brainstorming. And because soccer is such a fast-paced sport, we believe that stop-action slides of soccer players in action will be ideal for this program. So we will produce a slide presentation with an accompanying audiotape. The program will follow a team through an entire soccer game, showing how teamwork, passing the ball back and forth, and building on each other's abilities and opportunities, leads to a win. Interspersed with action shots of soccer, we will use shots of a brainstorming session at work, showing the similarities. . . ."

The creative approach can include an outline of the program, such as a manual's contents page or the main sequences within a film or videotape. But avoid locking yourself into details and locking the minds of the people who read the treatment sheet or proposal into expecting those specifics when they review the final production.

## Schedule

Set realistic and accurate schedules for the program within the treatment sheet or proposal. One way to do this is by working backwards from the date at which the program must be completed, such as when the annual stockholders' meeting is held or when the new product will be in the field. Based on this date, work toward the present, setting interim deadlines and approval points along the way.

Approval points are especially important. One of the greatest unnecessary expenses in any program is the cost of revisions after supposed final deadlines. The way to make sure things are done right the first time is to set deadlines and to stick to them as well as you can.

On the other hand, most schedules should include a "fudge factor"—a few additional days designed to give you catch-up time. Be careful, though, not to pad projects so much that no one believes your deadlines any more.

Avoid being on optimist about schedules. Be a realist about the time it takes to do things. Obviously, this advice becomes easier to follow as you do more and more programs. So you may find that you are padding too much or too little at first. It's a good idea to give yourself as much time as possible. This time is like money in the bank when you find you have underestimated the time it takes to do part of a project.

## Budget

Don't pad the budget excessively, but don't discount it. One of the worst things that can happen in business communications programs is to overspend the budget before you reach the final stage, and then have to cut back on the finishing touches. It's also uncomfortable when you have to explain why you went so far over the estimate. Accurately and realistically setting a budget up front is better than trying to rationalize overspending after the fact.

One place business communicators run into budget troubles is when they forget "add-ons," like sales tax or messenger services. Another is in the cost of alterations or changes. Although it doesn't happen often, every producer can tell stories about a program in which the changes and alterations cost more than the original program. The way to avoid both problems is to create a realistic and detailed original budget . . . and stick to it.

There are two basic budgets: "bottom-line" and "line-item" budgets. A bottom-line budget simply states that the total cost of the project will be "x" dollars. Or that the total cost of each major element, such as typesetting or soundtrack recording, will be "x" dollars and the bottom line total will be "y" dollars.

A budget like this allows the business communicator some latitude in allocating money. If photography costs more than anticipated, perhaps the money can be made up in soundtrack recording by using fewer music cuts. Or a few illustrations can be dropped because the cost of printing will be higher than anticipated.

There's no problem with a budget like this if all you are concerned about is the final cost of the project. As long as the production meets stated objectives for this cost, it's fine. This budget is especially useful for programs that are being done with extensive in-house support, and with the business communicator in overall control.

But sometimes the business communicator will be using outside vendors for a project, perhaps receiving bids from several different firms. In this case, a line-item budget might be better. In a line-item budget, each specific element is listed and described, with the cost for that item identified.

This is a more complex budgeting procedure, but it is often the only way to make sure you are comparing apples to apples. You may find, for instance, that it is better to pick and choose among vendors, using one for sound work and another for photography, based on their estimated costs for each line item. Or you may find that you are paying a premium price for something you could do in-house. And you could well find that one vendor's bottom line cost might be higher than another's, but that you are getting far more for your money.

Many vendors dislike line-item budgets, and with good reason. It forces them to spend a great deal of time estimating costs and listing things in detail. It may also force them to bid higher than they would for a bottom-line budget because they have to make certain they can do any part of the project and still make money.

### Conclusion

The conclusion of a treatment sheet or proposal should be a summary of main elements. But part of your task while writing the document is to sell the idea. Another part is getting the project moving, by asking for a certain action. So the conclusion should be a brief review plus a motivational message, such as:

> "Once the audience has seen this program, they'll be far better equipped to serve our customers effectively. It will result in an image of difference between ourselves and our competition. We'll be known as the company that cares... and that will be more than a slogan, it will be part of our work life. The sooner we begin this project, the sooner this valuable selling tool, our image of difference, will be visible to our customers."

## CONCLUSION

We began this chapter with the statment that time spent in front-end analysis is time saved later in the project. An additional statement is frequently true: time spent on front-end analysis of one project leads to shorter time spent on front-end analysis of the next similar project. As with anything else, experience leads to expertise and productivity.

However, don't become complacent, especially concerning audience interviews. Audiences change, even within the same firm. So it is sometimes necessary to look for a fresh approach, and to take a fresh look at the audience to see what new approach might work best.

The crucial concept within this chapter is that the more information you can gather and the more you can focus your plan, the easier it will be to produce a planned program that accomplishes the statement of purpose.

# 3

# Choosing the Correct Medium

## INTRODUCTION

During our discussion of the communications model, we mentioned that a message can fail to communicate due to problems within the communications channel, as well as problems within the message, transmitter, or receiver.

That is why the choice of a communications medium is crucial to the success of a business communications program. If the message is strong enough, of course, it can overcome a poor communications channel. But sometimes the message is not strong enough, or the communications channel is so poor for that message, that a great deal of time and money is spent in futile efforts to communicate.

In this chapter we will discuss some advantages and disadvantages of common business communications media. This is not meant to be a comprehensive discussion of production methods nor a description of each medium. Rather, this is an overview of the media choices and of the considerations required to make the right choice for a specific program.

## THE MEDIUM IS NOT THE MESSAGE

For some communications, as Marshall McLuhan said, "The medium is the message." We may watch a lousy television show, or at least use it as a night light, rather than turn the set off. We may reread a book rather than having nothing to read on an airplane. In these cases, the message doesn't matter; the medium is important.

But that's not true for business communications. Time is too valuable to waste and so are budget dollars. For business communications programs, the medium is not the message. The medium must, in fact, be carefully chosen to enhance the message. And the medium must be cost-effective as well as effective in presenting the message.

These decisions can't be made without an understanding of what each medium does well, and what each can't do well. So we'll look at some common business communications media according to two major considerations—cost and creative effect.

## AUDIOVISUAL MEDIA

Audiovisual (AV) media include filmstrips, film, videotape, slide presentations with synchronized soundtracks, and multimedia presentations involving several projection sources. We'll look at each of these later, discussing individual differences, but begin by discussing things common to all AV media.

Audiovisual programs are excellent for evoking a mood and for presenting general information. They aren't as effective as print for presenting detailed information that must be retained and reviewed. This is because AV programs are paced by the producer, not by each audience member; reviewing parts of an AV program is not as simple as skipping back a few sentences or pages in a book or manual.

Although AV media aren't extremely effective for retaining detailed information, most audiovisual formats aid retention of basic concepts because they use high-impact elements, such as dramatic visuals, sound effects, music, and strong narration. When an audience member sees thirty color slides of happy people at work and hears a symphonic score including lyrics that shout the joy of working for the firm, chances are that he or she will get a very strong message about that firm being a good place to work.

Film and videotape have the highest impact of all audiovisual media because they present motion. It is one thing to show a still photograph of the firm's president on a screen while he or she "voices-over" a message to the audience. It's quite another thing—much higher in impact—if the audience can actually see the president talking and gesturing while delivering that message. Further, media such as film and video allow a person's personality to come through, if the person knows how to communicate effectively through that medium. As a result, film and videotape are more personal media than, for instance, a printed bulletin or brochure.

On the other hand, film and videotape are generally the most expensive audiovisual media to produce. Because of this, some business communications programs that require AV are better presented as sound-slide programs, filmstrips, or multimedia programs. It all depends upon the amount of impact required of the program, whether motion and color are required, and whether the program must be compatible with equipment throughout the nation or perhaps throughout the world. A series of trade-offs must be considered. We'll begin by looking at the basic trade-off of cost versus impact.

### Cost Versus Impact

There are two ways to calculate the cost of a program: One is total cost—what the bottom-line cost of producing and distributing the program will be. The other way is in terms of a "cost-per-viewer" ratio. A motion picture that has a total cost of $50,000 and reaches an audience of 100,000 people is actually less expensive per viewer than a $2,000 slide program seen by 1,000 people. The film will cost just $0.50 per viewer while the slide program will cost $2.00 per viewer.

However, a high cost-per-viewer is sometimes justified because of the expected outcome. For example, an elaborate multi-image sales presentation on a new high-rise office building might cost $40,000, yet be seen by just fifty prospective tenants. Even though the cost-per-viewer is $800, that program could bring the office building developer millions of dollars in rent.

Rarely is it possible to produce a program without concern

for costs. Looking at costs from both a total cost standpoint and a cost-per-viewer standpoint creates a realistic idea of what it will cost to bring a mesage to each viewer.

### Ease of Revision

Production and distribution costs are often only part of the total cost of a program. Although some programs will be used for a period of time and then discarded, many other programs can and should be revised now and then. In this way, the program's useful life is extended, while its impact is kept high because the program appears current. Another key consideration is the time between revisions of an audiovisual program. Some audiovisual media are far harder to revise than others, in terms of both costs and work involved. For instance, revising the visual portion of a slide presentation is quite simple. You simply replace old slides with new ones. But revising the audio portion of a sound-slide presentation frequently involves a great deal of work. For example, changing one paragraph of narration on a soundtrack would require rescripting and rerecording a narrator, then inserting that change into the master audiotape and remixing the soundtrack. Finally, the program would probably have to be resynchronized so that the visuals can be changed by an audio pulse on the soundtrack tape.

Revising films and videotapes also involves more time and costs than for a slide-program visual or audio revision. With film, a revision to either the picture or the sound will involve several expensive procedures. With videotape, a revision to either picture or sound is somewhat similar to revising audiotapes, but the process is a bit more complex. In either case, the cost is higher than for revising sound-slide programs or multi-image programs. Filmstrips, by the way, fall on middle ground. The audio portion of the program can often be revised in the same way as for slide shows, but the costs are higher because filmstrips are frequently produced in large quantities, and each audiotape must be replaced. To revise the visual portion of a filmstrip, either individual frames of the filmstrip must be spliced into each distribution copy or the master copy must be revised and reduplicated.

So it makes sense to use an easily revised medium, such as a sound-slide show, if there will be frequent need for revision. This is especially true if the business communicator can write the slide show script so that facts, names, and other data are shown on slides, rather than stated in words. In that way, the visuals can be replaced without the added expense of changing the soundtrack. On the other hand, a film or videotape program that will be seen by millions of people just once, and then require revision or replacement, may still be the best choice for a specific message, because the cost per viewer is so low that the cost of revision or replacement (per viewer) is nothing compared to the impact of the medium on those viewers.

### Motion and Color

In most cases, color or motion add to the cost of a program, so it is a valid question whether these creative elements are needed or not. Some programs demand motion, others demand color. Some can be done without either creative element, although it's rare that a film, videotape or slide presentation will be produced in black and white. Most viewers are conditioned to seeing color television, color films, and color slides. However, some programs could be done without color, and many can be done without motion. In fact, there are times when the lack of color and motion emphasizes the message.

For example, a training presentation concerning nonverbal communications will most probably be done as a color videotape or film, because gestures and other motions would appear to be necessary parts of the program. But those gestures are just as obvious in black and white as in color. For that matter, color might distract from analysis of the gesture. For the same reason, perhaps stop-action analysis of the gestures might be better than full motion.

On first consideration, a program such as this would appear to be an obvious candidate for full color film or videotape. But further thinking may show that a slide presentation, overhead projection transparencies, or even a print piece might do the job better. Before you make up your mind about that, consider some other criteria.

### Audience Perceptions of AV Media

Many of the considerations we've discussed so far relate to money or production difficulties. But the most important consideration concerning various types of audiovisual programs has more to do with psychology; that is, how do people perceive the medium?

Some people think of slide programs as boring and dull, and of filmstrips as being even worse. Obviously, this isn't always true. Some filmstrips and slide shows are far less boring than some films or videotape programs. But it is the perception, not the reality, that is important. And if your audience members perceive a slide program or filmstrip as boring, you're fighting an uphill battle from the beginning of production. Finding out about this perception during the front-end analysis is essential.

Some people think of television as a familiar and entertaining medium. As a result, they're comfortable with viewing programs on videotape and assume they'll be somewhat interesting. Again, this is a broad generality, but it is something that should be considered. If your audience feels comfortable with television, and you want them to feel comfortable with your program, then perhaps videotape is the best medium for this program.

Some people think of motion pictures as a powerful and important medium. Some also think of motion pictures as fantasy, when contrasted to the reality of television. As a result, you might want to choose videotape for a documentary program but choose film for a high-impact important message.

Sometimes a specific business communicator may have an audience that doesn't fall into these categories, one that thinks filmstrips are more entertaining than television or a slide show has much more impact than a motion picture film. The point is that an analysis of how the audience feels about various media will give the business communicator some indication of the best medium to use to impart a certain message. By beginning with a medium the audience respects and enjoys, the business communicator can at least know that he or she is not starting the process of persuasion with one strike against the program due to the medium.

### Universality and Compatibility of Equipment

A very important criterion for choosing one medium over another is the presentation mode and environment. Another is compatibility between various types of equipment and environments.

There are, for example, several incompatible formats for

film, filmstrips, videotapes, and videodiscs. Sometimes this is no problem because everyone within your audience has access to the same type of equipment or because you always provide the equipment to show the program. But it can be a problem, especially for multinational programs.

Different countries have different systems for electric power and for television signals. Further, some equipment readily available in one country will not be available in many other countries. So programs that must be presented in many countries should be in a universal medium format.

One format that is almost always available in any country is 16mm. optical-sound motion picture film. The 35mm. slide projector, too, can be found in most developed countries, as can the standard Philips audiocassette recorder. Overhead transparency projectors are also found throughout the world, or overheads can be viewed simply by looking at them against a light.

But video systems aren't as universal. First, there are several incompatible formats, such as VHS and Beta in half-inch cassette size. Second, videotape depends upon certain electronic pulses for stability and color correction. These pulses aren't always the same from country to country, so video programs recorded with one country's equipment may not always play back on another country's gear.

Even within one country, such as the United States, there are difficulties in making certain that compatible equipment is available in every locale. For example, a common standard for sound-slide programs involves an audiocassette recorder capable of recording and playing back an inaudible pulse of 1,000 cycles per second. This "1,000 Hz, separate track, inaudible pulse" standard is found on most audiocassette recorders with an "AV" designation somewhere in their name or model number. But that is not the only pulsing standard. Some machines use an audible pulse far lower in frequency. Others use an inaudible pulse that is higher or lower in frequency or is based on some digital code. So compatibility doesn't always exist within a certain class of media equipment, such as audio or video recorders. You have to take into consideration what equipment is available, what standards and formats that equipment uses, and how important compatibility is to the specific program.

## Ease and Effectiveness of Presentation

No message is of value to an audience unless it can be seen and heard. So it's important to consider ease and effectiveness of presentation when choosing a specific audiovisual format.

One of the first factors is the viewing environment. If the room will be darkened, almost all audiovisual media can be effectively presented. But photographic media, such as filmstrips, films, or slide presentations, are less effective in a lighted room, as would be the case if you wanted trainees to take notes while looking at a program. Video projection systems, too, often work better in a darkened room, although they can be seen with some effectiveness in rooms with slightly reduced lighting. If the room will be brightly or semibrightly lit, an overhead projector program can usually be seen well, as can an image from a television receiver. You must, therefore, have an idea of what the final environment for viewing will be before determining the medium.

Sound is also important to many presentations. Consider sound from both loudness and intelligibility aspects. A program that relies heavily on words requires a quiet room or some way for listeners to shut out extraneous noise, perhaps through headphones. A program that relies heavily on massive sound effects and great music requires a speaker system capable of reproducing those sounds effectively.

Finally, ease and effectiveness of presentation often depend upon the presenter. A person who can easily load a videocassette into a player may have great problems threading a 16mm. film onto a projector. A person with little or no AV experience may be unable to resynch a sound-slide program that goes out of synch during a program. So the experience level of the presenter must be considered.

Incidentally, the importance of the program should also be considered. If a program absolutely, positively must be presented with no hitches, look for a reliable presentation medium with built-in fail-safe features. For instance, a multimedia program may involve a dozen or more projectors, each with a bulb that can burn out at an inopportune time. If losing a projector's image during a presentation would destroy that presentation, it might be worthwhile to invest in an automatic bulb changer or at least to put new bulbs in all the projectors just prior to the important presentation.

Although every type of equipment can fail, and probably will fail at some time during an important presentation at least once in a business communicator's career, certain media equipment is more reliable than others. A videocassette machine and television set, for instance, don't involve projection bulbs or special synchronization equipment. Of course, the tape may be flawed or damaged or the videocassette recorder or television set may develop a problem. But it is less likely that these problems will happen than that a projector bulb will burn out. That's not to say that videotape is always the most reliable medium, but just to illustrate that, once again, trade-offs must be considered.

## A GUIDE TO AUDIOVISUAL MEDIA

In addition to the factors mentioned above, and equally important in terms of program effectiveness, audiovisual media can be analyzed on the basis of the communications channel, the message, and the audience.

The simplest form of audiovisual medium would be a group of slides or overhead transparencies used to accompany the spoken word. Having both an audio and a visual component reinforces the message more than one sensory input does. Another benefit is that of personalization, of an informal or formal presentation that can be modified to suit a specific audience. It's also reliable and universal, in the sense that you do not need specialized equipment except for a slide projector or overhead projector and the program is based upon a live presentation.

However, you pay a price for this flexibility and personalization. This medium does not offer consistency nor does it have high impact. It doesn't, in short, have the show business elements common to more complex presentation media.

The next step up in audiovisual media is canning the audio portion of the program by making an audiotape. There are several reasons to do this, especially if the program will be repeated many times. A live presentation may be fresh and interesting the first time it is given, but it rapidly loses that feeling if the presenter begins to give rote recitals. And if the same program must be given by several presenters, the program's effectiveness depends entirely on their ability to keep it exciting and to hit the key points.

A prerecorded soundtrack ensures that the same message will be presented every time, and that it will be presented in a concise and competent manner, if the soundtrack is prepared correctly. Also, a prerecorded soundtrack allows the business communicator to take advantage of other sound sources to add interest and information to the presentation. For instance, some of the points could be made clearer through the use of special music or by recording sound effects. These extra sound sources can also be used as bridges to make transitions between main thoughts.

A prerecorded soundtrack also often shortens the time it takes to deliver a message while lengthening the time audience members will retain that message. By writing a concise and clear script and having that script recorded by someone with a good speaking voice and few "umms" and "you knows," the message will usually be clearer and shorter than if it is delivered live.

Soundtracks can be used in conjunction with slides or overheads in a nonsynchronized system, such as one in which the visuals are changed according to a written script or to an audible beep on the soundtrack. But most audiovisual programs use some means of synchronization so that the soundtrack and the visuals are linked together automatically. This is usually done through an electronic "synch signal" applied to the soundtrack. A synch program is usually developed only with slides or filmstrips, because it would be quite difficult to mechanically change overhead transparencies with the soundtrack.

As we mentioned earlier, a potential disadvantage of these synchronized audiovisual programs is that they can get out of synch. For instance, an unskilled presenter could start the show at the wrong place on a slide tray or at the wrong frame on a filmstrip. Or some flaw in the slide tray or filmstrip sprockets could stop the visual from advancing properly. Fortunately, new innovations in programming and playback equipment make this less of a disadvantage every year.

A more disconcerting disadvantage of these simple audiovisual formats is the loss of fluidity that occurs each time a slide or filmstrip frame advances. The brief period of time when the screen goes blank during the visual change can be somewhat distracting.

By stepping up to a multiprojector presentation, this problem can be prevented. If you add a second projector and a device to gradually fade out the image on one projector as the image on the next projector fades in, you can keep a visual on the screen at all times. Also, you can develop some dissolve effects so that images seem to flow into each other.

You can step up even further by linking together several two- or three-projector dissolve systems, usually through a computerized programming device. Now you can put more than one image on the screen at a time, plus overlap and dissolve and flash images, to produce a program with high impact.

However, the number of projectors and associated equipment involved in these multimedia, or "multi-image," programs increases as impact increases. So does the opportunity for error. Multimedia programs tend to be used in situations where there is a need for high impact yet the program doesn't justify the cost of a film or videotape. Also, multimedia programs tend to be used where frequent visual revisions are necessary. For instance, a growing corporation may produce a multi-image corporate capability presentation that can be shown in the main conference room. As long as the soundtrack remains fairly general, new products or services the corporation offers can be included simply by adding or changing slides.

Many multimedia programs can cost just as much as a professional videotape or film. Although they have the disadvantages of requiring a great deal of set-up and can sometimes go out of synchronization, they can be extremely effective for certain types of presentations. For instance, a program that would benefit from fast-paced visuals yet involves the need for visuals that can't be filmed or videotaped, such as historical photographs or drawings, can be produced effectively as a multimedia program. And so can programs where the relationship between visuals shown on the screen at the same time is important. In addition, multimedia programs lend themselves well to wide presentation screens, so an entire wall of a room can be filled with fast-moving visuals.

Videotape and film are the next step up the ladder. They are similar in that both media permit full sound and motion and both physically link sound and picture together so they can't get out of synch. But they are somewhat different in application and in the costs and techniques of production and presentation.

The major advantage film has over videotape at this stage in video technology is that video projection systems designed for large-audience viewing are costly and cumbersome. That's changing all the time, however, as new electronic technologies are adapted to the problem of creating a massive video image for large-audience viewing; but current projection equipment within the budget of many firms isn't as sharp or as easy to use as most motion picture projection equipment. The video systems that are superb in quality are also so high in cost that motion picture projectors are inexpensive by comparison and can produce an image of sufficient size and quality for almost any audience size. But, in general, motion pictures are more expensive to produce than videotapes because they require several intermediate production steps.

One major advantage of videotape over film is that "instant replay" is possible. You can immediately see whether or not you've made the shot you needed. Motion picture film, in contrast, must be processed before you can tell if you've correctly exposed the film and composed the shot. Because of this instant replay capability, videotape programs can sometimes be produced faster and less expensively than equivalent film programs.

Some film cameras, incidentally, allow the director and cinematographer to attach a video monitor into the system. These "video-assisted" devices combine the best of both worlds: using film but seeing the shots on video as they are created. This is especially helpful for situations in which it would be very difficult or costly to re-create a scene in the event of poor composition or poor film exposure.

Both videotape and film require more equipment for field production than sound-slide or multimedia programs. Film might be slightly more portable now, but that's changing as new videotape systems are developed.

Although some videotape programs—for instance those involving a role-playing situation between a sales trainee and sales trainer—can be shown without editing, most other types of programs require editing together the best of several takes or putting together sequences shot at different times and in different locations. Film is edited by physically cutting the film. Video is edited through an electronic duplication process. Both require more professional training and experience than simply sorting and loading slides into trays, and both require fairly sophisticated editing systems.

Disregarding these production elements and the problem of

showing videotape to large groups, the major difference between film and videotape is in the audience's perception of the medium and in the universality of the medium. As we've discussed, many people perceive television as a familiar medium and one with a great deal of realism. Film, on the other hand, is perceived as an entertainment medium and one with more "importance" than videotape. Although these may be vague terms and not applicable to all people, they serve to show one difference between videotape and film; that is, videotape may have a different impact than film, although both will have more impact than most other audiovisual media.

Returning to the problem of compatibility, in the United States, there are four common videotape formats. Most producers use either the ¾-inch cassette (also called "U-Matic") or 1-inch reel formats for master taping and either the ¾-inch cassette or one of the two ½-inch cassette VHS or Beta formats for duplication and playback. New entrants to the video field include videodisc systems plus other tape systems, such as Kodak's 8mm. tape system. If a business communicator wants to make certain that his or her videotape program can be viewed by the widest possible audience, the program would have to be made available on at least the three most common playback formats. In many cases, this means that the communicator must estimate how many of each type of playback tapes to duplicate, and it means extra work and extra cost. If the business communicator selects just one of these formats, he or she may be limiting the potential audience or forcing those who do not have equipment in that format to rent equipment.

Two common motion picture formats used in the United States for business communicators are 16mm. optical sound and Super 8mm. The latter can be used for professional productions, but is used far less than the other format. As a result, 16mm. film production and playback equipment is available almost anywhere in the nation and the world. It is a very universal medium.

Although film is sometimes more expensive to produce than videotape, it has some advantages for specific applications. If the highest possible impact and prestige are required, film is probably best. Motion pictures can be shown almost anywhere there is electrical power, so programs that will be seen by many people from outside of the business communicator's firm, are often best produced on motion picture film.

However, there are exceptions to this rule caused by the rise in cable television and UHF television systems. Both provide a large number of outlets for videotapes, including videotapes produced for business communications. In fact, some large companies are already experimenting with the use of these relatively inexpensive television systems for training, sales promotion, and other business purposes, either for internal consumption for the organization's employees or for external consumption to customers or dealers.

One final note about slide-based, film-based, or videotape-based programs involves conversion. It is conceivable to convert from any medium to any other medium. But it is far easier to convert from a photographic-based medium, such as film or slides, to an electronic medium, such as videotape or videodisc, than it is to convert the other way. In fact, this transfer can be done by projecting the image onto a wall and photographing it with a video camera. Of course, many more elaborate ways to make these transfers may be used, all at higher cost than this method and with higher quality. For instance, converting from videotape to slides would require shooting still pictures off the video screen; converting from videotape to motion picture film would require some process to film the videotape, either off the screen or through a computer conversion process. However it is done, videotape to photographic conversion is typically more expensive and less effective than the reverse conversion of film or slides to videotape. So if conversion may be required, it's better to start with a photographic medium than to start with video.

## AUDIO

Audio should be treated as a separate category from audiovisual because it has no visual component. Although that's a disadvantage for some programs, it can be a great advantage for others. For one thing, it allows the listener to create his or her own imaginary visuals. Also, audio productions can be done rapidly and with less expense than many other media. On the other hand, elaborate audio productions using sound effects, special music, and talented narrators can create an entire world, a new environment, without the need to recreate that whole environment through photography or videotaping.

Audio is also a portable medium, both in terms of production and playback. It's simple to pop a cassette into a player and listen to a program while driving to and from work. And it's almost as simple to make a recording.

But audio has some drawbacks, too. Audio is not perceived as an important information medium by most people. They think of audiocassettes as entertainment, not as sources of information. And audio programs must often compete for attention with all sorts of visual stimuli, from traffic on the road to a fly on the wall.

One of the best uses of audio is as a "leave-behind" or "take-home" review of material presented by other means. A copy of a speech can be recorded on cassette, for instance, or copies of an audiovisual show's soundtrack can be made for later review. Another good use of audio is as part of a program that involves a print element, such as a manual. The audio expands upon the information contained within the manual and can serve as a review in environments where the manual can't be read.

## PRINT

Print media include a wide variety of formats, ranging from one-page photocopied handouts to hardcover books filled with color photographs. The common denominator is that all these media can be held in the hands and read or viewed without electronic or mechanical assistance.

Print pieces can have just as much entertainment value as audiovisual programs, but most don't. Of course, a blockbuster novel or popular magazine is entertaining and provoking, but most printed pieces developed for business communication don't have the built-in advantages of plot, heroes and heroines, and interesting topics.

The most important advantage of print material over AV or audio is that the audience members can set their own pace for the absorption of the message. A second advantage is permanence. A videotape produced twenty years ago may have been produced in a format that no longer exists, or the tape may have been destroyed by an electromagnetic field or some physical hazard. But printed material can be reproduced as long as one copy exists, and it can be read despite moderate damage from water stains or age.

Print materials are also easy for the audience to retrieve and review. This is especially important when the audience's need to know is not simultaneous with receipt of the information.

Employee orientation programs are classical examples of this benefit. When a new hire views an audiovisual program outlining retirement and insurance plans, or procedures for filing grievances or other detailed information, he or she usually has little need to know. The new hire is not planning on retiring for quite a while, usually had to be healthy to get the job, and rarely has an immediate grievance. But all these things could become important in the course of a person's employment. When they do, the best way for an employee to review the information he or she needs is by referring to a pamphlet or handout containing the information.

The best way to handle an employee orientation program is by using an audiovisual program to reinforce main concepts and to give the new hire a good feeling about the company and company benefits. Additional print materials should supply the details of policies and procedures that an employee will need to follow when he or she takes advantage of a benefit or service.

Incidentally, one benefit of putting this sort of information in print is that it can be revised easily, especially if the print material was originally created in a format, such as three-ring binder, that makes revisions fast and inexpensive.

## Cost Considerations

Many of the same decisions and considerations we discussed for audiovisual media hold true for print. Cost, for instance, is still a factor and should still be amortized by the number of audience members who will use the material. The cost of print materials, however, should be calculated differently from audiovisual costs.

Most print materials involve two distinct cost considerations—the cost of producing master materials and the cost of reproducing those master materials. Although this is often true for audiovisual programs as well, we are usually dealing with far larger volume for print materials.

The cost of producing master materials is a "fixed cost." Whether you do one or one thousand, the cost of producing the first copy is always the same. The costs of duplicating those master materials is a "variable cost." If you print one copy of a book, it may cost $3,000. If you produce 3,000 copies, each may only cost $1.00.

When you first set up a budget for a print program, include both fixed and variable costs. Each additional run will probably use the same master materials, so the fixed costs will be very small on succeeding print runs. At a certain high volume level, in fact, the cost of the master materials will become insignificant when compared to the cost of printing.

### Content

When determining how much to spend on a print project, one major consideration is content. If the president of the firm is going to announce 30 percent pay raises, it really doesn't matter how he or she does it . . . the message will be received and appreciated. But if the president of the firm is trying to generate more capital from outside sources, the material should be presented in the most professional manner possible, so that the audience perceives the firm in the best possible light.

As usual, there is a trade-off—between packaging and content, between keeping fixed costs low and predicting the number of copies to be printed, between the need for durable binding and the need for easy revision. Making those trade-off decisions depends upon a number of factors, but the most important factor is the purpose of the material.

### The Purpose of the Program

Some print materials have no other purpose than to impress audiences. Some annual reports, for instance, contain just a few pages of necessary stockholder data and forty pages of fluff about the firm's potential. You could say, in fact, that the entire purpose of some print materials is to be perceived as important rather than read for important information. In these cases, the packaging may be costly, but that cost is justified by the purpose.

If the purpose of a program is to produce material that can be read and reread, then durabilty is important. Here, too, the program will cost more to produce than one with planned obsolescence, but that cost is justified by the purpose. The prime means of ensuring durability is the binding method chosen for the material. A stapled handout will be less durable than a handout bound in a three-ring binder, and a softcover book won't take as much abuse as a hardcover book.

Further, the purpose of some programs is more important than that of others. Again, one quick way to make a program appear more important is to spend more money on packaging. As with other considerations, the purpose of the program will lead to any number of trade-offs.

## The Audience

Just as some people are overqualified for certain jobs, so are certain media overqualified for their purpose and their audience. This is not much of a problem when using audiovisual media because most people are fairly sophisticated auditors of audiovisual media. It is, however, a problem when determining what level of quality and sophistication to use for a print program.

For example, if the audience is composed of people who have a certain amount of reverence for printed materials, a training program designed to encourage trainees to jot their own notes in the margin should be packaged so that it does not appear too expensive or too formidable. But a program designed to convince rich people that they should invest in a certain company's stock should look quite expensive.

Look at the way audience members prefer to receive information. If you walk into a department's coffee room and find a pile of hardbound books, you can probably create a similar volume for that audience. But if you see a few picture magazines and a television set, you might want to reconsider your plans to use print for this audience. And if members of your audience subscribe to a specific publication, with a specific look, it might be effective to use a similar look as a guideline during the production of your program. In that way, you'll build on the audience's perception of that respected publication.

## A GUIDE TO PRINT MATERIAL

At the most basic level, a letter or memo is a form of print communication. This form has a very strong advantage—it is personal. As a general rule, the more personal you can make the message, the more the audience member who receives it is likely to react strongly.

However, even at this most basic level, you lose something—a form of immediate feedback. So you still have to be aware of the audience's opinions, attitudes, and beliefs and to couch your message accordingly to persuade them to act as you wish.

A letter or memo has some obvious drawbacks as a communications medium for many messages. Unless you are willing to address each audience member individually, writing a separate letter or memo for each, you have created a form—hardly a personal form of communications. Many messages just don't fit into the letter format; they require illustrations, graphics, or other elements not found in standard business letters.

The next step up might be called a bulletin or handout. In general, this describes a print piece of very few pages, typically with few illustrations. These materials are often photocopied or printed by an inexpensive process, sometimes on special bulletin or program letterheads.

Although a bulletin is easy to revise and can be personalized to the extent that it deals with a specific issue for a specific audience, the prime advantage of this form of print communication is that it has a greater impact than a business letter or memo, simply because it goes to a wider audience and may involve some typesetting or multiple-color printing. On the other hand, some bulletins or handouts have no impact at all on most of the audience. A direct mail piece, for example, or a sales bulletin may not appeal to everyone to whom it is mailed. It all depends on content. As an example, a stock analyst's newsletter gains importance from its success, not from its graphic style, expensive paper stock, or printing method.

For more important messages, most communicators would choose a brochure format. At its most basic, a brochure is simply a piece of paper folded into three or more sections. A brochure may also use several colors, a special paper stock, or a more elaborate graphic treatment than in handouts or bulletins. Also, a brochure may often be typeset rather than typewritten and printed by a means other than photocopy.

A brochure can add a degree of importance to a message and can be quite interesting if it is designed well. But it has some limitations, especially involving space. The format of most brochures is better suited to bite-sized particles of information rather than long and detailed presentations of information. Brochures are normally used in this way, to present general concepts in an interesting manner.

However, one specialized brochure used to provide detailed information is the pamphlet, an inexpensive and easy-to-revise multi-page brochure. Pamphlets are used to present information in a condensed and easy-to-use format, such as a pocket-sized guidebook. One possible way of determining whether something should be called a "pamphlet" or a "manual" might be that pamphlets are often read and discarded, rather than retained for reference as would normally be the case for a manual.

A manual or book normally contains a number of pages. A pamphlet of more than 48 pages could arbitrarily be called a manual and one of 96 or more pages could be called a book. This is partly a mechanical distinction; a printed piece of 48 pages would probably require a heavier cover and more substantial binding system than one of 16 pages. But it is also a distinction based on the purpose of the medium—a manual or book will probably be read and retained for later review.

Traditionally, we look at a book or manual as something of permanent value. In some cases, they are bound in such a way that revisions require reprinting and rebinding of the entire volume. But as our business world changes rapidly, more and more books and manuals are being designed so that individual pages or sections can easily be replaced.

Three-ring binders, for example, make revisions a simple matter of replacing individual pages. Spiral bindings are slightly more difficult to remove for page revisions, but they at least make revisions possible. On the negative side, some people do not perceive these binding methods as being "real book" formats. In addition, custom three-ring binders are rather expensive in small quantities. So these books and manuals are often reserved for printed material used as part of training programs or other internal organizational programs, not for materials provided to the general public.

## ELECTRONIC BOOKS AND VIDEOTEXT

Electronic books or text displayed on television screens (videotext) are among the first new media categories to be developed in the computer age. As the number of such systems increases, we'll be able to store and access entire libraries of information at the touch of a button.

The advantages of electronic books and videotext are not just concerned with saved space on bookshelves. With some skill at a computer keyboard, you can access an enormous amount of information from one source or you can access very specific information from a wide range of sources. It is, or will be, almost as if you had a library—and a skilled reference librarian—at your fingertips.

There is a charge for this, of course. Most electronic publishing firms or libraries charge by the minute. If the system is not located nearby, you will also pay long-distance telephone charges. But the speed of the computer often makes it possible to "dump" a great deal of data into your system at the speed of light. You can then call it up in "real time," at a rate and speed comfortable to you.

Information with wide general appeal can be accessed in certain cities through various "videotext" systems. These are an offshoot of cable television in many cases, operating like a "pay TV" channel that provides text displays rather than movies or special events. As the system develops, most people in the United States will be able to call up a great deal of information simply by punching the right buttons on a television console.

Also, several computer networks use home computers to access data and distribute publications. A few books, including both novels and nonfiction, have been written specifically for network users; some books are even being written chapter-by-chapter by network users. There's little doubt that this trend will continue, and perhaps reach the world of business communications sometime soon.

But there are problems with electronic publishing. For one thing, "out of sight, out of mind" sometimes holds true. It's far easier to pick up a book sitting on a shelf or table than it is to call up an electronic network, tie in the computer, and go through a number of computer stages just so you can read a few pages. Also, video display screens are less portable than books and some people report headaches and eyestrain after using these electronic systems for a period of time.

Finally, some people simply enjoy reading print on paper. It seems more real, more permanent, than flickering lights on a television or video display.

## CONCLUSION

Many factors are involved in the correct choice of a medium for a specific business communications program. Although many of these factors are objective, such as cost or quantity or ease of revision, others are subjective, such as creative considerations or impact or personalization. We've included a chart that outlines some of these considerations, but not all of the subjective criteria fit into a chart format.

### FACTORS IN SELECTION OF A MEDIUM FOR A BUSINESS COMMUNICATION SYSTEM

(L = Low. M = Moderate. H = High.)

| Medium | Cost | Revis-ability | Impact | Retention | Personal-ization | Dura-bility |
|---|---|---|---|---|---|---|
| Audio | L | M | L | L | L | H |
| Slides | L | H | M | M | L | H |
| Sound/slide | M | M | M | M | M | H |
| Filmstrips | M | L | L/M | M | M | M |
| Multimedia | M/H | L | M/H | M | L | M |
| Films | H | L | H | H/M | L | M |
| Video | H | L | H | H/M | L/M | M |
| Letters | L | H | H | H | H | L |
| Bulletins | L | M | L | L | M | L |
| Brochures | M | L | M | M/L | L | M |
| Pamphlets | M | L | M | M/L | L | L |
| Manuals/books | H | L | H | H | L | H |
| Electronic publishing | M/H | H | M | M/L | L | H |

Weighing all of these factors sometimes becomes quite a balancing act. But it's a necessary part of creating effective business communications. As we said at the beginning of this chapter, "The medium is not the message." The correct choice of medium can help you present your message in the most cost-effective and professional manner possible.

# 4

# Some Business Writing Concepts

## NOT THE FIRST STEP, BUT A BIG ONE

Many people who produce business communications think of writing as the first step. We have shown in the first three chapters that a lot must happen before word one reaches the paper. But all of those early steps are aimed at this point—at beginning to write the communications. In most cases, with the exception of a presentation done completely with visuals, the words become the main focus of the communications message.

That's not to say that the words must carry the entire message; they don't and they shouldn't, because we receive and retain information best when we receive it through several senses at the same time. But words generally provide a framework, and words are almost always used to describe all the elements involved within business communications.

In this chapter, then, we'll discuss words, and how words are linked together into sentences and paragraphs, scripts, and print copy. We won't discuss basic rhetorical concepts or grammar. We would most certainly emphasize, however, that a certain knowledge of these basics is mandatory for effective communications.

We'll also briefly discuss a new tool for improving writing productivity and creativity—the computer—and especially the computer used as a word processor.

## WHAT MAKES GOOD WRITING?

Good business writing is usually simple writing. Clarity and readability are vital. This differentiates business communications from literary writing, such as poems, plays, or novels.

In part, that is because most novelists, poets, and dramatists want to entertain so that people will purchase their writings. Business communicators, on the other hand, usually have information and persuasion as their primary purposes.

Part of entertainment, for some people, is the act of interpretation—trying to develop a clear picture of what the writer is saying. Although we may enjoy spending time to analyze a poem or a character in a novel, in business we want our information clearly presented, without any possible misunderstanding or a great deal of interpretation.

Any time we, as communicators, make the message more complex than it has to be, we're not communicating effectively. We're forcing the audience to work, to translate communications instead of simply absorbing them. A complex message causes faulty translation of information, because we can't be sure that the audience will share the same experience and education used to create a certain sentence or paragraph.

This is not to say that business writing must be dull; in fact, business writing must often be "brighter" than novel writing because we don't have exceptionally interesting topics. Nor does business writing have to be wordy, filled with adverbs and adjectives that precisely modify every noun and verb. In fact, business writing must often be very concise because we don't have enough of the audience's time to expand upon topics.

The real key to effective business writing is choosing the correct words and presenting them in a manner that delivers them intact to the audience member's mind.

## SOME BASIC WRITING CONCEPTS

Writing for the print media differs from writing for the audiovisual media, but both have some similarities. We'll discuss those similarities before describing the differences between them.

## Use the Active Voice

Almost every form of writing benefits from the use of the active voice. Active voice simply places the "doer" first, then describes "what the doer did." For instance, "She threw three strikes in a row" is written in the active voice. "She" is the doer, and what she did was "threw three strikes." The passive form would be, "Three strikes were thrown by her."

At times the passive voice should be used. For example, suppose that the person doing the action isn't known, as in "All the windows were broken by someone." In this case, it is probably more important to stress that "all the windows were broken" by using passive voice. Or suppose that "The president was hit by the ball." In this case, passive voice emphasizes who "the ball hit," and that is more important than "the ball." In the active voice, "The ball hit the president," the ball is emphasized.

Passive voice often leads to very awkward sentence structure: "An exceptional sales year was expected by all departments, but 10 percent sales were predicted to increase by none of us." This is not only awkward, it is weak. What the sentence is trying to say is "All departments expected exceptional sales, but none of us predicted a 10 percent sales increase." Now the sentence is shorter and stronger, and follows a logical pattern that makes sense to most people.

## Use Conventional and Simple Sentence Structure

Most active sentences are also simple sentences. The subject is placed first, followed by the predicate. The subject is that part of the sentence about which something is being said or done. The predicate is that part which says or does something about the subject. You can determine the subject of a sentence by asking, "Who or what is being talked about?" You can determine the predicate by asking, "What's being done to the subject?" This follows a common-sense pattern—we usually want to know who or what we are talking about before we find out what the subject is doing.

Although it is not always the case, most writing benefits from simple sentence structure. As a case in point, "Most writing benefits from simple sentence structure, although that's not always the case" presents the most important information first and in simple order.

In this example, the dependent clause "although that's not always the case" is given less prominence because it deserves less prominence. It's stating an exception, not a normal state. The concept "most writing benefits from simple sentence structure" is the message we are trying to impart to our audience. The dependent clause just clutters up that thought and will be ignored most of the time.

In business writing, dependent clauses should be converted into sentences if they can't be dropped. Or, "Drop dependent clauses. If you can, convert them into simple sentences." And notice in this example, how important the comma is to understanding. Especially in writing audiovisual scripts where you can't see a comma, converting dependent clauses into simple sentences is often the only way to ensure clarity.

Clarity, after all, is what you are trying to achieve. Simple sentences are clear. Each sentence contains one thought. Each is easy to understand and absorb. Little translation is required.

## Avoid Unusual or Polysyllabic Words

If you write something using polysyllabic words, and find yourself "translating" those words in your own mind, consider translating them to simpler form for the audience. The word "polysyllabic," for instance, translates to "having many syllables." For clarity, the translation is better even though it is longer.

The same thing happens if the words we use aren't immediately understandable to the audience. If we force the audience to translate a word or phrase, they either skip the task or get so involved in the task that they lose the next few sentences. This is especially important in writing audiovisual scripts, of course, because there's no way to stop the show while the audience digs out dictionaries.

Most Anglo-Saxon or English words are simpler than their Norman or French counterparts. Use Anglo-Saxon words like "great," rather than the Norman "magnifique." Also, Anglo-Saxon words are normally more precise compared to similar Norman words; there aren't as many translations possible. Norman words tend to be high on "the ladder of abstraction," with many possible meanings.

The ladder of abstraction has the most concrete word on the bottom rung and the most abstract at the top. For business writing, try to stay as low as possible on the ladder. For instance, don't say "workers" when you really mean "senior supervisors in the data processing unit," and don't say "device" when you mean "electric motor." By staying low on the ladder of abstraction, you again limit the translation required by the audience.

## Organize Material into Small Segments

To see how others do this, scan several magazines or listen to the narration on a network documentary. Notice that the writer usually breaks the words into fairly short sequences, each containing a main thought and just a few support statements to reinforce that thought. He or she will link a few of these sequences together into a larger segment focusing on a slightly expanded idea. Then the writer links several of these larger segments into a slightly larger topic area, and so on until the program is completed.

This "building block" system works for almost any topic. Tie things together into small self-contained paragraphs, and then tie a number of those paragraphs into a subsection. Then tie those self-contained subsections into a section, and finally tie all those self-contained sections into chapters or into a single-topic brochure or pamphlet. Each individual part supports itself, yet all build together to create a substantial construction. Normally, each will conclude with a review of the main topic and provide a stepping-off point to the next small segment.

These stepping-off points, or "transitions," are the nuts and bolts that hold the construction together. They tie one small segment to another, and create a flow to keep the audience moving forward.

This bite-sized approach works for several reasons. First, it organizes material into a logical pattern, making it easy for the audience to follow the reasoning process you've used. Second, many of us have limited attention spans; we get distracted or daydream. By using small segments, we can cut our losses from daydreaming or distracted audience members. And, third, small segments are easier to absorb at one sitting; they give us breathers, at frequent intervals.

## Maintain a Consistent Style

Most of us dislike routine, but routine has a valuable purpose. Something done routinely is done with little cost in thought or energy. We "get into a routine" and find that certain aspects of our life are simpler, if not as exciting. In the same way, our audiences are probably locked into several routine ways of receiving information. If we break that routine, we may have trouble imparting our message to the audience.

If your audience generally receives information presented in one specific writing style, they'll have to work harder if you shift to another style. You'll be breaking their routine. If, for instance, a group of supervisors has completed four segments of a training program that uses simple sentences, many short quizzes, and frequent illustrations, they will not do as well if you present the fifth segment in academic language, with one major test, and no illustrations. You're breaking their routine of learning.

Even worse, don't change style in the middle of a communications program. "Style" embodies all the elements that create a certain method of presentation. If you've been using first- and second-person (I, we, you), don't suddenly shift to third person (he, she, it, and they). If your style has been conversational, don't suddenly become pedantic. If you do, you'll break the audience's routine, and they'll lose your message while they try to re-establish that routine.

Maintaining a consistent style is difficult when writing long communications. One way to improve consistency is to reread everything you've written before beginning the writing process again. Another way is to write a first draft in bits and pieces, but write the final draft in one sitting, if possible. However you do it, do it. If you don't get into your own routine, you'll jar the audience members out of theirs.

## Use the Proper Level of Language

Many researchers have developed formal readability and listening indexes to aid writers in producing materials that are neither too complex nor too simple for a certain grade level. This is fine for textbooks used by young people, but it does not take into account the difference between a 13-year-old eighth-grader and an adult who may have an eighth-grade education, but who has twenty or thirty years of reading and listening experience.

Rather than rigidly adhering to one of the many reading-level formulas to determine comprehension levels, just use common sense. If you scan a sentence or paragraph and see too many polysyllabic words, simplify them. That's all most formulas do—divide the number of words in the sentence, or in a certain number of sentences, by the number of polysyllabic words. If you have too many polysyllabic words, you'll get a high number, or a high grade level required for comprehension.

Keep polysyllabic words to a minimum, especially when the "poly" means three or four syllables in a word. This also punches up your writing quite a bit, since it forces you to use the short words that normally pack a lot of action into a small package.

## Edit Ruthlessly

It's so tough to write well that we become extraordinarily ego-involved in the process. After spending long moments pondering a sentence, slashing that sentence out with a single pencil mark is difficult. But it is far better to die a thousand little deaths as you cut your words than to die one big death in the "bomb blast" from a dull program.

It's realistic to think that you can cut 25 percent of everything that you write, without losing content or style. That last sentence, for example, could have read, "Realistically, you can cut 25 percent of your writing, without losing content or style." We've just reduced a 20-word sentence to 14 words.

Many editing changes work exactly the same way, by making simple changes that improve the readability and retention of writing. It's a lot easier to think of editing in that way than as "butchering" deathless prose, and it's also a lot more accurate. The truth is, very few sentences any of us write are deathless, and those that are leap off the page and fight the editing pencil all by themselves.

## Use Analogies and Other Techniques

Many of the concepts and ideas we must present as business writers have one common problem: they are dull as dirt. Another problem is that we have no common audience demographics; we're trying to reach people of many different age groups, educational levels, and occupational specialties. If we could solve those problems completely, we'd be magicians, not writers. We're not, but we do have some suggestions that can help decrease these problems somewhat.

First, look for common analogies that will be understandable by all audience members. Analogies infer similarities; that is, if one thing is true, then something similar is probably true.

Analogies work because they build on existing knowledge. We know how a football squad works together as a team to reach a goal. Using that analogy makes it easier to understand the abstract concept "teamwork" in a business situation. Also, using analogies referring to things that the audience already accepts as true and worthwhile adds credibility to the new concept; it earns truth and worth by association.

Using analogies also can make your job easier. First, you have an existing vocabulary; the company president becomes the "quarterback" and the effort to get people working together better becomes the "game." Analogies also make visualization easier. There are only so many ways you can show people in offices working as teams—and few are very interesting visuals. But there are many ways to show a football team in action—and most are interesting.

However, not every audience, or every member of a specific audience, will be interested in football or find football analogies interesting and informative. That is why it is important to develop an analogy that will appeal to the entire audience.

Most important, be sure that the analogy you choose actually makes the point you want to make. A football team is made up of a number of specialists who work together . . . and the quarterback's often considered the "most special." So a bowling team or some other grouping of equals might be more effective as an analogy about participative management. Remember, an analogy is effective when the audience not only can identify with the concept you have chosen, but also can infer the new idea from that concept.

Analogies, incidentally, are especially effective for two purposes: First, if the audience is composed of people from a variety of disciplines with a broad demographic range, common analogies can help you speak to every audience member. An engineer may not understand "quality improvement," for instance, in the same way that a clerical supervisor does. One may think of it as reducing the number of bad solder joints made by a robot welder while the other thinks of it as making sure that no files are incorrectly labeled. If you use an engineering example or visual, the clerical supervisor may not relate to the situation. However, if you take a situation totally removed from either engineering or clerical supervision, both groups will understand the analogy and be able to relate the basic concepts to their work life.

Second, analogies are effective when the actual situation is touchy—one of those business situations that are understood but not discussed. At other times you will need to point the finger at someone as a bad example. It is always better if you can remove those situations or examples from actual people or places in your organization. Showing photographs of a football player fumbling a ball, as an example, is better than showing a photo or two of people from your organization making mistakes.

In some situations, it's necessary to go one step beyond analogy—to parody—to make your point. This is especially effective when you have several different messages or concepts to impart, but need some recognizable common thread to tie them all together. A parody is a comic imitation of some familiar concept or idea; it allows you to plug many different concepts or ideas into it.

For instance, a parody of a news broadcast gives you at least three distinct segments—news, weather, and sports. You can present basic information in the news segment, a motivational mesage in the "sunny weather" segment, and suggest an action step during the sportscast.

By using parody, you add humor to communications, and that's almost always sorely lacking in business messages. You're also providing a familar framework for the audience; because they know the framework, they can concentrate on the message.

Parodies are especially effective if you can write, visualize, or narrate programs using recognizable characters. The "Wide World Of Sportswear," for example, provides an excellent opportunity for a writer and narrator to parody the "Wide World Of Sports" television show. Within the "sports magazine of the air" format, many different segments could be used. They can be tied together by parodies of "Howard Hotsell," "Phyllis Gorgeous," "Mahatma Ally," and "Heywood Hale Brown"—all recognizable voices with specific characteristics.

Parody, like other attempts at humor, must be done well, or else done so poorly that it becomes a "parody of a parody." If it is not done well, it will bomb even worse than a straight program. Parody will often work where cartoon characters or other childish attempts at humor will not, because most people believe parody is a sophisticated form of humor. At the very least, it will be different from what people normally expect, and that will help keep their interest.

That is really the only reason to use any special technique—to add interest. Sometimes you can pick one example as an anecdote to illustrate and emphasize a specific concept. For instance, here's how an anecdote can be used as a "grabber" to capture the audience's attention:

> VISUAL OF A PLANT MANAGER, ON-CAMERA, SHOWING SMALL PART IN HIS HAND. HE SAYS:
>
> "This small part was worth $30,000 to our company last year. Not because it worked well . . . but because it didn't work at all."

By picking this example, the writer grabs the audience's attention and makes a statement. Few audience members will leave before they find out why that part cost so much and how it failed.

The grabber, or "narrative hook," is used frequently in entertainment programs. Often a television program begins with a strong action sequence, even before the title or the first commercial. You can use the grabber in business communications, too. One way is to present an anecdote before you present an introduction or background information. Another is to choose a "slice-of-life" approach that dramatizes a real-life situation as a case study for the program. The idea is the same in both cases—add interest by involving the audience in the situation.

There are many other ways of adding interest, and involving the audience in the communications. All revolve around the same basic concepts—find some common denominator for the audience, such as an analogy or parody, or find some interesting anecdote or example that will capture their attention and get them "walking a mile in someone else's shoes."

## SOME DIFFERENCES BETWEEN PRINT AND AV SCRIPT WRITING

Most of us have been reading since our first years in school, but we are still kindergartners in our ability to understand audiovisual messages. That's especially true for people who were raised before AV programs became commonplace. In some cases, these people remember the birth of television . . . because it happened well after their own nativities.

This significant difference is one we must recognize when producing copy for print or AV. We know how to speak "print," but few of us are facile in "AV." It's a foreign language, and we must treat it just as we would a foreign language when producing AV shows.

You learn to speak and to understand AV in the same way you learn to speak and understand foreign languages. By study, practice, and experience. If your audiences have seen several audiovisual shows, or are young enough to have been exposed to AV in school, you can produce a more sophisticated show than if your audience has had no prior exposure to AV. And you, as the producer, should follow the same pattern—start simply and work toward sophistication.

By the way, don't assume that sophisticated means complex. Some AV shows are very complex, but some AV shows are so sophisticated that they appear simple. This is especially true in terms of writing: it's actually easier to write four or five sentences to state a concept than it is to distill that concept into a single phrase or sentence.

That's the secret of effective AV script writing, however; say things in the simplest way possible, yet in a way that will be memorable. The more words the audience hears, the more words the audience has to wade through to reach the major message. If you wade through your scripts first, doing that work for the audience, they'll reward you by retaining your message.

Remember that an audiovisual program is ethereal; each word disappears as soon as it passes beyond the last pair of ears in the audience and each visual fades after it has been seen by the last pair of eyes. So the message must be presented in a form that can be retained without reference to the medium. In print programs, by contrast, you can sometimes assume that the audience will get only a vague idea of the message during the first reading, but will go back to pick up details when it is important to do so.

Fortunately, audiovisual programs have several elements that aid retention. Most obvious, of course, is the use of the visual element—slides, film, or videotape. The use of colorful and well-shot visuals reinforces the verbal message; in fact, sometimes the visuals will carry the entire message, as in cases where the audience members don't understand the language or can't follow the words. This is especially important when the audience includes people for whom English is a second language. They may be too shy or too proud to admit that they understand less of the language than you would expect.

But don't neglect the other elements involved in most audiovisual programs, such as music, sound effects, or the talents of narrators and actors. Black ink on white paper carries no intrinsic emotional content. It all has to come from the words or photographs on that inked paper. Music often does have emotional content, and the correct choice of music can greatly enhance the audience's understanding of the underlying emotion behind your words and pictures. A talented narrator can impart coloration and meaning to the words he or she reads.

Sound effects can also add emotional content to a presentation. But sound effects are even more useful in adding realism and interest. People recall things and events for many reasons, based on many different senses. One of those is the sense of hearing, especially as it relates to distinctive noises. The sound of a machine gun defines that weapon, not the way the weapon looks. By including those distinctive effects sparingly in the soundtrack you can provide far greater impact and retention of your message.

So far, we've emphasized audiovisual programs while talking about the differences between print and AV. However, there are some special considerations about print that should be discussed as well. First, print provides a means of emphasis for one word over another. (AV can do this, too, through narration or special music, but it's often more effective when certain words are made more important through large type or special graphic treatment.) Through the use of boldface type or underlining or special colors and sizing, you can make sure that the audience understands what key words and phrases are most important in your communications.

Print communications can also be produced in a variety of shapes and forms that carry out the theme of the message. A training pamphlet on ladder safety, for example, could include a foldout page showing the correct relationship between the ladder's height and the distance between the wall and the ladder's base. A sales promotion piece on a specific product might use a brochure shaped like that product. In both these examples, the benefit is that the medium itself becomes part of the message, bringing the sense of touch into play.

Perhaps most important, print pieces differ from AV shows in the physical involvement required of the audience. People may become involved in an audiovisual presentation, but people must become involved in a print piece. Sure, they can simply toss the printed material aside and never look at it, but if they look at it, they tend to at least remember a word here or there or recall a picture or graphic. It is entirely possible with any print or AV communications, that no one pays the slightest attention to what's being said or shown. It's far more likely, however, that a person will pick up a print piece and at least scan it—either upon receipt or later—than that a person will ask for another viewing of an audiovisual program.

More and more business communicators are finding that the best way to ensure that their messages are understood and retained is through the use of both print and audiovisual media. This is just common sense—taking the best of both forms of communication. But this creates a special problem for communicators, a problem similar to that faced by athletes who play two sports during the same season. A baseball player may find that he or she is swinging a golf club like a baseball bat, or vice versa, even though the muscle groups and motions are different for each sport.

A writer will normally use a more conversational style for audiovisual scripts than for written communications. AV "forgives" sentence fragments, poor punctuation, and other flaws that glare on the printed page because no one reads an AV script except the writer, approver, and narrator. As long as the audiovisual script sounds correct, it *is* correct. In print, on the other hand, grammar, punctuation, spelling, and construction flaws greatly detract from the message.

This basic difference demands a different approach to writing and editing messages for the two media forms. For AV scripts, it helps to mumble the words aloud to make sure that they sound right and that the sentences or phrases are short enough to be read without gasping for breath. For print pieces, it helps to edit the materials three times: once for overall content, once for unwieldy sentence structure or poor organization, and a last time—often word-by-word—for spelling and punctuation errors or typographical problems. Incidentally, it helps to record your AV narration and listen to it as the audience will, and to photocopy your print material, preferably in the column width and style of the final product, so you're forced to read as the audience will.

Within each medium differences in style are required in order to write effectively for that specific medium. A single-projector slide presentation and a motion picture are both AV media. But most slide presentations are viewed as separate "shots," with narration accompanying each shot, while most films are viewed as "sequences" of many shots, with the narration accompanying that sequence. You write a slide-show script shot-by-shot, providing some transition between each paragraph for organization. You write a script for a film or videotape sequence-by-sequence, not worrying as much about paragraph transitions as you do about major transitions between one sequence and another.

In print, the size of the paper and the number of separate main headings often determine writing style. A dictionary or glossary has a main heading every few lines with no transition between headings. A brochure may have several main headings on each page or panel, and each may be a distinct element without need of transition between elements. A book or manual may have several levels of heads, with each representing a change of thought. A short handout, on the other hand, may be just a compilation of data with no thought given to flow or transition and few headings or other graphic elements.

## THE COMPUTER AS A BUSINESS COMMUNICATIONS TOOL

Twenty years ago, no book on communications would include a section about the typewriter. Two hundred years ago, no pamphleteer's broadside would have discussed pens and papers. But today it's important to devote some time to a machine with the potential to improve your productivity and your writing ability: the computer.

Many of the processes involved in producing print and audiovisual communications programs are repetitive; that is, they are done, perhaps with some modification, on most projects. And repetitive tasks are one of the things a computer does extremely well.

Also, one of the best ways to develop accurate schedules and budgets is by reference to the real costs and times involved in similar projects. This requires you to use a data base and to manipulate that base to give you specific information. Again, data base storage and manipulation are strong points of most computer systems.

You can also access many data bases for information or scan current and past materials produced in a certain topic area. Given the correct type of computer and associated equipment, you can even create graphs, charts, or other computer-generated art based on your own data or imagination. Once these elements are created, they can be stored and retrieved or used as a basis for other computer-generated artwork.

Because computers work so fast and can store so much data, you can keep a running total of time and costs involved in every project and compare it to every other project you have done. In addition, it's very easy to call up past budgets and schedules, giving you some solid information upon which to base future budgets and schedules.

In chapter 8 we'll describe in more detail how computers can actually become part of the communications channel, via interactive programs. For now, let's look at a more common use of computers—as word processors.

## How Word Processors Improve Productivity

It's easy to see how a word processor can improve productivity. In the hands of an experienced user, everything from the first draft to the final copy goes faster because it is done at electronic speed. Instead of laboriously retyping copy each time a change is made, the word processor can make the changes required and retype fresh copy at the speed of light.

This is not extremely important if you are writing a one-page handout or a short script. But it can become important when you are writing and rewriting long scripts or books because word processors allow you to spend your time writing, not retyping.

Some of the other ways word processors can improve your communications process are somewhat less obvious. For example, some typesetting equipment accepts copy from your computer, either via telephone lines or directly from your computer's discs. Rather than typing final copy once at your office, then keyboarding it again for the typesetting system, you do the job only once. This also makes you responsible for the final typing job, and allows you to keep close watch for typos or other errors.

One common cause of errors in typing and typesetting is that the person doing the typing does not understand what he or she is typing. Because the typist is not reading for content, it's easy to drop a word or even an entire paragraph or page. And it's just as easy for you to miss the problem during a cursory review.

That's why a word processor can be especially helpful for communicators who create their own copy acting as their own typists. Many people who use word processing report that they will never step back to a typewriter or longhand because the word processor does more than just increase productivity, it also *improves* creativity.

### How Word Processors Improve Creativity

Many people who write think of writing as a creative act, determining what words to use and what order to use them in to impart a specific message. But there is a mechanical part of writing. The word processor can simplify that mechanical part so you can devote more time to the creative part.

For example, if a person writing on a typewriter accidentally hits the wrong key or begins to type the wrong word or syllable, it's sometimes tempting to try to recast the thought so that an erasure is not necessary. Taking the path of least resistance makes it easier to sit at the typewriter for a few minutes to come up with a different idea than to drag out all the correction devices to fix the error. The result is that the final copy doesn't say what you meant to say.

It's just human nature to take the easy way out. But the word processor isn't human. It's endlessly patient, never bored, and doesn't mind retyping and revising.

The creative release this brings to a writer can be enormous. He or she is free to change anything, right up to the last moment. So there's every reason to look at each word many times, to see if it is the correct word in the correct place. There's no reason to accept anything less perfect than you want it to be.

Also, writing on a word processor is easier than writing with a typewriter. When typing, you must break the flow of thought to change paper, to return the carriage, or to handle the other mechanical parts of the job. The word processor does most of those jobs for you.

Finally, when a microcomputer is combined with a good printer and a flexible word processing program, the business communicator can begin to create products that look very similar to final copy after typesetting. As a result, you can preview the way a specific column width or type style will work before going to the expense of typesetting and printing. In addition, some word processing printers are capable of producing camera-ready copy that looks almost as good as typesetting and that is certainly sufficient for many handouts, brochures, and other print communication.

### Some Problems with Word Processors

The word processor has some drawbacks, especially during the early stages when you are learning how to operate it. For instance, one wrong stroke, just one mistake can lose everything you have written. If you kick out a power cord, for instance, most computers will shut down, and you'll lose anything that wasn't stored to a disc or cassette prior to the power loss. And discs or cassettes can go bad, or can be handled badly. So most people who use word processors learn to make copies, both printed copies and extra computer cassette or disc copies, of everything they do. Without these backups, there's often no way to recover from a one-second mistake that destroys hours of work.

It's also possible to overwrite with a word processor, simply because it is so easy to write on a computer. If a communicator is used to gauging program length by the amount of pages of script or copy, it takes awhile to get used to thinking in terms of word count or of computer files that may be shorter or longer than typed pages.

Learning to use a word processor can also be a frustrating experience and a lengthy one. In addition to developing a feel for a different keyboard, the learner must develop a new vocabulary so he or she can command the computer correctly. Until the learner understands how the computer works and how to make it do specific tasks, the word process may actually cost time instead of saving it. But that soon changes, after training and experience show the best way to make use of the computer's versatility.

## Some Purchasing Advice about Word Processors

The computer revolution is happening too rapidly for any book to follow. So we will concentrate on some general advice, not on specific systems or hardware and software choices. And we will make the assumption that you have some knowledge of basic computer devices and terms, so we will define them briefly, if at all.

One of the first things to consider when buying a word processing system is understanding the difference between "hardware" and "software." A computer is made up of parts such as integrated circuits, video display tubes, and disc drives. These are the hardware elements. But a computer requires software to put that hardware to use. Word processing requires both specialized hardware and specialized software.

Software is the brain of any computer system. Every computer needs "operating system" software to tell it what to do. Without these instruction packages, called programs, the computer is absolutely unable to do anything at all. It needs to be told how to make the components work, what to do when keys are pressed, and everything else required to be an efficient machine.

Also, special instructions are required to get the computer to handle tasks like word processing. These are called "application programs," because they tell the computer how to handle a certain application. One of the keys to being able to use a computer for word processing is a good application program.

A word processing program should allow you to rapidly and easily change margins, add tabs, indent paragraphs, change line spacing, and do all the other things that you can do on a good typewriter. Also, a good word processing program will allow you to manipulate parts of the document by deleting or inserting letters, words, and paragraphs or moving blocks of text from place to place.

One thing to consider concerning software is the type of writing you will do. Not every word processing program can handle audiovisual scripts well. The process of creating two separate columns on the same sheet of paper seems to be beyond the scope of some programs. If AV scripts will be a major part of your work, ask for a demonstration of how the software will handle that aspect of your work. Actually, getting a demonstration is *always* a good idea.

Also get the name of someone to call at the computer store when you find it impossible to re-create the things that looked so easy during the demo.

Some firms combine powerful software and powerful computer systems into dedicated word processors. These tend to be expensive, but very good at one specific task—producing and printing word processing work. However, a standard computer system can also be used as a word processor, if it has the appropriate software and its hardware elements are designed for word processing work.

The computer keyboard and display screen are your links into and out of the computer. You will spend a lot of time looking at that display screen and typing onto that keyboard, so make certain that the computer you choose has a keyboard that feels good and a display screen that is easy to look at. Avoid, for instance, keyboards that use touch-sensitive pads rather than keys. And avoid keyboards that save space by keeping the keys close together. Both types of keyboards will make it difficult to type rapidly and accurately.

Perhaps the best type of keyboard is one that is detached from the rest of the computer. In this way, you can set up the display screen wherever it feels most comfortable and do the same thing with the keyboard.

Video display screens are susceptible to glare, which can create problems for people attempting to view small letters on the screen for a long time. Also, certain combinations of letters and background are hard to read. At the present time, nonglare screens with yellow/amber combinations are popular, as are high-resolution screens which provide sharply focused letters with high contrast.

The crucial consideration, of course, is comfort over time. So it is a good idea, if possible, to rent or borrow a computer for a trial period. Things that are no problem at all in the computer store can rapidly become a problem after an extended bit of typing.

Another consideration that doesn't seem important at first is speed. When you read computer specifications that say one computer operates at an average access time of "25 microseconds" while another operates at "25 nanoseconds," the difference seems insignificant. But the difference between a machine capable of operating in nanoseconds and a slower one operating in microseconds can become very significant when you stop to think about how a computer works.

A computer is not a smart machine. Actually, it is capable of doing only a few specific tasks. All computer applications are made up of these tasks. What makes a computer appear smart is that it can do these tasks so fast that it can do many, many of them in the blink of an eye. So a computer that can do 1,000 operations in a second will appear to be far smarter, and far faster, than one that can do only 500 operations in a second.

What this means to you is fairly specific: Less time spent waiting for discs to whir or for the computer to locate a specific file means less interruption to your work flow and thinking. So a fairly fast computer is helpful for word processing activities, especially since many word processing tasks involve specialized tasks that the computer must perform, such as searching through every line of a document to make sure spelling is correct.

A word processing computer should also have a significant amount of storage space. Computers actually use several different types of storage. One, called "ROM" or "Read-Only Memory," is built into the machine. It is often the storage space that holds the instructions directing the computer's basic functions, like making words appear on the display screen or making the disc drives work. ROM is designed so that it is always available, as part of the permanent computer system.

A second type of memory is called "RAM" or "Random Access Memory." This memory is also typically built into the machine, but it differs from ROM. When the computer is turned off, RAM disappears. This short-term memory is available only after it has been loaded into the machine.

A third type of memory is "outboard storage" through cassettes or discs. Think of these storage devices as being similar to desk drawers or file cabinets. You keep information you need at your fingertips on your desk top. When you don't need something you put it away someplace in a drawer or file. But you want to be able to get it from that file quickly and easily when it is required. Discs are far more commonly used for business communications word processing computers than cassettes because they are faster, hold more data, and are generally more reliable than cassettes. Both cassettes and discs operate in the same way. When you have completed your work on a specific document with the word processing program, you need some way to store it so that it remains intact even if the computer's power is turned off. You store such data on either

# SOME BUSINESS WRITING CONCEPTS

cassettes or discs in the form of digital information, a series of pulses that are either ones or zeros, ons or offs. Through a number of different programs and hardware systems, the computer can translate those digital pulses back into words and commands when you reload the document.

One reason discs are more practical for word processing than cassettes is that word processing documents take up a lot of space. For example, a typical manual chapter may run 20 pages or so, with 250 words on each page. If you think of a computer word or "byte" as equaling a written word, that means the computer disc must have at least enough space for 5,000 words. However, the disc also needs space for the program directions telling it what to do. So we're talking about a large amount of data, even if that data will be moved at computer speed rather than human speed. It takes a certain amount of time to transfer that data into and out of files. A disc system takes far, far less time than a cassette system.

Most word processing systems should have more than one disc drive. That's because one of the most vital tasks you must learn to perform, and perform without fail as frequently as possible, is "backing up" your discs. A backup is a faithful copy of your documents, made by duplicating from one disc to another. Backups can be made with cassette systems or with single disc drive systems, but they are far easier with two disc drive systems. And when something is easy, it gets done more often.

The reason backups are important is that any system is fallible. It's possible to accidentally turn off the computer or to do some strange sequence of commands that causes the computer to go temporarily insane. When either of these events, or several other events, happens, chances are very good that at least some, if not all, of the work you are doing at the time will be lost. If you have a backup, the most you can lose is whatever you worked on since that backup . . . and that's an especially good reason to make very frequent backups when working on important documents.

After you have finished working on these documents, you will probably want to get a "hard copy" of them. This job is accomplished by a printer. The printer works like an electric typewriter that uses computer commands instead of finger pressure on keys. The literally hundreds of printers available for computers generally fall into two categories: "daisy wheel" or "dot matrix." A daisy wheel printer is like a typewriter with an interchangeable type ball or wheel. The name comes from the similarity of the type wheel to a daisy, with petals containing the letters of the alphabet and other alphanumeric elements and the hub being similar to the center of the daisy. These printers work by lining up one of the petals with the correct spot on the paper, then striking the petal with a hammerlike device. This forces the petal against a ribbon, impressing the petal's letter, number, or symbol onto the paper.

Daisy wheel printers are electromechanical devices, using a combination of electronic pulses and mechanical movements to create letters. As a result, they are somewhat slow, ranging from far slower than most good typists to perhaps three times as fast as the best typist. They have one singular advantage over the dot matrix printer. That advantage is that the daisy wheel printer's output looks like typewriting—because it is. So the output is "letter quality."

A dot matrix printer, on the other hand, produces letters and numbers by squirting tiny bits of ink ("dots") out through jet nozzles in a pattern ("matrix") onto the paper. It's the printing equivalent of those light displays on digital watches. When the computer sends a certain signal to the dot matrix printer, for instance the signal that tells the printer to print a letter "t," the printer will automatically spray ink out of only those jets which will create a vertical series of dots up the center of the matrix and then a horizontal series of dots across the top of the matrix. The result will be a number of closely spaced dots of ink that look like the letter "t." The drawback of the dot matrix printer is that letters and numbers are made up of dots, not of solid lines. Some people find dot matrix printouts hard to read if they are used to reading standard typewriting.

Some dot matrix printers support a "double strike" or "letter quality" mode that will fill in some of the spaces between dots, making the printout look more solid. As this technology improves, and as people become more comfortable with the way dot matrix printouts look, these printers will become even more useful for word processing applications.

Dot matrix printers have several advantages over daisy wheel printers. They are far faster and have few mechanical parts to wear out. Also, because each symbol is created out of a specific number and pattern of ink jets, a wide variety of symbols can be produced, including foreign symbols and pronunciation symbols as well as unusual type sizes or styles.

## SOME BUSINESS WRITING CONCEPTS

The authors of this book, incidentally, use both printers. Our letter-quality printer is actually an electronic typewriter with a special computer interface. The dot matrix is a high-speed model. Because the letter-quality printer is so slow, chews up so much carbon ribbon, and destroys so many plastic daisy wheels, it is reserved for the final copy of programs that will go straight to the printer as camera-ready copy or for letters and manuscripts that must look as good as possible. But the dox matrix printer is the daily workhorse, used for all interim printing needs.

One reason to have both types of printers is that many people aren't comfortable reviewing and editing copy directly from a display screen. Review copies can be printed rapidly on the dot matrix, edited just as you would any other typed document, and the revisions put into the document prior to printing it out letter quality.

That brings up an interesting point relating to this modern technology. The truth is that the technology exists for us to do all our writing and revision at computer speeds, but many of us are not ready to do so. Just as it takes some time to learn to go from writing with a pen to writing with a typewriter, so does it take some time to learn how to write with light on a screen. Most people who have taken the time to become comfortable with word processors find it is far easier and more productive than typing or writing by longhand.

Finally, be sure to analyze the computer system you are considering in terms of being "user-friendly." User-friendly means that the system is easy for you to use—it provides bridges, not barriers, to use. Some computer systems provide symbols on the display screen that you can touch to tell the computer what to do. Rather than recall a keyword like "Save," you simply point at a file symbol to tell the computer to save a file. Other systems use software "overlays" so that you can speak to the computer in plain language and get your request translated automatically into computerese. We are nearing a time when we will be able to talk to computers and listen as computers talk to us.

The reason all these things are important is that any computer is only as smart as the person operating the computer. The easier the computer is to use, and the closer it can approximate the way we currently use tools, the more user-friendly it will be . . . and the more useful it will be.

## CONCLUSION

Early in this chapter we asked, "What is good writing?" The answer is that it all depends upon the message, the medium, and the need. We suggest, however, that there are few techniques you can use to make all your writing better.

Writing in short, conversational sentences helps. So does editing to make sentences even shorter and clearer. Keeping a picture of an audience member in your mind as you write, and writing words and concepts that audience members will understand and accept, are also important. But the real key to good writing is to write things the way you like to hear or read things . . . as long as you don't enjoy reading pedantic and unwieldy reports and theses.

# PART TWO
# Production Techniques

## THE ROLE OF THE BUSINESS PRODUCER

For most business communications programs, no individual is given the title and charged with the duties of the producer. But there is a producer... and it is usually *you*. That's because you are the person most involved with the project, with the most knowledge concerning program objectives—and the most to lose. It's actually not that different from the role played by Hollywood producers, although the resources you have available may not put your program in the "blockbuster" category.

A Hollywood producer often allows the "creative types" to handle the day-to-day shooting, recording and editing of a production. That's a luxury you normally won't have as a business producer. Whether the project is a simple print handout or a complex broadcast-quality videotape, you'll be called upon to make a staggering number of decisions.

Within this section, we can't tell you everything you need to know to successfully produce any media program. What we can do is offer some suggestions and some descriptions of typical elements you must be concerned with during production.

In each area of media production, there are some distinctive differences. We've broken production elements into some arbitrary categories: print, audio, photography, and motion media, and interactive or computer-assisted programs. However, the reality of being a business producer is that you can never segment your thinking to focus just on audio or just on photography. Instead, you almost always have to look at the entire program, and how the specific production element you are using will fit into the program's objectives.

## COMPONENTS OF A PRODUCTION

In any type of production—print, audiovisual or motion media (film and videotape)—you always find some common components. The reasons all programs do not look or sound alike is that the producer's talents and budgets ensure that the program does look different from other programs.

However, it is still useful to look at the common elements. Any print production, for instance, will include these main elements:

1. Copy that states a certain message. This includes headlines, body copy, and photo or illustration captions.

2. A graphic treatment that may include photographs or other illustrations, such as line art, drawings, and other artwork. It will always include some concern for margins, type size and style, relationship of headlines and subheads to copy, and similar decisions affecting the overall look of the printed piece.

3. Paper stock and ink/paper color decisions, including decisions regarding paper size and thickness.

4. A presentation and distribution decision that includes binding, delivery, and other publication considerations.

An audiovisual or motion media presentation will include the following elements:

1. A script that includes music choices, visual choices, and words to be spoken by a narrator or actors.

2. A soundtrack that converts the script into reality, including music, sound effects, narration, and voice-overs of people involved in the program's message.

3. A visual compilation composed of actual slides, videotapes, or film, shot on location or in a studio, as well as graphic elements and other "flat art" illustrations.

4. Some means of linking the visuals and audio together so that they can easily be presented to an audience.

## THE EVOLUTION OF A PROGRAM

The word "evolution" is used here because it implies something more specific than "development." It implies a progression, with each step growing out of the step that went before it. Just as a good architectural design evolves out of the site chosen and the occupant's needs, so does a good business communications program evolve out of the need to impart a certain message through a certain structuring of words and images.

You, as the producer of the program, are the master architect. Just as an architect's job begins long before the first foundation hole is dug and continues throughout the process of construction and furnishing, so does your job begin early and continue until the program is finished—and presented. And just as an architect can see his or her visualization ruined by an engineering or construction error caused by poor communications or poor monitoring of the work, so can the same thing happen to an AV or print producer. The solution for producers is the same as for architects: combine a superb understanding of the elements you use with a superb devotion to both detail and the overall picture.

The most difficult thing for a producer to do is visualize the final product. This is also the most crucial part of the job. You need not only to understand in your own mind what the final job will look like, but also to be able to make that clear to other people involved in the project. Over the years, this task becomes easier, and you have more samples to show. But, at first, it's extremely important to state clearly and precisely what you want the product to look like, and to know at least enough about the processes involved in getting that look so that you can explain it to your clients and your production support people.

## DO-IT-YOURSELFER OR GENERAL CONTRACTOR?

Unless you're one of the fortunate few who can do everything well, there are probably some things you do better than others. You may be an excellent writer but have trouble selecting music and mixing an audiotrack that enhances your writing. Or you may be superb at the technical elements of audio but have trouble visualizing things creatively. Know your strengths—and your weaknesses—so that you can produce effectively.

It is possible to put together a media presentation from start to finish with no outside assistance. But it's unlikely that you will want to do that as a regular job. A do-it-yourself carpenter may enjoy building one set of cabinets, or even one home, but he or she would probably not want to do it over and over again. In the same way, you may enjoy all the elements involved in a print or AV production, but some of those elements get pretty tedious when they must be repeated for several projects.

Many business communicators begin by doing the entire job, being do-it-yourselfers. As they gain experience—and as the newness of the tasks wears off—they find it far more productive to farm parts of the job out to specialists. In addition, their experience has given them the insight to see that a specialist can often add far more to a program than can a talented amateur. So they become general contractors, maintaining control over the production, yet hiring specialists to meet specific program demands.

Just as a knowledgeable homeowner can save a great deal of money by being a general contractor when building or remodeling a home, so can a business communicator save money and time by overseeing the work of professionals. In both cases, the best approach seems to be that professionals should be hired for those jobs that are very complex, require many specialized tools, or take a great deal of concentrated effort. Into this category we could place the process of printing and binding, videotape direction and production, programming interactive video presentations (including elements such as replicating discs or videocassettes), and mixing together many different sound sources.

Some other parts of production require little specialized training, few tools, and a lot of patience. Keylining text materials is one of these elements, as is the physical act of assembling visuals and programming presentations. Here it might be more productive to train some clerical support people or other assistants to do the job, with you acting as supervisor. In that way, you can free your time for your most important job—keeping everyone else on track.

Whether you are producing a major media program or a simple slide presentation, it's vital that you take an active role in the production process. That role must be as administrator, as well as a final arbiter of creativity and quality. Each individual working on the project will focus only on those elements affecting him or her—but those collective visions may not be the vision you have of how the final product should look. And, especially with major projects, it's very easy for people to slough off a day or two and miss deadlines. All it takes is a few of these missed deadlines, however, to put you days, even weeks, behind. So you have to watch time budgets as much as you watch actual dollars.

Finally, don't hesitate to feed your curiosity when you begin dealing with professional production people. Ask questions, even "stupid" questions. After all, you're paying for the privilege. Also, every professional you will be working with started once with no more specialized knowledge than you have. In some areas of media production, in fact, the equipment is so specialized that a top pro would have great difficulty walking into another pro's shop and using the equipment available. Most of us have learned how to use specific equipment through a process of trial and error—an apprenticeship.

Most of the staff members you will deal with in any production house will have served a similar apprenticeship in one form or another before gaining the title of professional. So think of the first few productions you do in any medium as your apprenticeship period. This helps for two reasons: It makes you feel better about asking questions, and it will make you feel better if you have to chalk up some misspent time or money to experience.

# 5

# Developing Print Programs

## SOMETHING OLD, SOMETHING NEW

Communicating through print media is almost as old as humanity. Cave paintings, messages scribbled on bark, documents chiseled into eternity on the walls of monuments—all of these are ways people communicated with one another and with those who would follow them on this earth. Throughout our history of using print communications, however, there have been many changes, many innovations that have made this communications medium far more powerful. It is interesting, though, that most of those changes and innovations have been in technology, not in creativity. Now we have high speed printing presses, accurate and simple cameras, computerized typesetting processes, and all the other systems required to rapidly convert words and illustrations into documents that can be read and retained by an audience.

But we have developed over all these centuries of using the print media, a certain set of standards and acceptable design criteria. And those elements continue to work, even if we are using production systems far removed from chisels and caves. That's what we will be discussing in this chapter—not much about the technology of print media, but a great deal about the systems and techniques that work with any form of print media to create an effective program.

## PROGRAM DESIGN

When you first start thinking about a print project, you probably already have some idea of how you would like the final product to appear. You may have already decided upon a general format, such as a one-page newsletter, a booklet or a book. You will probably also have some general guidelines which you must follow. For instance, you may know that the company logo must be in a prominent place, that you need to use four specific color photographs, or that the particular program you are doing must follow a format developed for previous programs in the same series.

So you are really beginning with some ideas. Many aspects of the design process have been completed before you even begin.

One way, incidentally, that you can aid that process is through a "swipe file." This is simply a collection of examples of print pieces that you like and think might someday work for you. If you see a photograph that effectively illustrates an abstract concept, it should go in the swipe file. If you see an annual report that manages to avoid a dull listing of financial facts and figures, pop that in the file.

It's surprising how fast this swipe file fills up; and how useful it becomes later, when you refer to it while developing a program. It will give you ideas concerning the size and shape of the material, what format might work, how color and photos can be used, and how type styles and paper stocks work together.

Don't just collect things you like, however. Also collect those you hate, so you don't make the same mistake. In short, do anything you can to gather actual examples of various print materials. You'll find it enormously effective to visualize what the final product will look like before you've invested a great deal of time and money in preproduction work.

## SOME BASIC LAYOUT IDEAS

When professional designers lay out print materials, they often use "greeking" to simulate body copy. Greeking is simply lettering in a specific type style and size that means nothing. It's usually typeset in Greek or Latin, hence the name, and it is used so that people can get an idea of how a layout looks without getting so involved in the copy that they forget to view the other elements involved.

Now, of course, there are certain type elements that must be considered in light of the words being used. For instance, you don't want a column or two of type to be placed near a picture unless the type somehow refers to the picture. But the concept of looking at the layout without looking at the specific words will help you get an overview of the program. Later, you can make sure that a particular section of type doesn't contradict your layout.

There are a number of rules and techniques for designing print materials. The most basic technique is to simply go with what you like. Few of us are inspired designers who can come up with a truly original design each time we face a blank sheet of paper. But all of us have some intuitive sense of what looks right and what doesn't. So trust your intuition.

You'll find, for instance, that most of the "rules of composition" learned by designers are basic common sense. Concepts like not jamming all the major elements into one corner of the page or being careful to balance illustrations with copy just naturally occur to most people when they begin laying out print material.

You'll also find that most professionals involved in print production have looked at literally hundreds of programs such as yours. They will have many alternatives or suggestions for improvement, if you ask them for help.

### Keep It Simple

If there's any single rule that seems to work for all media production, it's this: Keep it simple and straightforward. If you are designing a multipage booklet, design one page and repeat the basic design on succeeding pages. Not only is this easier for you, it also helps the reader. Just as you don't want to disconcert the reader by changing your writing style, you want to avoid changing your layout style in midstream. Keep it consistent.

One of the best ways to do this is through a "grid" design. As the name implies, a grid is a set of lines that establish boundaries and positions on the page. You'll find grids used in many forms of print communications, including this book. Each page begins and ends at a specific spot and each has the same margins.

Many large corporations set up a grid system for all print material created anywhere within the firm. It becomes part of their corporate identity program, so that their specific audiences learn to expect a certain "3M" or "IBM" look. This is very helpful to designers, although it does set boundaries and limitations for their work.

If you choose to set up your own grid, it's fairly simple to begin by considering the mechanical limitations of the printing process. For instance, most printing processes require a "gripper edge" along at least one side of a page. This edge is used to move each piece of paper into position and to hold it in place on the press. On an 8½ × 11 page, for instance, you may need a ¼-inch gripper edge on one side of the page. For continuity, you'll probably continue that same edge along all sides of the page so things look symmetrical. You may also need space at the top or the bottom of each page for header or footer information and page numbers. And you may need a certain amount of space on the right side of left-hand pages and the left side of right-hand pages so that the pages can be bound together without making it impossible to read information near the center, or "gutter," of the book.

You now have a border around the page. Within that border, you can set other lines and boundaries. For instance, you might decide to use a two-column design. This means that you will split each page into halves. You may decide that the heading of each chapter or section in the material should drop down one-third of the page and continue across both columns. In addition, you might give yourself more flexibility for illustrations by setting up lines that will border pictures or drawings. Maybe you'll give yourself the options of using one-column, two-column or one-and-one-half-column illustrations and setting the top, bottom, and side limits where those illustrations can start and end.

When you have finished these considerations, you have a gridwork of lines. You also have the basic design elements you need to keep the layout simple and consistent. You can ensure that this grid is kept consistent in several different ways. You could, for instance, measure each element on each page of your design to see that it conforms to your master grid. Or, if you have an extensive number of pages to lay out following the same pattern, you could create a transparent plastic overlay of the grid for use as you lay out each page. More likely, you will either photocopy the grid page or have enough grid pages printed up for the job.

# DEVELOPING PRINT PROGRAMS

You should be aware, by the way, that most printing preparation processes "ignore" light, or nonreproducing, blue. So you can draw your grid in light-blue pencil or print it with light-blue ink and the grid will not show up on the final printed piece. (Just so there's no confusion, you *can* use light-blue ink as one of the colors in your final product. That's a different part of the process than creating the camera copy, negatives, or master plates for photocopying.)

The benefits of a grid system or a similar system which makes sure that the layout remains consistent are worth the effort of setting up the grid. For instance, limiting the sizes of pictures or illustrations to one of three or four options allows you to "gang" several shots together during the processes involved in creating print-ready visuals. This is more economical, since several shots can be reproduced at the same time. And you can sometimes save on typesetting costs because all the type will be set to the same dimensions. But, perhaps most important, setting up standard dimensions allows you to make many creative decisions concerning the layout just once, freeing you to concentrate on details during the rest of the layout process.

## Balance

We've all seen things that just "don't look right"; a photograph that contains so much blue sea that the foreground beach or people on the beach appear to be out of proportion, or a person's clothing that has too much of a dark color on top and too little on the bottom. These examples simply illustrate that visual balance is something you must think about if you want your print materials to look right, to be pleasing to the eye, and to be easy to read.

Balance can be "formal" or "informal." You can precisely and consistently measure and place each element on a page so that it is in perfect balance with every other element. That is, you can make sure that you have precisely thirty lines of type in each column and that the total area of two small pictures in the right lower part of the page equals the total area of the large picture in the upper left of the page. That's formal balance, and it's found in a number of print materials.

Informal balance, on the other hand, is making sure things look right, using your eye as a guide and following common sense. You might, for example, have a small picture in the upper right, but a very dominant picture—maybe one including a great deal of red or with a very strong close-up image of a person. To balance that little picture, you may need a much larger picture in the lower left of the page—but a larger picture without the dominant color or subject matter.

All balance, however, depends on how our eyes perceive visuals. This has to do with basic eye movements and with colors and shapes we tend to emphasize or de-emphasize.

Our eyes normally move from left to right as we read or as we view something. And we normally start at the top of the subject we are viewing. As a result, it is best to put the most important thing on the page in the upper left corner, and then give the eye a "clue" as to where to travel next. For instance, if you want the readers' eyes to look at a person's picture in the upper left corner first, and then go to the lower right corner where that person's biographical information is listed, you might want to make sure that the person in the picture is looking to the right and down. Your readers' eyes, then, will follow the path suggested by the subject's eye.

Sometimes you may want to break the rules and put the most dominant element in the center of the page, or in the lower part of the right side. If so, make sure that the material in the upper left (or along any edge, for that matter), is relatively unimportant. Once a person's eye is focused on the center of the page, it is difficult to attract attention away from the focal point.

If the print material you are designing will involve more than one page, you'll probably have "two-page spreads"—materials that will be spread out before they are read. In this case, you have to consider both pages in the spread as one element as far as eye movement is concerned. Avoid placing a strong element in the upper left of both pages, for instance, because the eye will skip from the right to the left page, ignoring what is below the strong element. Position a very strong element top left, and a slightly less powerful element bottom right of that page, then an element of almost equal strength to the one on the bottom right at the top left of the next page in the spread. In this way you are creating a stream of eye flow. What you want to avoid, of course, is any "dams" or "branches" to block eye flow or take it away from the main stream.

When we speak of balance or design, we're not just speaking of illustrations or type. All the elements on a page are part of the design. And this includes elements "left out," such as space between paragraphs or around illustrations. This "white space" is a significant design element. A page with the correct amount of space will be more appealing, and more readable, than one in which elements are jammed together or spread too far apart. When balancing a page, remember that white space can be a strong balancing element because it is a major block of space in one color. So a large, but relatively low-impact, drawing can be balanced by a small amount of solid white space.

## STANDARD DESIGN ELEMENTS

In general, you have four major design elements to consider: Type style and size, illustrations and graphics, placement on the page, and paper and ink.

The actual print elements you will use depend upon the type of project you are doing. If it is a promotional piece, you may use many photographs or large headlines with a great deal of white space surrounding the elements. A detailed report, on the other hand, might use just a few illustrations or photos and have very little white space except where required to separate headings and columns. We'll discuss general concepts, therefore, rather than concentrating on the design of each specific type of print media.

### Type

We'll discuss type styles in detail later. At the layout stage, the most important thing to remember is to use a consistent type face throughout the program, and keep it simple. The exact proportions you use will depend upon the importance you want to give to certain typeset words or sentences; normally you will follow a consistent pattern throughout the piece. As a general concept, you might want to set proportions so that the major headline is always three times the size of body copy, while each level of "minor head" is 50 percent smaller than the major headline. So a one-inch headline will call for a half-inch minor head and a one-third-inch body copy size. (We'll give you more precise information about this later, too.)

At the layout stage, you'll be using approximate values for the amount of copy, number of heads, and similar type-related elements. This is another of those "chicken-and-egg" situations: Do you write and edit all the copy before doing the layout, or do you do the layout before doing all the copywriting and editing—or do you work on both simultaneously?

What seems to work best is splitting the job into three stages: First, write the copy that should go into the piece. Second, do a rough layout to see if there is too much or too little copy. And, third, juggle the layout and the copy to fit the space available and the overall design.

## Illustrations and Graphics

The next major element to consider is the graphic treatment. Will you use photos, line drawings, elaborate artwork, charts and graphs, or a combination of these illustrative visuals? In most cases, if all graphic elements are the same size, the "order of impact" is that a color photograph, will have the most impact. A chart or graph will have the least. Artwork and drawings fall into the middle. As you begin designing, therefore, you should have some indication of what visuals will be used. If you have a stunning photo, plan on using it large on a page. If you have a simple chart that must be run large for readability, position it within the layout so that it becomes the major focus of attention.

If you must use a number of small photographs or illustrations, make sure they are readable and effective. A mountainscape won't be very effective if it is run very small on a page next to several other photos. It needs physical size to encompass the scope of the mountain. So you would be better off choosing a close-up of a mountain wildflower with the mountain out of focus in the background. If the illustration is of people, keep in mind the limit to the eye's ability and the mind's willingness to distinguish between objects. If a person's head size in the finished print piece will be less than the size of a penny, you're probably wasting space.

There's also a cost consideration involved in selecting photos or other illustrations: A large photo or illustration will cost you less than an equivalent area filled with small photos or illustrations. This is because the technical aspects of handling one photo require less time than several photographs. So cost may lead you to use fewer illustrations, but larger ones.

## Placement on the Page

We've discussed placement on the page in some detail earlier, but it is worth some expansion here. Placement becomes a design element in many ways, but the most important is in the adjacency or linking between various other elements. The mind tries for linkages at all times, so it is best to provide clear links when doing a layout. We don't usually expect, for instance, to see a photograph placed so that its top, bottom, or sides wind up in some random relationship to the text beside the photo. Instead, we expect either the top, bottom, or sides of the photo to line up with some edge of the type or we expect to see the photograph bleed off the edge of the page. We don't expect one column of type to start an inch down from the top of the page and end two inches from the bottom of the page, while the adjacent column starts two inches down and ends one inch from the bottom. We expect, in short, that the placement of elements on a page will result in some part of each element on the page lining up with some part of another element on the page.

## Paper and Ink

Finally, ink and paper are part of the design considerations during layout. You may not know precisely which colors of ink you will use nor exactly upon which paper stock the final product will be reproduced. But you should have some idea of how the paper and ink will work together. For example, you should know that the illustrations you will be using require a coated stock or some other excellent paper and that the ink must be laid down thick to make sure the illustrations snap off the page. Keep in mind that shiny coated paper will make white space more prominent while deep ink on illustrations and text will make those elements vibrant and dynamic.

A critical consideration should be the look and feel of the final product. One thing that separates print communications from electronic or photographic communications is that the product can be held. If you want to create an image of substance, you'll probably want to use a heavy paper. If you want to save money and imply that this information should be read and tossed, you may want to use newspaper-quality paper and inks. You may choose from a variety of papers and inks, and you should begin thinking about your options early.

You should also think about how the paper you may use will fold. Will it provide a sharp edge or will the roughness of the stock result in an imprecise fold? Based on this information, you might choose to avoid any design elements that will result in the need for precision near the fold, or incorporate a design element that takes advantage of precise folds.

That's really the concept behind reviewing all these design elements when you begin layout. You want to make sure that you are taking advantage of all the potential available from these elements—and avoiding as many pitfalls as possible.

## THE ROUGH DRAFT OR THUMBNAIL SKETCH

Whether you plan on doing the final design yourself or not, it will help you visualize the final results if you learn to use rough drafts or thumbnail sketches effectively. Since so much of design work is visual, and based upon what looks right in relationship to everything else, any means you can use to visualize those relationships and elements is extremely helpful.

You can do this in several ways. You could, for instance, photocopy many layout pages that have the grid or basic parameters already inked in. Then you could begin to pencil in your layout on these pages, erasing or revising as needed. Or you could begin at an even more basic level, with a thumbnail sketch.

A thumbnail is a miniature layout sheet. For a multipage brochure or training manual, each page might appear as small as your thumbnail, hence the name. The basic purpose of thumbnails is to put each page in relationship to all the other pages. In this way, you can begin to pattern your design and to see how the pages relate to each other. You can tell, for instance, that you are relying too much upon a strong upper-left visual or that some sections are sparsely visualized while other sections are too heavily visualized.

The thumbnail is especially helpful when you are dealing with a specific number of pages or a specific type of fold. There are certain restrictions and procedures required for various printing processes and print material configurations. At the rough layout stage, you often need to be aware, for example, of which pages could most cost-effectively include color or which final pages will actually be adjacent to one another when a large sheet of paper is folded. By carefully juggling the pagination plan used by the printer, you can make full use of color on every available page, if you start at this rough-draft stage to make sure that your photo selection, copy size, and design will result in the correct location for color elements. In the same way, you should think about how the paper will be cut or folded. Again, this will affect the way in which you design the piece. Make sure that things which must run next to each other do, in fact, end up next to each other when the final product is folded or collated.

Also, if you are not going to do the final layout yourself, the rough or thumbnail becomes your main form of communication to the designers and printers with whom you will be working. You'll find that it is far easier to show them what you mean through this format than it would be to write up the directions. Also, it's a lot harder to misinterpret a drawing than it is to misinterpret a statement like, "I want the picture on the left to line up with the picture on the right."

The thing you should consider at this rough-draft stage is the overall look of the material. Place the rough or thumbnail several feet away from you and view it as an entity without words or pictures—just blobs of shading. If there appears to be a good balance, you probably have created a good design. You may find, instead, that something doesn't appear quite right. If so, you've just found a problem at the earliest—and cheapest—stage.

## WORKING WITH TYPE

After you are happy with the design, it's time to get precise, to begin final layout. In most cases, you'll begin this precise step with a very imprecise juggling process. You'll start by guesstimating how much copy you have and how much space that copy will take based on the size and type selected. Then you'll determine how much space is left for illustrations and white space. Finally, you'll start making trade-offs between size and number of illustrations and size and amount of copy until you have the right fit.

## Typewriters Versus Typesetting

The method you use to present final copy depends upon both budget and objectives. Professional typesetting is expensive, but it usually looks good. Typewritten copy is inexpensive, and erratic in effectiveness as a print element. You'll make your choice based on how much you can spend, how important it is that the type appear perfect, and the number of copies required.

We recommend typesetting whenever it is feasible. That's because we've found that it saved both time and money in the final analysis. To understand why that's true, contrast typewritten copy with computerized typeset copy of the same material.

You start in the same place for both methods. That's with rough copy that has been typewritten or handwritten double-spaced on sheets of paper. You will have edited the copy and be fairly certain that this is the way you want the final words to read. And you will have already specified the size and column width and other needed data concerning the final type.

Now you hand the copy to a typist. He or she makes sure that the typing element is clean and that a fresh carbon ribbon has been installed. Using plain photocopy paper or, better yet, special extra-white heavyweight "repro" paper, the typist will begin typing the material onto the paper. (Avoid bond paper with visible watermarks or a speckled finish that may show up in the reproduction.)

The typist is limited to certain type sizes and styles, with the variety dependent upon what's available for the particular typewriter used. The typist must correctly set the typewriter controls for a consistently dark carbon ink impression on the paper. Finally, the typist must be extremely careful not to make a mistake, especially not in the middle of a sentence or paragraph because that would involve expanding or contracting the space used. The reason is that the method of correction can leave a residue that could be picked up as a smudge by the printing process. So the typist may have to go back and retype the entire paragraph or entire page.

When that typewritten camera-ready copy is sent to the printer or taken to the photocopy machine, the print quality is entirely dependent upon whether the typewriter made consistent impressions and how black they are. A weak impression on a light ribbon will result in poor contrast on the final printed piece, and may even make the piece unreadable. If the typewriter happens to have cracked or damaged letters, those letters will appear cracked and damaged on the final copy.

Incidentally, one benefit of the word processor is in this area. With a good printer, a word processing system can consistently and precisely produce final copy that will be satisfactory for many business communications programs. Because it is so easy to reprint a page with a word processor, correction problems do not exist.

In contrast, when using a typesetting system you could mark up that first typewritten version to your heart's content. You can add pages, subtract lines, or do whatever you want to do to the page. As long as you follow the standard copyediting and proofreading symbols, the typesetter can work with your copy. (These symbols are found in most dictionaries and a number of journalism books or are available from most typesetting houses.)

You may select a type style and size from a wide variety of available fonts. In most cases, you can specify any size you want, from two- or three-inch heads to minute footnote copy. And you can specify precise column widths and methods of justification.

Justification deserves further explanation. A "justified" line of type has an even margin on both sides, like a newspaper column or this book. An "unjustified" line will have columns that are flush on only one side, but ragged on the other. Here are some examples:

This is a paragraph with a justified left margin.
It is easy to read and easy to typeset. This is
the most common format for type.

This is a paragraph with a justified
right margin and a ragged left margin.
It is difficult to read.
Although it is easy to typeset, it
is often difficult to type.

This is an example
of a centered paragraph.
This is not used very often.

And this is an asymmetrical paragraph.
That means that no predictable
pattern is used in the justification and placement
of lines.

These are difficult to read
and disruptive to
the
reader.

With typesetting equipment, all of these methods of justification are possible. Also, you can often change your mind after you've seen one method. All it requires is a few simple computer commands to reformat the type. The same feature, by the way, is possible with many word processing computers. It's a good feature to look for it you intend to create final copy on your own word processing printer.

In a computerized typesetting system, you're essentially using a glorified word processor with a lot of options. All the copy is converted to computer data and can be easily changed with a few simple formatting programs. Computerized equipment usually doesn't add mistakes to the process, and it is easy to fix any mistakes made. The computerized typesetting system can also frequently "handshake" with your word processing system. This means that you can create final, revised, checked, proofread, rerevised copy on your own machine, then simply send the final disc to the typesetter or even deliver the text via telephone lines. So you can correct all the mistakes yourself, lowering the expense of typesetting.

Finally, the finished typeset product will reveal dense black letters on very glossy paper called "galleys." The density of letters, letter quality, and paper/letter contrast will be as good as you can get. When the typeset copy is finally printed or photocopied, the results will be excellent.

To determine if typesetting is worth it for your application, just calculate the cost per hour of a typist (adding in fringes and expenses) plus the cost of typewriters, ribbons, paper, and similar equipment or materials. Subtract that from the cost of having the same copy professionally typeset. You may find you are actually saving money, and you most certainly will find that you aren't spending as much as you thought when you first got the typesetting bid.

However, even if you cannot afford to typeset everything within a business communications program, you can still improve the look of some jobs by judicious use of various professional type styles and systems. For instance, you can buy press-on lettering pages in a variety of type styles, ranging from standard popular text type to unusual and offbeat specialty types. It's rather time-consuming to press each letter into place, but the results look very professional for headlines and other important lines of type.

You can also have headlines and similar important type typeset. This is especially effective if you have the type set in a style similar to that of your typewriter.

## How to Size Type

When you first begin working with print, especially with typesetting, throw yourself on the mercy of a good typesetter. Get some advice about how to determine the correct size and style of type for a given objective and how to fit it into a given space.

Start by understanding how type is measured. There are two basic measurements—the "point" and the "pica." There are 12 points in a pica, and 6 picas in an inch. So type that measures one inch in height is "72-point type." Within that 72-point type you'll have 6 picas. You can use a special ruler called a "pica stick," which is sold at art supply stores, to determine how many picas will fit in a given space. On a sheet of 11-inch-deep paper, for instance, there are 66 picas from top to bottom, or 72 × 11 = 792 points. If you were using a typewriter-sized type, in 12-point size, you could fit 6 lines or 6 picas per inch (because 12 points equals one pica or 1/6 of an inch). On the entire page, you could fit 66 lines of type.

Next, determine line width, or column width. Again, you'll use the pica, with 6 picas per horizontal inch. So a column that is two inches wide would be a 12-pica line. A column six inches wide would be 36 picas.

Given those two measurements, you can specify type sizes. If you are working with a standard 8½ × 11 sheet of paper and want to have a one-inch margin on all sides, the available space is 6½ inches wide by 9 inches deep. In picas, that's 39 picas wide by 54 picas deep. If you jammed the type together, you could get 54 12-point lines on the page, each 39 picas wide.

In practice, you won't jam the type together. Instead, you'll use spacing between lines. This spacing is called "leading," recalling the time when most type was set in lead molds with solid lead spacers separating lines. It's typical to have leading equal to 20 percent or so of the total line height. So, a line of 10-point type would have two points of leading, making the total line height 12 points. This is specified "10/12" for the typesetter, and it simply means that the typesetter will put two points of space between each line of 10-point type. If the type is too far apart, the lines are harder to keep track of when reading, and space is wasted. So the 20-percent rule helps, regardless of type size; you might use 72/86 for major headlines and 36/42 for subheads. As is often the case, your eye will be the best judge of what spacing looks right. (By the way, this book is set in 11/13 type.)

Of course, you count the leading when calculating how many lines will fit on a page. So a line of 10/12 type is counted as a 12-point line. And, to calculate the number of lines per section or chapter or program, you'd simply multiply the number of pages by the number of lines per page. But you have to add a little fudge factor to account for special lines, called "widows." Widows are those very short one-or two-word lines that result when a sentence doesn't end on a normal line. In most cases, you try to avoid having widows at the start of a page, so you keep a little extra space at the end of a page to handle an extra widow line.

In some designs, the space between paragraphs is equal to two lines of type in the type size being used (this book, however, is set without space between paragraphs), so a page of copy set in 10/12 type will have 24 points of space between paragraphs. All of this space must be considered when calculating the number of lines available.

Next, determine how many characters will fit on a standard line. A character is any letter, numeral, punctuation mark, or space on the line. Most type-style books (and all typesetters), will give you a count per pica for their type. You can also determine it by counting several sample lines of type, then dividing the average number of characters per line by the pica length of that line.

Actually, calculating the number of characters per line is more difficult than it may seem. That's because not every character is the same width. Some letters, like "M" and "W" are wider than the average, while others, like "t" and "i" and "f" and "l" are narrower than average. So you normally count wide letters as 1.5 and narrow letters as 0.5. This gives the three-letter word "the" a count of 2.5 characters, while the four-letter word "meow" has 6 characters.

Based on that information, count the characters in this headline:

## PROFITS SHOW UPWARD TREND

You'll find that it has 25.5 characters. That's including the spaces between words. Suppose you are using 72-point headline type, with a character count of six characters per horizontal pica. You must have a column width of more than four inches (24 picas) to set this head on one line.

When you are trying to determine the amount of space required for a certain amount of copy, you'll almost always use approximations. You might know that you normally get 250 words per double-spaced page of copy and that you have 10 pages of copy. That's 2,500 words. If you further guesstimate that the average word has five characters and that each word is followed by a space, you now have 1,250 letters and 250 spaces, or 1,500 characters per page. Ten pages means 15,000 characters. If you are using a type style and size that give you 20 characters per 12-pica line, you know that you need 15,000 ÷ 20, or 750, lines to hold all those words. If you're getting 50 lines per page, that means you'll need 15 pages to fit the copy. And don't forget the necessary fudge factor for paragraph spaces and widows.

But here again, one of the beauties of computerized typesetting shows up. Suppose you miscalculate, perhaps by writing copy with very few paragraph breaks or writing copy with a lot of "M" and "W" characters. Your sizing might be as much as a full two points too big or too small for the space. Although you try to be more accurate than this because any change costs money, you can tell the computer operator to reset the type one size different from that specified. (Tell a typist to change from pica to elite and retype, and see what happens.)

Be aware that you can change the number of characters per line in a couple of different ways. One that we've already discussed is justification. If you allow the typesetter to hyphenate words as required so that every line is crammed with as many characters as possible, you'll get more words in the same space than you would get if you carefully spaced words so that each line has a solid margin. You can also close up the spacing between words and between letters to save space. Conversely, you can use "proportional" spacing to reduce the number of words on each line. Proportional spacing means that the spacing between each character is adjusted so that the letter looks balanced, not just placed a measured distance from the previous character. In the same way, you can proportionally space each line so that the lines are all the same size (justified left and right). You'll have some lines with a lot of space between words and some with just a little space between a few words, but the overall effect should be to expand the amount of space used by the type.

### Type Families and Styles

You should ask the firm that does your typesetting for a type-style book. This book gives you a complete set of sample lines set in every typeface the typesetter has. You can also buy type-style dictionaries from art supply stores. These will include most of the type styles available from all sources throughout the world. Using these books, you can choose from many options for each print project you have.

You may, in fact, find there are too many options. So it might help if we suggested some ways to limit the choices. First, you'll normally want to select either a "sans serif" or a "serif" type face. Serif faces have extra lines on the letters, like the text of this book, which is set in Caledonia type. (Note that the heads are a sans serif type, Optima.) And then you'll want to choose either condensed, italic, expanded, bold, or medium. In general, for most business communications, you'll be wise to avoid novelty types or script that looks like handwriting or calligraphy.

If you want variety in the type, such as when you want to emphasize something or signal a change in thought, you should add variety by changing type size or by using a variation of the major type face. In design terms, that's called staying within the same "family" of type. So you might use Helvetica Bold for headlines, Helvetica Medium for body copy, and Helvetica Light Italic for special emphasis items. You wouldn't use Helvetica Medium for body copy, but then choose an elaborate Gothic style for headlines and handlettering for emphasis items. If you really want to call attention to some copy, one way to do so while staying within the same type family is by distorting the type. Some phototypesetting systems can bend, twist, expand, or condense type into special shapes without losing legibility or the basic type style.

## DEALING WITH PHOTOGRAPHS AND OTHER GRAPHIC ELEMENTS

Many of the techniques and ideas we will discuss in this section are just as applicable to other forms of illustrations as to photographs. But we will discuss them here as they apply to photographs since photographs tend to be the most common illustrations used in print materials. We've already talked about some placement considerations involving eye movement and balance. Now we'll concentrate on sizing and preparing the graphic elements for printing.

### Sizing Illustrations

When you work with illustrations, you need a sense of proportion—in more ways than one. You need to think about how strongly the illustration should be played and how it will fit into the rest of the layout. You also need to know how the illustration can be proportionally increased or reduced until it fits in the spot allocated for it.

There are three main ways to size illustrations: First, you can use a proportion wheel. This inexpensive device is like a slide rule. It allows you to plug in two or three dimensions and read out all the other information you need to accurately fit an illustration into the space available. You could measure the length and width of a photograph, for instance, then measure the width available for that picture on the page. You might get figures such as 5 inches by 7 inches for the picture and 3 inches available in the new column. You can then use the proportion wheel to determine how many column-inches deep this 5 × 7 picture will be when you reduce it to 3 inches wide. The wheel will also automatically give you a percentage, such as 45 percent, that tells the printer how much to reduce the original photo while shooting it for printing.

You can do the same thing through algebra. In this case, the formula is: The original height/original width is proportional to new height/new width. So $5/7 : x/3$. By solving for $x$ ($x = 3 \times 5/7$), you can determine the new height of the image.

And you can do the same thing through geometry. You simply trace a diagonal line from lower left to upper right corner of the original artwork. Now you measure along the bottom edge of that picture until you have the new width dimension. By going up to the diagonal line and moving over to the vertical dimension, you can then measure the new height of the picture.

What you are doing in all these cases is manipulating the size of the illustration without changing the proportion of the illustration. And this is an important concept, as you'll see the first time you try to fit a horizontal illustration into a vertical space. You can make the illustration bigger or smaller, but you can't make something that is essentially a long narrow visual into a square or into a broad image. You can, however, try various cropping options to see if you can take a portion of the illustration rather than the entire illustration.

Cropping sometimes allows you to make a long narrow image out of a short wide image. You simply enlarge one part of the image. Instead of taking an entire 5 × 7 horizontal photograph for the illustration, you simply take a 1-inch by 5-inch vertical slice out of the shot. Of course, enlarging that small a portion of the picture will sometimes result in a fuzzy, grainy picture. But it may be the only alternative available to you if you are stuck with a specific space that must be filled with a specific photograph.

### Selecting the Correct Type of Illustrations

When deciding upon what illustrations to use, there are several factors which must be considered. They all cluster around one central consideration: Which methods of illustration that are within the budget will fit the program objectives and the printing process and the paper and ink chosen? This is one of those areas where some experience is vital; you have to know what the process and materials will do to specific forms of illustrations, and you won't know that until you see the final product.

A top-quality color photograph, for instance, may seem an ideal centerpiece for a handout, even if the photo will only be seen in black and white. However, the process of converting that color photo to black and white could well destroy its impact. Further, unless the handout will be printed by an expensive process, chances are the photograph will appear as a muddy, fuzzy blob on the page. In this instance, it would be better to create a simple line drawing; although the line drawing may appear to have less impact when

# DEVELOPING PRINT PROGRAMS

viewed side-by-side with the color photograph, it will have more impact when viewed as part of the final product.

To make an intelligent decision concerning the best sort of illustration for a specific application, you have to have a fairly good knowledge of the processes used to convert original art and photography into materials that can support the printing process. To understand that, you need to understand the printing options available.

The least expensive of all modern printing processes is photocopying. That's because no interim materials are required. You create a clean original copy, then place it in the machine. It becomes your "printing plate." Of course, there are many limitations to this process. Even if the photocopier you intend to use supports color, the color you will get from this process can't match that from other printing processes. And the photocopy process tends to create a lower-contrast duplicate; that is, something that is solid black against white may be photocopied to dark gray against a very light gray. Perhaps most important of all, many photocopy devices demand an original that is the same size as the duplicates required or at least fairly close to the same size.

Photocopiers also handle photographs and other nonline illustrations poorly. They are basically designed to reproduce lines, whether those lines are lines of typewriter type or lines on a chart or drawing. "Continuous-tone" materials, such as photographs or artwork, won't reproduce well unless special work is done to convert the continuous tones into dots or lines.

Even if this special work is done, the process of photocopying normally won't result in the same quality of illustration possible with other processes. So, if illustrations are an important part of the project, plan on printing by a different method.

The first step up from photocopying is printing with paper plates, using an offset process. You can think of it as a version of the process used to transfer an impression from a rubber stamp to a piece of paper, although there is a significant difference. That difference is that the plate—the device used to convert the material you want to print to material that the printing process will easily accept—is not made up of raised letters, as is the case with a rubber stamp. Instead, the plate uses the principal of chemical differences between oily ink and water to make sure that ink adheres only to those areas on the plate that are covered with words, images, or other things that should be printed. At the least expensive stage, as we have indicated, plates are often made of heavy paper. In more expensive processes, the plates may be rubber or metal. The differences are primarily in durability over long print runs.

All the lines, dots, letters, and numbers are converted into very slightly raised bumps on the plate. (This corresponds to the rubber stamp.) When ink is applied to the plate, it sticks to the bumps. When paper comes into contact with the plate (or with a roller assembly that takes the ink off the plate and puts it in correct proportion onto the roller), the paper will be inked in the same spots and in the same density as the original plate.

A problem occurs with some illustrations that are not composed of simple lines and dots but instead are composed of a continuous series of shadings and tones. The precision possible with this offset process is not high enough to allow the illustration to be converted to the printed page with any level of clarity and resolution.

The continuous tones and shadings of the illustration, artwork, or photograph have to be converted into lines or dots that are not continuous, but broken into a pattern. Otherwise, there's no way for the ink and printing plate to differentiate between levels of shading. You can think of it as the difference between sifting flour with a flour sifter and simply dumping flour out of a can. With the sifter, you are able to control the flow of flour so that various lump sizes are allowed to pass through. Without the sifter, the flour is simply poured out of the can, with no discrimination between sizes.

This conversion is done through a screening process. The original drawing is photographed through a transparent screen. The result is exactly the same as looking through a screen at the outside world. The closer you get to the screen (or the coarser the screen material), the more the outside world looks broken up into separate bits.

The screen breaks continuous tones up into dots. Tones that are very dense are translated into areas that have a lot of dots. Tones that are very light translate into areas that have very few dots.

You can envision the result. Areas that have a lot of dots will have a lot of ink on them. Areas with few dots have far fewer areas to accept ink. Now the printing process will reproduce the tones in the original line art.

## DEVELOPING PRINT PROGRAMS

Further, the finer the screen, the more variations that are possible. To check this for yourself, look very closely at an illustration in the newspaper (coarse screen) and an in expensive magazine (fine screen). You'll see that the dot pattern is far more detailed in the magazine. You could count the number of dots per inch, if you'd like. But take our word for it. You'll find about 65 lines per inch in the coarse-screened newspaper and about 120 lines per inch (or more) in the fine-screened magazine.

What all this means to you is simple. You can't just slap a photograph or a continuous-tone drawing down on a piece of paper and expect it to print well. Instead, you have to take an intermediate step to make the illustration "camera-ready."

This gets somewhat confusing because the interim process required to get something camera-ready also involves a camera. Basically, you photograph the illustration or photograph through the screen. At the same time, you can reduce or enlarge the illustration to fit the space allocated by your layout. Then you take that screened print and place it on the final layout sheet along with type. (Because type is made up of lines, it doesn't need to be screened.) Then you often photograph the entire thing again, creating a final printing plate.

The object of all this discussion is to explain why it is important to understand the limitations of each printing process when choosing illustrations. Unless you plan on spending the money to create a fine-screened interim material (called a "screen print" or "halftone"), there's no sense in planning on using top-notch photographs. And if all the illustrations you plan to use involve line art, you may not need to spend money on specialized printing operations. Instead, you can go with a less expensive process using few intermediate steps.

When you add color to the equation, costs increase geometrically. That's because you are now dealing not only with differences in shading, but also with differences in the shading of each color. So you end up with several interim steps.

Two types of color are used in print work: One is called "flat color." In flat color, you simply state that this area of the work will be Color A, that area will be Color B, and so forth. You could say that headlines will be red, body copy brown, illustrations will have green lines and blue borders. Your choice is unlimited. Well, actually, there are limits—money and space available on the page for various colors.

The second type of color is called "four-color." This is the process used to accurately reproduce color photographs or drawings. It's called a four-color process because just four colors are used to reproduce the entire spectrum of colors possible. This is accomplished through a filtration technique that separates any image into four color ranges.

Let's take a simple example: a photograph of a lush golf course under a deep blue sky. On the course, golfers are wearing yellows and reds.

The process would begin with the same sort of steps used to convert a black-and-white illustration into a screen print. You'd create a black-and-white screened separation negative. Then you would photograph the same scene through a filter that allows only those elements which are cyan to pass through to the film. (If that doesn't seem like a common color, don't worry. It is a common color in print work, because it is a primary color that encompasses about one-third of the color spectrum.) You'd do the same thing with the other primary colors, magenta and yellow. By carefully registering each shot, so that all the elements line up, you will end up with all the elements within the original photograph separated into their component primary colors. If you look at each of these separations, you'll be able to see that primary color. You might, for instance, look at the blue (cyan) separation. You'll see some totally clear areas, such as where the golfers' clothing includes no blue at all. You might see some light shaded areas, perhaps where the Kentucky Blue Grass on the greens and fairways has a bluish hue. And you'll see some dense areas of sky where the blue is very heavy.

During the four-color printing process, each piece of paper will pass through four different press plates. That's one for each primary color and one for the black-and-white original separation, because everything has some amount of white and/or black in it. At the conclusion of the process, the original photograph will have been reconstructed, with all the shades intact. (If you want to see an example of this process . . . and a bad example . . . scan the newspaper for awhile until you spot the printer's nightmare—a color photograph printed with one of the separations out of register so that the various ink passes don't end up in the same spot.)

Flat color, incidentally, also involves multiple passes through printing plates. The place you save money on flat color is in the separations. Because you are specifying color of a specific tone, and not expecting it to look true to life, all you have to do is create a printing plate with nothing but headlines on it. Then all the headlines will come out in a selected color. You're avoiding the separation costs and that additional step in the process.

## PAGINATION AND FOLDING

Pagination refers to ways in which the printer lays out pages of your project for printing so that they fit on the press in the way that will let them be printed most economically in terms of paper size. Let's suppose that you want to create a training manual that is 8½ × 11 inches in page size. One way to print this manual would be on individual sheets of paper, each 8½ × 11. This means that each page requires a separate printing plate, a separate print run, and, if color is used, separate print runs for each additional color of ink.

There is an alternative: Use a larger paper size, so that several pages can be run at the same time. The key is to choose a paper size that will result in the least waste of paper and to paginate the work so that similar pages are run at the same time.

Your printer will be able to tell you which standard paper sizes are readily available, but one that is almost always around is "book paper." This comes in several standard sizes, such as 23 × 35. If you want an 8½ × 11 final product, this 23 × 35 sheet of book paper will print eight pages at a time (four across, each 8½ inches wide, for a total of 34 inches, and two deep, each 11 inches, for 22 inches).

The actual eight pages placed on each plate for printing depend upon the total number of pages in each manual and the method used by the printer to cut, bind, and print two sides of the pages. But you'll usually find that each group does not include adajcent pages.

What this means is that you can select certain pages to contain, for instance, two-color or four-color illustrations. Then any page on the same printing sheet as those selected pages can also include color with very little additional cost to you. So if you know that you must include a full-color picture on the center page of a booklet, you can find out where that center page will be in terms of pagination and also include color on the other pages printed at the same time.

Conversely, you may find that the cost of adding color to a page will be prohibitive, because it falls on a pagination schedule that includes all one-color printing except for that page.

It becomes, as you can imagine, a real challenge to make the best use of color. You do it with thumbnail sketches, and with a knowledge of the pagination available on the particular printer's press and paper size chosen.

That's also why you should shop around a bit when choosing a printer. Sometimes a large shop can give you a far better price than a small shop, simply because they can run many pages at the same time. As a side benefit, you may be able to run color on several more pages because several more are included on each sheet.

Pagination is also an important consideration when you are thinking about how the final product will be folded. Folding is reserved for short print pieces, of course, because the number of folds involved in a project of many pages would be prohibitive. But folding can save money for these short pieces because it involves less hand work and fewer steps than many binding methods. For instance, a binding method called "saddle stitching" involves nothing more complex than putting staples into the pieces of paper. Typically, you'll use about three staples per unit of bound material. So each volume must be printed, then each piece of paper must be cut, then the pages must be collated into the correct order, then a cover page might be added, then the book will be brought to the saddle-stitching machine and three staples will be put in place.

Contrast this to a folded piece. First the sheets of paper will be printed, then they will be folded into the correct form. That's it. Two steps.

There are two basic ways to fold paper. The first method is a parallel fold. This fold runs parallel to any previous fold, such as when you put two folds into a sheet of stationery to fit it into a standard business envelope. You'll see this type of fold used on many brochures; in fact, an 8½ × 14 or 8½ × 17 brochure is often called a "three-fold" because it fits into a standard envelope size with just three parallel folds.

The second type of fold is called a right-angle fold. You fold each new fold in the opposite angle to the last fold. So you could fold an 8½ × 11 sheet in half, to 8½ × 5½, then fold it in half again, to 4¼ × 5½. You are making the same number of folds that you would use in a two-fold parallel-fold application (like a letter), but the result is a different shape.

The important message within this section is that the mechanical limitations and considerations involved in screen prints and illustrations and folds and paper size and pagination—and a dozen or so other things we have not discussed—can have a great affect upon the creative possibilities you have. That's why we have discussed them before spending time on some basic creative concepts that relate to print materials.

## CREATIVE CONSIDERATIONS

Under this general heading, we're going to discuss some things that don't fit into any other categories, yet can strongly affect the effectiveness of your print product. These include color selections, type of illustrations, format and size, and similar decisions.

### Color and Format Choices

As a general rule, the concept that you should go with what you like still holds true. But you should also consider what the audience will like . . . and how the audience perceives various materials, formats, and color choices. For example, it's not accidental that restaurants are often accented with red and that restaurant menus tend to use red covers. Red has been found to be a color that encourages appetite. Nor is it accidental that most annual reports look similar to one another. By following an accepted format, the firm is showing that it understands what is expected of a business document.

What we're really talking about here is the psychology of media production. In some cases, it's good psychology to create something completely different—a training manual that looks like a comic book or a brochure die-cut to the shape of the product it is selling. But in many other cases, it's smart to build upon the work done by others, creating media materials that are similar in format and appearance to other materials designed for the same purpose.

The *Harvard Business Review* is a prime example of this latter concept. If you are designing a case study for executives, you probably want them to treat it as a serious and useful business exercise. So following the format of a respected business journal's case studies is a simple way to lend credibility to your work.

You could also emphasize the importance of the print material through your choice of color. A print piece using a "classic" color combination such as light-brown paper, deep-maroon type and gold accents will be perceived as more important than one using garish colors or pastels. To pursue this idea just a bit further, you might also want to choose colors that have a special meaning to a special group; in Minnesota, for instance, a bright purple color might appeal to sports-oriented groups who are fans of the Minnesota Vikings.

You probably already have a pretty good idea of what effect certain colors have on you or on those who make up your normal audiences. Black is normally a somber, serious color; white is equally formal, yet not as somber as black. Reds and greens are festive; grays are conservative. Pastels are restful and soothing; primary tones are vibrant and exciting. There's been a lot of research on color, but all of it really comes down to common sense: A color that makes you feel a certain way will probably make most people feel that way . . . unless it is a color which you specifically associate with an event or a person.

When you are choosing color combinations, one important consideration is contrast and legibility. You'll frequently see advertisements or promotional communications that use "reverses," where type is lighter than the background color. But you'll rarely see reverses used for communications involving long stretches of copy. That's because while the impact of large dark areas is useful for attracting attention, it makes the product very difficult to read. Also difficult to read are printed pieces in which there is little contrast between copy and background, as when something is written in light-red ink on a light-blue background.

The best way to improve legibility is to use a very light, very plain background and very dark, good-sized lines of copy or illustrations. White paper with black ink, obviously, is the extreme case. But the same legibility occurs with any very light background contrasted with any very dark foreground. The difference in contrast is important.

Also, you can improve legibility by making sure that the type of paper effectively reproduces the material you want to communicate. Newsprint absorbs ink, making it fairly difficult to get sharp lines of text or sharp edges on illustrations. As a result, newspaper photos and drawings tend to be a bit fuzzy. The way newspapers improve legibility is by using large type and fairly coarse screens for photos. They avoid things that require fine lines. Contrast this to an annual report or a book that reproduces photos or paintings. You'll normally find that the paper stock is very glossy and has a very hard surface. This allows fine lines to be reproduced well and also provides an underlying sheen that makes contrast high and gives the ink an undercoating of luminance.

On the other hand, glossy papers sometimes reflect light, making it tough to read the text on the page. You'll notice this whenever you have to carefully position a magazine so that light doesn't glare at you as you read. So you may decide to use an uncoated or a matte coated stock, accepting the fact that you might lose a little sharpness in return for improved reader comfort.

### Shape and Size

Unless you are willing to spend extra money to have print pieces cut to specific shapes and sizes, you'll normally use standard and accepted formats. These range from large posters and tabloid newspapers to vest-pocket books or business cards. In practice, we expect certain sizes and shapes for certain applications. Although some of these applications are based upon ease of handling or storage, more are based upon what's been done before. So it's important to think a bit before deciding that a particular program should be done as a textbook or as a pamphlet. You may find that a change in format will make the program more effective.

We discuss several print formats within the section on case studies. For now, we'll just give one example. We did several training manuals for a large manufacturing firm, all in a standard 8½ × 11 format, using large type and plenty of white space. Then we got the job of designing an additional manual, aimed precisely at factory workers and and others who had no desks, no briefcases, no specific work area they could use to store reading material. After much thought, our client had a "Eureka moment" . . . he decided to produce this particular communications program in a much smaller size so it would fit in a workshirt pocket. All of us had some trepidation about this idea. It meant smaller type than we normally used and it meant that the book would run about four times as long as most other elements within the training series. But we went ahead and did it.

The results were excellent. Because the book easily fit in a pocket, it was available to people whenever they had a few spare moments to read. It was taken home, rather than stuffed into a wastebasket, and it was read. More important, the audience members realized that a special effort was made to match the communications program to their work environment, and they appreciated it.

We've also created communications specifically shaped to transmit a message. In one case, we created a brochure for a building contractor that was die-cut so that it could be put together into a house. On the outside of the house we printed a calendar. The idea was that the brochure would be retained as a desktop calendar by the audience, and serve as a continuing reminder of the contractor's abilities.

Of course, many of those brochures found their way immediately into wastebaskets. But that's always a problem with print communications. It's very easy to toss them away, sometimes without reading them. Unlike an audiovisual program, where you at least know that the audience sat through a program, you can't be sure that everyone will read material you send them. The best you can do is try to make the product as creative and effective as possible, to entice them to read and to retain the information. But you should also be aware that some people won't even make that effort. In those cases, you might still be able to impart some small message simply through the shape, the colors, or the headlines you use for the communications.

## CONCLUSION

The process of developing effective print communications is just like the process of developing any other media. Some people discount print, thinking it won't be as exciting or entertaining as other media. Others put too much faith in print, thinking it will be extraordinarily effective. The truth is that print communications won't be absorbed by osmosis; they have to be read and viewed and understood to be effective. So the most crucial task any print program developer has is to interest the reader and then fulfill that reader's interest with good information presented in a comfortable manner.

That's a difficult task. But it is made easier if you understand something of what is required by the printing methods you are using. Because you normally do not see the finished product until the end of the job, it's difficult to know how vibrantly the red ink will glow on the blue page or how poorly the photographs and illustrations you've chosen will reproduce on the paper you're using. We stress again and again the importance of experience. But we can't stress it enough in terms of print communications.

The real problem with print is volume. When you make a mistake on a slide show, you can usually change a single slide. When you make a similar mistake in print, you may have to change three or four thousand copies. That's why we suggest three basic guidelines for every print job you do:

First, look at similar jobs, both bad and good. Try to do the good parts even better and to avoid those bad things that don't seem to work. (They won't work any better for you this time.)

Second, try to make changes at the lowest possible level. Use thumbnail sketches and a rough layout and be certain that you like what you see at this stage before progressing to final layout.

And, third, try to make your intermediate steps look as much like the final product as possible. If you are using color, ink the colors in on the layout sheets or on a tissue paper overlay. If you are using a specific type style, try to find another print piece using that same type style and paste it into your layout so you can see how it will work. If you are using illustrations or photographs, always keep in mind that the final product will not appear the same as the original. It will be altered by whatever process is used to put the illustration onto paper.

Finally, what is the future for print communications? As writers, we hope it is a solid future. But we are seeing some changes. We're seeing fewer lengthy manuals and workbooks, more use of print to accompany other media. We're seeing far more disposable programs than ever before; that is, programs deliberately printed inexpensively because the client knows they will be read and tossed. And we are seeing far more concern about the ability and willingness of people to read anything. But, in fact, we still find that print communications can do jobs that no other media can handle. Not the least of those jobs is providing reference material that is easy to store and easy to recall.

# 6

# Soundtracks: The Right Side of the Script

## INTRODUCTION

One difference between print and audiovisual programs is pacing; an audiovisual program must be paced by the producer so it is neither too fast nor too slow for most audience members. Pacing is usually set by the soundtrack. Unfortunately, it's often very difficult to tell exactly what pace the soundtrack will have until it is completed. That's because most audiotracks are created piece-by-piece, and are heard together only after a final mix at the very end of a project. So a script that reads okay, music that sounds okay, and sound effects that work okay may result in a total soundtrack that is not the least bit okay. And you usually won't know that until you've gone through the time and expense of creating a final soundtrack.

Knowledge comes from experience and from listening to a number of soundtracks, both business and entertainment tracks, to begin hearing what works and what doesn't.

Incidentally, we won't always spend the time to explain small differences between creating an audiotrack for film or videotape and creating an audiotrack for filmstrips or slide programs. The concepts and processes are basically the same for all types of audio production. The major difference is that you must be concerned with using certain technical processes to synchronize a person's voice and lip movements on film and videotape.

## AUDIO PLUS VISUAL

Although we treat "audiovisual" as one word, you should look at it as two words. What often happens, however, is that you or the people who are approving your AV project don't see the entire project until it is nearly finished. Instead, you see scripts and slides and other separate elements. As a result, many programs emphasize the "A" a little too much. They are word-heavy and use visuals as repetition, not as an alternative means of imparting the message.

A novice producer will usually write a script that says everything that must be said, then find music, sound effects, and visuals that fit those words. But the truth is that visuals, music, and sound effects can sometimes carry the message better than words. More important, when all elements are used together, you create a whole greater than the sum of the parts.

This synergistic reaction is called the "third effect" when it is used by journalists. You'll react to a certain photograph differently when you read different captions to that photograph. If you see a photo of a child hugging a dog while an adult looks on, you might think it's a happy family group . . . until you read the caption that says the landlord is allowing Johnny one last hug with Fido before he takes the dog to the pound because no dogs are allowd in the rental unit.

In business communications, you can use this third effect to your advantage. Any time you write, "as this slide clearly shows," you're probably making a mistake. If the slide is clearly showing something, use the other program elements to add something that is not clearly shown.

That's why it is important not to focus exclusively on any single aspect of audiovisual production to the exclusion of other elements.

For a given message, the length of narration in an AV presentation will probably vary inversely with the experience of the writer and producer. A novice will write more words. A master will use other elements to reduce the number of words. By using fewer words and more visuals, you'll generally increase the effectiveness of your message, because you are creating impressions through several senses and making it easy for the audience to retain those impressions.

# WHERE DO YOU BEGIN?

For communicators working with print, the first step in production is simple. You put words on paper. For AV, it's not that simple. That's because the words on a printed page need only respond to their own internal rhythm. The paper doesn't demand a certain sentence structure and tone. But an AV show does. The type of music and other sound and visual elements selected will often demand a certain writing style.

For instance, moody photographs of seascapes and dark forests will require, perhaps, a narration using poetic sentence structure and many adverbs and adjectives, plus a lyrical orchestral score. But simple, action-oriented sentences would be more fitting for a new product introduction show that uses an upbeat rock score and visuals of your newest product in use.

A good place to begin any soundtrack project is by looking at the options available to enhance the message. You have a wide variety of alternatives, and soundtracks give you one enormous opportunity that is not available in print or in visuals. It's the imagination of the audience, plus their personal backgrounds and experiences with similar sounds. You can literally bring in an entire world of music, sound effects, and narration to create an effective message.

All AV media are nothing more than a series of stimuli to the eye and the ear. They can't be stored like a book or a handout. If they are stored at all, it is in the mind of the viewer, not in a desk drawer or on a bookshelf. However, AV reaches the minds of the audience through more than one sense, so there is a greater chance that a message will be retained—as long as the message is shaped in a way that most people will accept.

What this means is that the message must concentrate on impressions, not information. People view a photograph or hear a musical passage as a series of small impressions leading to an overall impression. And not every person will get the same impression from any given stimuli. So part of your job is making sure that you give the right impression; one that carries your message and one that will be understood by everyone.

We all have a certain impression of "red," for instance. But it is very difficult to describe "red" with words. And it is even more difficult to describe a certain value of red. The same thing holds true for sound effects and music. It's possible to give a technical description of a certain musical passage, even possible to precisely describe that passage using notes on a scale. But that description is not the same as hearing the passage because the description can't add the coloration possible with a musical performance. But, here again, many novice producers fail to be very specific in their thinking, and their communications, about the type of narrator's tone they want, the impression they want to give from music or sound effects, or what overall impression they expect to be retained by the audience members. As a result, they give vague directions on the right side of the script and leave a vague message in the minds of those who are helping them produce the program as well as in the minds of those who view the program.

## SCRIPT FORMAT AND DIRECTIONS

When you write an audiovisual script, you'll normally break the page into two vertical segments, titling one "visuals" and the other "audio." The title of this chapter refers to the positioning of the audio segment on the right side of the script. Typically, you will write the audio portion of the script in such a way that it refers to visuals presented on the left side of the page, adjacent to the audio. For instance:

| | |
|---|---|
| MAIN TITLE: "HOW TO PRODUCE A SOUNDTRACK FORMAT" | MUSIC UP FOR TEN SECONDS. |
| LS RECORDING STUDIO | NARRATOR BEGINS: Today we are going to |

Begin each page of the script with a new paragraph, and try not to split paragraphs, sentences, or words on a page. You want the narrator to be able to read the script easily, without unnatural hesitations as he or she shifts pages. For the same reason, write narration in upper and lower case, not all caps. And double-space narration so the narrator can add notes or can easily write in changes that occur during the production process.

Directions for engineering the program should also be clear and simple. You may not be involved in the actual recording session, or you may be involved so much that you can't afford the time to reconstruct your thinking process during scriptwriting. Either way, be very specific in your instructions. And this is especially important concerning music. You might specify a "sounds like":

> FADE UP MUSIC. SHOULD SOUND LIKE THE KIND OF MUSIC USED WHEN LASSIE RUNS THROUGH THE SNOW TO GET HELP FOR THE LOST PUPPY.

You can also specify certain types of music, such as:

> ESTABLISH LIGHT ROCK, GUITARS AND DRUMS PROMINENT or USE SWELLING INSTRUMENTALS, STRONG ON STRINGS AND FLUTE.

If it's important, specify the kind of tone you want, such as POIGNANT or PATRIOTIC. And you should also specify what you want the music, sound effects, or narration to do. For instance:

> ESTABLISH MUSIC FOR FIFTEEN SECONDS BEFORE VOICE BEGINS. BEGIN VOICE IMMEDIATELY AFTER SFX OF CRASHING CANNONS IS HEARD ON MUSIC. FADE DOWN MUSIC AND NARRATOR FADES UP.

You may also want to specify a SEGUE; that is, a transition in which one music source fades out as the other sources come in:

> SEGUE FROM LIGHT ROCK TO HISTORICAL SONG.

Most standard audio directions are just common sense, like FADE IN or FADE OUT to signal that a sound source should be brought in or out. However, using the correct terms is less important than getting your message across. There's always a temptation to write sparsely, giving terse directions. But the time it takes to explain a direction more fully in writing is usually far less than the time it takes to fix a program that has been incorrectly produced due to miscommunications.

## COMPONENTS OF A SOUNDTRACK

The basic components of any soundtrack are about the same. You will have some voice source, some music source, perhaps some special effects or location sound sources, and you will have a mix that emphasizes one or more of these sources at any one time. We'll look at each type of source separately, then talk about the recording process used to put them together.

### Narration and Other Voice Sources

In most business communications, the major sound source you will use is the human voice. This can be either the voice of a professional or an amateur narrator or the voices of people recorded on location. We distinguish between these voice sources by calling narration "voice-over" (VO) or "on-camera talent" (O/C) and by calling location recordings "sound bites" or "actualities." We'll contrast these alternatives while explaining some basic concepts necessary to effectively use both narration and location recordings in business communications programs.

A professional narrator provides three major advantages for business communications. First, a pro can often add meaning and drama to words that enhance the audience's understanding of those words and the impact they have upon the audience. Second, a narrator's voice sets a certain tone, a certain level of quality, that is important in lending prestige to the program. Third, a narrator can often give you an almost flawless reading of a script in one take, saving you editing time and studio costs.

On the other hand, most narrators *sound* like narrators—like trained professional spokespeople. Unless they are exceptionally good actors, it is unlikely that they can take on the role of an employee or customer or whoever else they are supposed to represent. So it is sometimes hard for audience members to identify with the narrator. How many sales representatives, for instance, have perfect diction and a mellow voice? How many factory supervisors sound as if they belong on the stage? More to the point, how many business communicators have the skill and patience it would take to write and direct a narration that would accurately capture the words, mannerisms, and attitudes of the person being played by the narrator?

It's when this realism is important that you would consider using amateurs. But there's a trade-off, as usual. And that trade-off involves both time and money. Some people choose to use amateurs because they think they will save money by not paying a narrator's fees. This is true, but it does not take into account the time the producer will spend getting a decent recording. If the producer is paying for recording-studio time or for technical help, and is taking the amateur (as well as the producer) away from work for a period of time, the cost can be significant.

When working with amateurs, there are some ways to reduce the time involved while improving the quality of the final product. Begin by putting yourself in the amateur's place: directly in front of a microphone, maybe with all sorts of lights glaring down so the scene can be filmed, and reading something off a script. It's no wonder that the first few readings a person does are terrible. A better way to handle the situation is to give the person a chance to get acclimatized to the script and to the environment at two separate times. Let them look the script over a day ahead of time. And ask them to show up a little early on the day of recording. Before the person shows up, have everything set up. Don't turn on massive studio lights or flit around adjusting cameras and props while the person is trying to read through the script a couple of times. Encourage the person to rehearse, and then quietly turn on the recording system sometime during the rehearsal. (You may get lucky and accomplish the recording without ever having to tell the person, "This is a take.")

If it is at all possible—and it may not be if the amateur is the president of your firm or some similar high-level type—try to take the script away from the person and ask them to use their own words or to refer to a short list of main points based on that script. It may not turn out exactly as you wrote it, but chances are the message will get through and it will sound more natural.

And that brings up an important point—make sure the recording sounds natural. Don't necessarily cut out every "you know" and "umm," or retake a sentence that seems somewhat ungrammatical. Just make sure it sounds normal and natural; let people "tell it like it is." The reason you are using an amateur, in most cases, is so that the audience identifies with that person. If you airbrush out all the flaws, the person won't sound real.

### Music Sources

The easiest way to get music for a program is to take it from popular tapes or records. This is done all the time, and it's illegal as well as unethical. It's exactly the same as reaching in the pocket of a performer and pulling out a few hundred or a few thousand dollars. And, if you are caught, a copyright-infringement suit may cost you hundreds or thousands of dollars.

Moral issues aside, it's not a good idea to use copyrighted popular music for most business communications. The fact that the music is popular means that people enjoy it and may listen to the background music rather than the foreground words.

In addition, popular music is not designed for use as background music or as emphasis music for business communications. There are better sources, including music libraries and custom-designed scores.

Music libraries either purchase or produce music specifically geared for the enhancement of soundtracks. For instance, they provide background music selections that go on for eight or ten minutes, not two or three as is common in popular music. And they provide "bridges" or "main title themes" that run thirty seconds or a minute, and have a definite beginning and end. These selections create a sound track that is much more professional than simply fading the middle of a popular tune up and down. Libraries also provide "stings" that can be used to emphasize a particular sentence or visual. You hear these all the time on television. They are the little five- or six-second crescendos that accompany the hero's deathless dialogue or that are included at the end of a commercial after the product has been identified. In business communications, they are frequently used as emphasis elements, too:

". . . so there's really no reason to have health insurance, is there?"

DRAMATIC STING UP. CHOOSE STRONG HORN CRESCENDO. SEGUE FROM STING TO SOUND OF AMBULANCE SIREN.

"There's no reason, that is, unless you get sick or injured...."

The sting serves as emphasis and as a transition element. It says that something important has been stated and will be stated. And it provides a brief but complete transitional music element.

Music libraries frequently provide an entire "family" of selections, including long and short themes, stings, and various other commonly needed music pieces. By choosing selections from within the same family, you can create a score that sounds almost as if it was written precisely for the presentation.

You can also commission a score to accompany your presentation. It's not as costly as you may think. That's because modern musical instruments and recording equipment emphasize individual performances. A person with musical talent and a couple of thousand dollars worth of keyboard synthesizers and multitrack recording gear can create a professional score. It may not sound like a forty-piece orchestra, but it will be music, and it will be the type of music that provides a subtle and unobtrusive "bed" upon which to lay voices and sound effects.

Most music libraries charge a "needle-drop" fee each time you use a selection from their library. Usually you also pay for the recording itself. So you may have spent $25 to $50 per volume for music library materials. And you may need to use six or eight needle drops to create the music track you require. A needle drop fee, as the name implies, is charged each time you use a selection within a program. In other words, if you were to use the same music piece four times in a production, you would have to pick up and move the needle (or rewind the tape) four times. Each of those would be a separate charge. If the needle drop charge is $50, you've just spent $200 for background music, plus the money you paid for the music source.

If you do many programs, let's say more than half a dozen each year, you might be better off paying an "annual use" fee to a music library. This allows you to use any selection you have on your discs or tapes as often as you would like to use it.

In contrast, you might pay $2,000 to $4,000 to have someone create an original score. But that score could be far more individual and useful than the music library music. (Also, you won't hear "your" music also being used as the background music for a shaving cream commercial.) You can, for example, add lyrics that precisely fit the theme of your program or the slogan used by your firm. And you can have the composer create a score that is precisely correct for each segment of your script. You can also use the score several times, for different programs, and get the benefit of the music aiding participants' recall of a previous program while listening to the present program.

So your choice of music sources really depends upon the number of productions you do each year and upon the audience for those productions. The fee will be based upon the type of use; obviously, a television commercial will cost you more than an industrial slide presentation, just as it would probably cost you more money to produce that commercial than to produce an industrial presentation.

There are two other music sources worth mentioning: One is location recording of music being played "live." You could, for instance, record someone playing a piano arrangement of some music that is in the public domain, such as an old folk song or classical score on which the copyright was never filed or is no longer applicable. Or you could record a marching band, a barbershop quartet, or other musical group. As long as the music they are playing is in the public domain, not copyrighted, you're home free.

You can also pick up records that are specifically designed to be used as background music for slide presentations or amateur films. These records often contain a number of common sound effects, a few ethnic and regional music selections, and one or two tunes that can be used to accompany slides of the summer vacation or birthday party or other common event. These are extremely inexpensive... and worth just about what they cost. However, they can provide some music and effects for those programs that don't demand much quality or specific music enhancement.

### Sound Effects

Another way to make things sound real is to add sound effects. Unfortunately, the actual sound of something may not record in such a way that it does sound real. A cannon's boom, for instance, is as much a physical feeling as it is an auditory feeling. And that's hard to capture on audiotape. So you may find that you need to enhance sound effects somewhat, or purchase sound effects records. These records are not very expensive, and are certainly not expensive when you consider the years of experience it takes for a person to be able to create a sound effect that works.

If you require a very specific sound effect, perhaps one unique to your firm or industry, you may have to record it yourself. Suppose you want the president of your firm to give his or her message while standing near the firm's latest product—a special

## SOUNDTRACKS: THE RIGHT SIDE OF THE SCRIPT

ultrasound machine that gives off a high-pitched whine when it operates.

If this is a motion medium production, you may want the president to speak on-camera, to be seen actually saying the words. In that case, you would record "lip synch" sound and keep the picture and the sound in synchronization during the sound mixing process through a special procedure that ensures that the visual of the person's mouth moving is precisely linked to the sounds that person is making. If you are showing the president doing something, like operating the machine, while his voice accompanies the activity but it is obvious he is not speaking as he works, the sound of the machine is called "wild sound" and his voice track is called a "voice-over." But, for both lip-synch and voice-overs, you would usually try to record the person's voice separately from the sound effect source. You might, for instance, record the person with the machine turned off, then separately record the machine in operation. In this way, you get the best possible voice quality and the best possible sound of the machine. If, at a later time, you want the president's voice without the machine, or the machine without the president's voice, you have that option, too.

Don't go overboard on sound effects. Use them when it is necessary to emphasize important elements, not just to provide background noise. Suppose, for instance, that you are producing a safety program on videotape for workers who use band saws. It's tempting to have the sound of the saw "under" throughout the program, because that's what the show is all about. In fact, though, the saw will soon become a mosquito drone that irritates instead of enhancing the program. It's far better to use the saw sound effect only when it adds something to the program:

MUSIC DOWN AND UNDER AS NARRATOR BEGINS:

Each year five of us take early retirement from our jobs. Not because we have lost our willingness to work, but because we have lost fingers... even entire hands... in a band saw accident.

FADE OUT MUSIC. BRING SFX OF BAND SAW UP FOR FIVE SECONDS, THEN OUT. NARRATOR CONTINUES:

Band saws are great time savers for us. But this program can be a life saver. So please take the time to listen to the ways you can use the time-saving band saw more effectively.

BRING BAND SAW SFX IN AGAIN, BUT LOW. KEEP IT UNDER DURING FIRST TWO SENTENCES OF BAND SAW OPERATOR'S VOICE-OVER:

I've been using this machine for thirty years . . .

Notice that the band saw sound effect is used only for emphasis or to establish the purpose of the presentation. If this program were actually produced as a film or videotape, it would be important that at least now and then the sound of the saw was present while we were viewing saws in operation. But if this program were presented as a slide show or filmstrip, we may not want to run the band saw sound. It may be disconcerting to see the blade of the saw stopped for a still photograph while the soundtrack includes the sound of a running saw. The real key is motivation for the effect.

## MOTIVATION

Many novices make the mistake of bringing in sound sources without motivation. They bring in music or sound effects without a reason to do so. The program is nearing the end, so they pop in some music. There's a band saw shot, so they bring in a band saw sound effect. There's a better way to do it.

. . . so we always keep a sharp band in the saw. A sharp band is actually less dangerous than a dull one.

OPERATOR'S VOICE-OVER ENDS. FADE OUT SOUND OF SAW. BRING IN MUSIC AND ESTABLISH FOR A FEW SECONDS BEFORE NARRATOR BEGINS CONCLUSION:

Band saw safety is part of everyone's job description . . .

Motivation is crucial in the effective use of music and sound effects. Nothing sounds worse than a show with music and effects brought in and out at random. In addition, insisting upon motivated sound effects and music will reduce the likelihood that a soundtrack will become so cluttered with sources presented simultaneously that none will be heard.

Motivation can come from the words, or from the visuals. We have all seen dramatic shows on television where the star enters a car and the music begins. He or she has changed environment, made a shift in the action. In addition, we expect that the person in the car will have the radio on, so hearing music won't surprise us. And we expect that the music will change in tempo if the star suddenly spots the bad guys in the rear-view mirror. But we don't expect that the tempo will suddenly shift just because the star turns a corner.

Sometimes, though, we can anticipate something that will soon happen. We may bring in the sound of the band saw at the last sentence of the narrator's statement, so the effect is fully established when we see the operator using the saw. This is a motivated action, too, because we will soon answer the audience's unanswered question concerning the new sound source.

The way to determine what will sound right and what sort of motivation will work is fairly abstract. If just seems to occur naturally during the process of soundtrack development. But one way to think about it is by putting yourself in the actual environment you are trying to create with words, visuals, and sound sources. If you were in a factory, talking with a person, wouldn't you hear the machinery around that person for a few seconds, then wouldn't your hearing system and intellect "fade down" that noise so you could concentrate on the person's words? And if you were on a scenic river trip, wouldn't the sound of the rushing water soon disappear as you concentrated on other sounds that were not so consistent? Also, if you were in the office working, would you expect the background music to be hard rock or something a little less demanding of your attention?

What we're saying is that you should make the sources appropriate to the environment you are trying to create. And, in terms of sound effects, you should try to capture the feeling of the sound, then get rid of it, because that's what we do after we have heard a repetitive sound for awhile. If, instead, you keep the sound effect or the music strong and vibrant, what do you do for an encore? How do you add even more impact to the presentation when the next spot that needs emphasis comes up?

## INTELLIGIBILITY

If there's any single thing to keep foremost in mind when producing or supervising production of a soundtrack, it's the ultimate purpose of intelligibility. Now this doesn't always mean that every note of music, every word, every nuance of a sound effect must be heard. But it does mean that the audience must be able to understand the message being presented without working very hard to do so.

When sound is presented by an artificial medium such as a speaker system, we can't expect the artificial medium to operate exactly like the human speech and hearing system. But we can use the human speech and hearing system as a guideline because that system generally results in the most intelligibility possible.

When we listen to something "live," location aids our understanding. We have a "binaural" hearing system: ears on opposite sides of our heads. So we can determine distance, location, and volume level by comparing what we hear through each ear. This system helps us isolate several sources from one another so we can deliberately block out certain repetitive sounds while we concentrate on other sound sources.

Our ears are also well-tuned to receive sounds across a broad variety of frequencies, but those frequencies are typically ones created by the human voice or by things naturally found in our preindustrial past. We couple our brain's intelligence to our hearing system and are able to hear and identify sounds that range from about 20 cycles per second (audio engineers call this 20 Hertz or 20 Hz) to about 20,000 cycles per second (20 kHz, where "k" means 1,000).

Further, our ears can pick up a broad range of volume levels. We can sometimes pick out the sound of a pin dropping on carpet and we can sometimes distinguish between the boom of a cannon and the crack of a rifle, although both are at very high volume level. In addition, we can filter out loud noises or soft ones, so that we can ignore cannon sounds in the distance and still hear pin drops in the local area.

We can also distinguish among a wide variety of similar voices or similar sounds because we never hear just one frequency. When people talk, their voice boxes vibrate at a certain prime frequency, based upon their physical structure. But each person has a slightly different physical structure, a slightly different way of forming words. As a result, that prime frequency is accompanied by many other frequencies that "shade" a person's voice. The same thing happens with musical instruments or other sound sources. When a violin string vibrates with an "A" note, it also vibrates with many multiples of the prime note, called "harmonics." When a bass drum booms out at 400 cycles per second, the drum skin also vibrates at double that frequency, or 800 cycles, and at triple that frequency, or 1200 cycles, and so on up the frequency scale. When we hear those sounds with multiple harmonics, our ear can separate the sound of one bass drum from another, simply by hearing the harmonics that accompany the prime frequency.

Any audio equipment has to approximate our human speech and hearing system to be effective. The better that equipment approximates our built-in high-fidelity system, the more intelligible will be the sounds that we hear through that system.

In soundtrack work, we are concerned about four basic types of audio equipment: Individual sound sources are recorded through microphones. Those recorded sounds are put on records or tapes. The strength of recorded sound is beefed up through amplifiers. And we hear the final result through speaker systems or headphones. At every stage in the process, the closer the audio equipment approximates the human system, the better the soundtrack will sound. And the system is no better than the worst part. So good microphones and great recording equipment won't aid intelligibility if the final product is played back through poor amplifiers and speakers.

In terms of audio equipment and recording techniques, you are concerned with a number of specific parameters that have corresponding human parameters. We'll discuss the most important ones in general terms, focusing on how they relate to intelligibility.

### Volume Level

Our ears have a "dynamic range" of sounds that we can hear. The softest sound we can hear is at the "threshold of hearing." It might be a pin on a carpet or it might be a dripping faucet heard at midnight. The absolute value of that threshold of hearing depends upon the individual, but most of us can hear very soft sounds. The loudest sound we can hear is at the "threshold of pain." It might be a jet engine's roar that still allows us to discern the sound of the turbine in that engine whirring around. It might be a rock band at close range, where we can still pick up individual tones. Again, this depends upon the individual, but most of us can hear fairly loud sounds without feeling pain.

Our dynamic range can be stated in terms of "decibels" or "dB." A decibel is a sound volume measurement that is logarithmic in proportion. In other words, the difference between a certain weak sound and one twice as large will be smaller than the difference between a loud sound and one twice as loud. This measurement system reflects what we can observe ourselves. If you have the television sound level very low, it doesn't take much of a twist of the knob to increase the sound a lot. But if the sound level is loud, you have to really crank up the volume knob a lot to get the audio to sound much louder.

We can generally hear sounds over a dynamic range of 130 dB. So we can hear a very low sound, and also hear one that is 130 times as loud as that low sound. Few audio recording and playback systems can match that.

The problem is that we are dealing with electronic and mechanical equipment with far less flexibility than the human ear. For a speaker to be able to send out a signal of one small level, then immediately send out one 130 times as large is difficult. It takes time to move a speaker's sound cone in and out. Also, the size of speaker that will accurately reproduce a small signal is minute in comparison to the size of speaker required to reproduce a large signal. So we generally end up making compromises.

The major compromise is that we focus on the mid-range sounds, because those are the most frequent. We accept the fact that the speaker system or amplifier may not handle very small or very large sounds well. For normal speech or music, this works out just fine for business AV communications. But problems occur when we have the need to reproduce a very large sound or a very soft one. The system just isn't designed for it, in most business AV equipment. So we must limit our dynamic range.

This is done by reference to a meter, the "volume level" (or "VU") meter. A VU meter reads out in decibels so you can determine the volume level of one sound in relationship to another. This is an important concept for soundtrack work, so we'll explain it in a bit more detail.

If you look at a VU meter, you'll typically see an area to the left that includes a green arc and an area to the right that includes a red arc. At the junction of those two colors, you'll usually see the number "0", for "0 dB." Zero decibels is the basic reference for most audio equipment; that is, 0 dB provides the optimum level of sound possible without distortion. If your volume level exceeds 0 dB, you will probably hear distorted sound, as if the ear were operated past the threshold of pain. On the other hand, if you can't get the needle on the VU meter to register at all, you are at too low a volume level, below the machine's threshold of hearing.

When you are recording important information, you want the peak sound included in that important information to reach 0 dB. And you want most sounds within that bit of information to register somewhere fairly high on the VU meter. For example, you might want any voice-overs to register very near 0 dB all the time, so that they are heard at maximum undistorted volume. Still, you might want the music you are using in the program to vary from 0 dB to far lower in volume, yet remain loud enough to be heard.

The central idea here is that a soundtrack has to be adjusted so that the volume levels are different than they would be in real life. In real life, we can have music rather loud and still hear a person talking. But we are also usually looking at that person, unconsciously adding information we may not be hearing by watching the person's lips and gestures. And we may turn our head so that we can put the music behind our ears while turning one ear directly to the person speaking. On a soundtrack the audience can't do that, so we must adjust the levels so that the relative proportion of sound is correct for the message we are trying to impart.

In most cases, this means keeping major sound sources high and background sources low. Just as we subliminally hear the very low background music present in offices, so should we normally just subliminally hear the music and sound effects used for background. We will keep them low in relation to main program material, only bringing them to higher volume when it is necessary to make specific points or to provide transitions.

One problem that occurs more often with amateur narrators than with pros, by the way, is that they cannot control their voice level to keep the average level at 0 dB most of the time. In these cases, you have two choices: You can manually "ride the gain" of the recording equipment so that you increase or decrease volume when needed. Or you can use electronic devices that compress, limit, or otherwise automatically control the signals coming in so the voice always records at higher volume levels.

A lot of this, of course, is information that the audio engineer already knows. We're telling you because it's so important to intelligibility. If the volume levels are wrong, it doesn't matter what else you do. It will be difficult, or even impossible, for the audience to understand your message.

## Frequency Response

We've already mentioned that the human ear is capable of responding to a range of frequencies from 20 Hz to 20,000 Hz. But the human being can also respond to other frequencies, above and below that limit. We may not hear a very low frequency change in sound pressure, like the very lowest rumble of a bass drum, and we may not hear a very high frequency, like a dog whistle or high-pressure steam escaping from a kettle, but we feel these pressure changes. In fact, an explosion doesn't jangle and upset us just because it is a loud noise. Part of our response is based on the change in air pressure, the sight of smoke and dirt clods, and other non-audible results of the explosion.

But audio equipment does not include all these other senses. So we are limited in what we can record onto audiotape and in what we can play back. The sound effect of an explosion may have little power when it is reduced to flickering volume levels on a VU meter. And, more important, some of the high and low frequencies that add coloration and strength to music will be totally lost through most audio equipment.

Only the very best audio equipment has a frequency response approaching the human ear's. Most of the equipment used by business communicators doesn't fall into that category. Again, it emphasizes the mid-range. You can test this out for yourself by listening to a high-fidelity recording of a popular music group played through a stereo system with good full-range speaker systems and a high fidelity amplifier, then listening to the same song played on monaural television by the same group. You won't get the same sound from the same television speaker, because that speaker is small in size (not capable of high volume levels) and is designed to emphasize the mid-range sounds of speech. That's the same size and type of speaker found in many audiovisual recorders or projection sound systems.

What this means is that you must be aware that what you will hear on the final soundtrack is not what you may hear through the elaborate sound equipment in a studio. Choose music, sound effects, and voices that fall within the middle of the frequency spectrum. That's the normal frequency response of audiovisual equipment. A cassette recorder's specifications may say that the frequency response is from "400 to 14,000 Hz," and that could well be true. But the best sound you will get through that recorder will be somewhere around the center of that range, perhaps at 1,000 to 5,000 Hz. This happens to be the range at which most voices operate, so this is not much of a problem for standard business communications.

### Signal-to-Noise Ratio

The last important parameter you must be concerned with when thinking about audio is the signal-to-noise ratio, or "S/N." It's also the easiest to understand, because it is an electronic parameter that has a close human parameter.

We've all experienced situations where we don't hear something that we should easily hear simply because other noises drown it out. For instance, our car radio is so loud that we don't hear the sound of an emergency siren, or we are running a saw and can't hear the telephone ring. In audio terms, the "noise" is very loud in relationship to the "signal" we want to hear. As a result, the difference between signal and noise is small, and we can't pick out the signal from the noise.

Audio equipment has some built-in noises, as do most forms of audio recording material. Tape hisses, and that hiss has a certain volume. Tubes and semiconductors within amplifiers have a certain amount of hiss, too, based on the movement of molecules within these components. You can hear these noises by turning up the volume on your audio equipment.

Engineers try to get rid of these noise sources by carefully designing equipment. But they can't totally stop all noise. The best they can do is get the noise so low in level that any signal will be strong in relationship to the noise. When you crank up the volume level, the noise will be amplified, too, but the signal will be much stronger in proportion to the noise.

Years ago, most producers always ran music under soundtracks because the music would mask the noise present in the tapes and equipment they used. Today, that's not really necessary. Modern equipment has a very good signal-to-noise ratio. Of more importance is the fact that the sound level of whatever you use as your audiotrack should be kept near 0 dB most of the time, so that it rides far above the noise inherent in the equipment. If it does not, and if you are forced to crank up the volume control when you play back sounds, then the inherent noise may well be a distraction for the audience.

## Common Noise Sources and Presence

You should also be aware of some standard noise sources that your ears may ignore but that audio equipment won't. Air control system hiss is one of these noises. It's "white noise" to us; that is, a noise made up of no specific frequency or pattern, so we ignore it. But the audio recorder won't. It will become an irritant on the track.

On the other hand, the absence of all noise can be an irritant, too. Most rooms have a certain ambience called "presence" in audio engineering terms. This is the sound of the room itself, as it is heard through a microphone. Most good engineers will record a bit of presence before and after recording other information in a room. They do this by simply allowing the recorder to run for awhile, "listening" to the noise of the room.

This comes in handy especially when the script calls for a ten-second pause between sentences. The narrator may not provide a pause of the precise length required. Let's say he or she pauses only four seconds. To expand that pause to the required ten seconds, the engineer could put in blank tape or leader. But this blank tape would have no presence. When you listened to the segment, you'd be aware of a sudden "drop-out" of all sound, as if you were listening to someone on the telephone and then the connection was suddenly broken. So a good audio engineer will generally splice in some of the tape he or she has recorded that includes room presence.

This may seem like a small, perhaps unimportant, detail, but it does make a difference. What happens is that people hear a problem, then spend the next few seconds thinking about what they just heard, and ignore program information. Also, people learn to expect a certain background sound and will notice the lack of that sound. For instance, people expect to hear some background noise when listening to someone talk in an office or a factory environment. So don't cut it out. Also, be consistent. Don't try to splice a segment of a person's voice that has background noise with one that doesn't have background noise, then go back to one with noise again. It's better to put a noise SFX or room presence under the noiseless segment, because people will get used to it and ignore it until it suddenly disappears.

## SOME CREATIVE CONSIDERATIONS

At the conceptual stage, and surely at the script stage, you have to make some creative decisions that will affect all these latter mechanical processes. We've talked about some already, but one of the most important is how you are going to open the soundtrack.

### Music or Voice

Basically, your choice is between music or voice, because you are usually going to open a show with either a person's voice or a musical selection. The decision really rests with the type of program and type of information. Sometimes, for instance, a voice-only opening will be best:

OPEN WITH NARRATION, NO MUSIC. NARRATOR SAYS:

People in the northland have a legacy . . . something they have received from the past and something they must pass down to the future. This legacy is a golden legacy . . . the golden legacy of the aspen tree.

BRING UP MUSIC FOR TEN SECONDS DURING TITLES, THEN UNDER AS NARRATOR CONTINUES:

Yes, the aspen tree is a golden legacy. But it is not a legacy that should be put aside in a vault. Rather, it's one that should be used. In fact, if we don't use it, we'll lose it.

MUSIC STING AT END. BRING IN LOCATION SOUND OF LOGGER.

Because there is one basic thought in this show—that aspens have worth—a narrated lead-in makes sense. Even if the audience members fall asleep immediately after the opening, they at least have heard the main message of the program.

However, sometimes there will be several thoughts in a show. In these cases, it may be better to use a music opening to set the theme for the program:

OPEN WITH THIRTY SECONDS OF MUSIC UP. UPBEAT INSTRUMENTAL, WITH REGULAR BEAT ALLOWING SLIDE CHANGES EVERY FOUR BARS OR EIGHT SECONDS. FADE MUSIC DOWN AS NARRATOR BEGINS:

Welcome to Widget Corporation. We're glad you have decided to put your talents and energy to work for us. Today we'd like to tell you a bit about the company . . . *your* company . . . and how we can all work together to secure your financial futures.

MAKE MUSIC SHIFT FROM TITLE MUSIC TO LOWER-KEY INSTRUMENTAL WITH A HISTORICAL FLAVOR. KEEP BACKGROUND MUSIC UNDER AS NARRATOR CONTINUES:

Widget Corporation began in a garage in Newark, New Jersey, back in 1903. At that time, Charles Widget was an out-of-work painter . . . and a full-time inventor. It was Mr. Widget who invented the process that today bears his name.

In this instance, there will be several facts presented, and the only real connection they all have is that they affect new hires of the Widget Company. So one good way to open the program might be a montage of faces of Widget employees who work in many different areas. Another way might be to select slides or film from various topic areas to be covered and preview them at this point in the program.

You might choose to open the program with sound effects, of course, but you should think long and hard before doing so. That's because some sound effects require establishment through visuals or through other words. If they are not correctly established, they can be misheard or misunderstood.

## Method of Transition

A second important consideration involves transitions. You can make abrupt transitions, such as a direct cut between the last note of the opening music and the first word of a narrator's introduction. Or you can make very fluid transitions by gradually fading down one sound while you are fading up the other sound.

As a general rule, an abrupt transition will give a program a more "documentary" flavor. It will sound like the urgent, fast-paced presentations we are used to getting on television news. A fluid transition will have more "entertainment" flavor, like motion pictures and television drama.

## Sound Levels and Relationships

When you put programs together, it seems obvious that you want the sound loud enough to be heard but not so loud that it irritates. Within that continuum, however, you have several other considerations. For instance, a program that will be viewed in a study cubicle and heard by a person wearing earphones should probably not be as loud in overall volume level as one designed to be presented in a ballroom to a thousand people.

You also want to think about the volume level as it will be perceived with the visuals. If you are viewing two people in the middle of a forest in a very long shot, it might be disconcerting to hear their voices as if they were two feet from you. On the other hand, a close-up of a person's face should be accompanied by sound that also is close up. Again, you can adjust this in the mix to make sure it works right. So try it a few different ways to see which combination of volume level works for each picture in the show. But don't go overboard with this. Perhaps just select one or two combinations. And make sure that the difference between these combinations isn't great. You want to suggest that the sound is coming from close up or from far away, not to make it sound the way it would sound in real life.

## DIFFERENCE BETWEEN MOTION AND STILL MEDIA

We've said that soundtracks are similar for films, videotapes, slide programs and filmstrips, and that's true. But there are differences, too.

One major difference is mechanical, the way the soundtrack is tied to the picture. In film and videotape, the picture and sound are "married"; that is, linked on the same piece of material. In slide shows and filmstrips, the sound and pictures are "synchronized," or tied together through some electronic system although they are on two separate pieces of material.

This results in both creative differences and technical differences. For example, a motion medium has a certain flow based on the fact that there is movement within scenes. So abrupt changes in sound may disturb the continuity of that flow. A still medium, in contrast, has a built-in disruption—the change from one still visual to the next. So you can get away with some abrupt transitions. (We could also make the opposite case: That the very fact that there are abrupt frame changes means that the soundtrack should be more fluid to smooth out the continuity of the show.)

About the only way to get a feel for the way visuals and sound will go together is to try out some options. Maybe run some music with a set of slides to see how they work together or maybe see if an abrupt switch from exterior sunrise to interior moonlight on film works well with an abrupt change between the sound of a rooster crowing and the sound of an owl.

When working with film or videotape, it is possible to be very precise in the placement of words and other sounds in relation to visuals. In fact, you must be very precise so that the sound relates directly to the visualization of that sound. In still media, however, you can't be that precise and don't have to be. But you do have to be concerned about the length of time it takes for various filmstrip or slide projectors to operate.

For example, it takes about two-and-one-half seconds for a slide projector to recycle. So the fastest you can make a single-projector show go is one slide each two-and-one-half seconds. You can't, therefore, specify that slides will change after every two words of narration unless the narrator is taking two-and-one-half seconds to say two words. In fact, you usually want to add a little pad at either side of the specific slide/sound combination to anticipate projectors that change too fast or too slow.

As a way to wrap up the differences between motion and still media, think about the way you would normally view each type of media. When a slide or filmstrip frame changes, it takes a certain space of time for your eyes and mind to react to the change. You may also have a certain amount of clatter as the change occurs. So you might want to make sure that a specific sound effect or other precise sound element occurs a second or so after the change occurs. In contrast, in film or videotape, the transition between visuals is less dramatic. So you might be able to call for the sound element immediately after the change occurs.

## PUTTING IT ALL TOGETHER

In most cases, you will not be doing your own audio work. That's because audio equipment is fairly expensive and, unless you are doing many hours of programming each month, you can't justify the capital expense. Instead, you'll be working with audio engineers in professional studios.

On the other hand, there's no reason you can't do your own audio work, by renting the equipment you need or buying an industrial-grade system. So, within this section, we'll try to cover both options; that is, we'll explain the process of putting together audiotracks as if you were doing it yourself. Although this detailed explanation may be more than you need if you will be using pros, by understanding the process in some depth, you'll be better equipped to enter the arcane world of audio engineering.

### The Multitrack Recording Process

The heart of any modern recording system is a multitrack recorder. This device allows you to record several separate "tracks," or channels, on the same length of tape. Each is a discrete sound source and each can be recorded separately without ruining what's on the other channels. That's in contrast to a standard cassette recorder, for instance, where any time you press the "Record" button you destroy whatever was on the tape. On a multitrack system, each track has its own Record control. Therefore, you can re-record over a track without affecting anything but that track.

You can see the advantage of this system. You don't have to do everything at once and do it right the first time. You can record each source separately. For example, you could put music on track one, then rewind the tape and find the perfect spot in relationship to that music to bring in a voice on track two. You'd then begin recording voice on track two at that spot, without affecting the music on track one. When you accomplished this, you would have music and voice in correct relationship with each other.

But suppose you find a mistake in the voice track after you've gone through the entire process of recording and mixing a soundtrack. Well, with a multitrack system, you can go back and record a new voice track on track two, yet not disturb what's on any other track. As a result, you don't have to go back to square one if you make a mistake or just want to make some changes.

## Overdubbing

Overdubbing is a multitrack capability used all the time in popular music. It's the way in which one singer can become a quartet. That singer would simply continue to overdub separate tracks. In other words, the singer would first lay down a voice track on track one, perhaps while listening to a full orchestration of the sound recorded on tracks five through eight. Then the singer would rewind the tape and overdub his or her voice on track two while listening to the music and to the voice on track one. You can see how the process continues, limited only by the number of separate audiotracks available.

In business communications work, we rarely use more than four tracks. So we use four-track recorders. But sound studios will frequently have eight-track, twelve-track, or twenty-four-track machines.

We'll limit ourselves to four tracks during this discussion. Understand that the concepts are the same for more tracks—you just pay more money for equipment and do the same processes more times.

## How to Produce a Soundtrack

You will usually follow a three-step process when producing a soundtrack: Step one is gathering original materials. Step two is compiling those original materials into a multitrack master. And Step three is mixing that multitrack master into a final soundtrack that has all the sounds required for the presentation in the correct physical relationship and with the correct proportion of volume.

As we discuss the soundtrack production process, we will be using several unfamiliar terms; that is, terms that will be unfamiliar until you've actually worked on a few soundtracks. The first of these terms is "master." A master is any material that will be used to create other materials. You'll also see this word combined with other words, such as "multitrack master" or "final mix master" or "master voice track." Next, you'll have "source" materials. A source material might be a record, a sound effects tape recorded in your factory, or an edited voice track. It's easy to confuse "source" with "master." In fact, the words can and will be used interchangeably. But a master is typically some original material, like the original tape recording used by a record company to produce millions of discs. The sources on that master are the voices and musical instruments.

Finally, we will be talking with "source recorders" several times in this section. A source recorder is used to play back a source so that the source can be duplicated onto another machine. If, for instance, you hook two cassette recorders together so you can make a copy of a program, the recorder you put the original cassette on is the "source recorder." The recorder on which you make the copy can be called several things, such as "slave recorder" (because it is dependent upon the source—or master—recorder for sound) or "dubbing recorder" (because it is the recorder on which you are making a duplicate or dub).

Step one in the soundtrack production process involves locating music and sound effects records or tapes plus making original recordings of narrators or other people who will be heard on the production.

You would normally record the narrator and other voices on tape, then edit that tape into an "edited voice track." This tape will have physical splices in it where you have removed bad takes. (A "take" is the term used to describe a section of either visual or audio material. You would begin a program, for instance, with "Page one, take one"; and you may well end up with "Page one, take twelve" before you get a take that contains the proper emphasis on words and no flubs over words.) Although you can do a dubbing process where you hook up two recorders and duplicate just those parts of the voice tracks that you want to save, the physical cutting method is preferred since it allows your editing to be much more precise.

Step two in the soundtrack process is the equivalent of taking one or two original documents and putting them together to be photocopied at the same time. It is the creation of a "multitrack master." The number of tracks depends upon the number of original sound sources you will have in your production. We are going to use four tracks in our example, so this step would be called "creating a four-track master."

The multitrack master is actually an interim step in the process. It allows you to put all your original sound sources onto one tape, in correct physical relationship to one another. But it normally does not involve putting the sound sources in correct volume-level relationship to one another.

The key to multitrack recording—in fact, to all soundtrack work—is timing. When you are working with music, for instance, a split-second beat can make all the difference in how professional the soundtrack sounds. Being able to bring in the narrator's voice at precisely the spot when the music swells to a crescendo and then shifts tempo to a different rhythm means that the narrator's voice is motivated to come in; it's not just haphazardly appearing after thirty seconds or so of music.

In most professional productions, several different musical selections will be used, or the same selection will be used several times, because one selection is not as long as the program. One way to handle this would be simply to link all the selections together, making sure you had a "music bed" long enough to cover all the information being presented in the program.

But a better way to handle it is to lay down each segment of the program separately. For instance, make sure that you provide enough of the opening music to adequately cover the time it will take for the narrator to say the opening words. But then, after listening to the combination of narrator and opening music, find a motivated spot to shift the music to the next selection. You might find that four or five seconds after the narrator has said the last words of the opening the music has a series of strong drum beats.

## SOUNDTRACKS: THE RIGHT SIDE OF THE SCRIPT

After the last beat, perhaps you can cut to another music selection that begins with a drum beat. Then, after establishing that new selection for a moment or two, you can bring the narrator or another voice source back in to begin a new thought within the program. The result is that the music doesn't just serve as background. Instead, it becomes a way to counterpoint and emphasize the words.

The multitrack interim master provides a vehicle for laying down each new sound source while listening to what's already on the tape. You'll find that it helps to have a stopwatch. In fact, many writer-producers will start timing music selections even before they begin writing program segments. In this way, they can write precisely enough words to fit into certain parts of a music selection. Again, the reason behind this is that it makes the program seem cohesive and well organized, with music used as an integral element and not as just something that's in the background.

Most programs begin with music. So you might begin by connecting a turntable to the four-track recorder. Now you would record the music you want to use to open the program from your record library. You'd record that selection onto one track of the four-track machine, let's say onto track one. And although you will be fading the music down so that it is "under" as background during many program segments, you'd record it onto the four-track at high volume level... 0 dB for the peaks. In this way, you can change your mind at any time concerning where you want music strong and where you want it under.

Let's say you want to let the music run for thirty seconds or so, then bring in opening narration. What you would do is listen to the music while looking at a stopwatch. As the watch hand nears thirty seconds, you'd look for a good transition point, like a spot where the tempo shifts. And you'd mark that transition point by noting the recorder's frame counter number.

Now you would rewind the four-track recorder's tape a few seconds back from that transition point. And you would hook up another recorder to the multi-track recorder. (Now you can see why most professionals hook all these separate sources up just one time, then use things like mixers and "patch panels" to connect one source or another to the output devices, like four-track recorders or cassette machines.)

On this source recorder, you'd put the edited narration tape and "cue it up" so that you have maybe two or three seconds of no sound or of room presence before the first word said by the narrator.

The reason you are backing up a bit on these tapes is so the tape machines can come up to speed before recording begins. That prevents distortion of voices caused by the start up of the machine's motor.

Now comes the beauty of multitrack recording. You can listen to the music on track one as you record narration on track two. So you can make certain that you have the precise relationship between the two sources.

Now you have two tracks recorded on the multitrack tape: music on one and voice on two. Let's suppose that you also need the sound effect of a machine, and that you want that sound effect to begin just as the narrator says the last word of the opening segment. You'd do this by either dubbing from a source recorder or a source turntable, just as you did for music and voice. And you'd locate the precise spot on track two where the narrator says the last word, then mark that spot with the frame counter, then begin recording the sound effect on track three when you reach that spot. As with other tracks, you'd record this at high volume level so you can make choices later.

When you are recording sound effects and music, by the way, you will normally start and stop the recording a bit before and after you think that you actually want the source to appear. In that way you leave some options open for later. For instance, suppose you want the machine sound effect to be established for a few seconds, then to bring in a voice-over by a factory worker. As the worker begins to talk, you want to gradually fade out the machine sound until it is totally gone. You'd do this by recording the SFX on track three. And you'd let it run longer than you think you will ever need. Now you'd put the voice-over of the factory worker onto track four, begining at an appropriate spot a few seconds after the SFX on track three begins. Later, during the "final mix," you can listen to the voice-over on track four while listening to the SFX on track three and decide precisely where you want the sound effect to fade out.

You can continue this process throughout the entire audio program. Typically, you'll always keep the same sort of sources on the same tracks—to make it easier during the final mix. But you can "checkerboard" the four-track in any way that you want. For example, you can make a music segue from one selection to another by recording the first selection on track one, then putting the second selection on tracks two, three, or four—whichever one is clear of

## SOUNDTRACKS: THE RIGHT SIDE OF THE SCRIPT

other sound sources. You would start the second music selection a bit before the spot that you wanted the segue to occur, so you have some latitude in the way you faded out the music on the first track while fading up the music on the second track.

You'll see why we stress the need for latitude when you begin step three, the "mix" to tie together all these separate sound sources. Step three is the equivalent of making a photocopy of several original materials. But the analogy falls apart a bit here, because you're not just making a copy. You're also adjusting the various levels of the multitrack recording during the copying process. This process is usually done through a "mixer" that allows you to individually adjust the volume level on each separate track and to combine as many or as few tracks as you want into a final "mixed master."

A professional mixer is often overwhelming to an untrained person. To understand what it does, you have to isolate one of the functions of the mixer at a time. Basically, all those switches and knobs on the mixer perform just a few functions. First, they allow you to control sound level on each channel "input" to the mixer without affecting any other input. So you can move the "potentiometer" or "pot" that is the volume control for channel one and just affect the volume of that channel. In this way, you can have a voice at 0 dB while you have music on another channel at -20 dB and then have a sound effect appear on yet a third channel at -10 dB. Each sound source can be adjusted separately.

Second, a mixer lets you combine various channels of inputs to various channels of outputs. You can have a wide variety of combinations, such as "8-in, 4-out" or "4-in, 1-out." For instance, a musical group may want to make a stereo, or two-channel, recording. They might want to have one vocalist's voice come out of the left speaker on the stereo system and the other vocalist's voice come out the right speaker. But they may want all of the four musical instruments to come out equally on both left and right speakers.

What we have here is a "6-in, 2-out" mixing situation. We are going to take six separate inputs—four instruments and two voices—and mix them together in various combinations so we get two outputs—one voice and all the instruments on output 1 and the other voice and all the instruments on output 2. This is done by switching various combinations of inputs to various outputs. If the voices are on channel one and channel two inputs, you'd punch a switch that sent channel one input to channel one output, and another switch would send channel two input to channel two output. If you had the instruments on channels three through six inputs, you'd punch switches on each of these input systems to send the inputs to both channel one and channel two output.

Third, mixers also frequently have a sound-shaping and enhancing function. So you could adjust various knobs to accentuate certain frequencies of each input channel. Let's say, for instance, that you've been forced to record someone speaking in a room in which there is a very loud hiss from an air-conditioning system. You can "notch out" a lot of that hissing noise by fiddling around with various "equalization and filtration" knobs on the mixer's input channel for that sound source until you find the major frequency of that hiss. By reducing the amount of volume you let through the mixer at that specific frequency, you can reduce or eliminate the hiss, yet still not hurt the rest of the frequencies that comprise that person's voice.

The final function a mixer performs is selecting the volume level and destination of outputs. You might not want to hear the same level of output in your engineering room that you put onto the final tape. So you can send one output volume level to studio monitor speakers and another volume level to the tape recorder. You can also select a "cue" function. This allows you, for instance, to cue up a record to the precise spot you want the sound to begin while you are recording something entirely different on the tape. This, incidentally, is the way disc jockeys can make those slick transitions from the end of one song to the start of another. As one song is going out on "program line" they are cueing up the next selection on the "preview" or "cue" channel.

In a very simple presentation, the mix may involve nothing more than running music up for thirty seconds or so, then fading it down while a narrator speaks for a while, then fading up the music to end the show. In a complex mix, you may be manipulating several tracks in terms of volume at the same time, and doing it throughout the program.

The problem is that you have to make all these decisions and manipulations in "real time." You can't stop and start the tape when you make a mistake unless you are fortunate enough to make a mistake during a time when there are pauses in all the separate sources. For example, if you have brought music totally out and you have no sound effects, you can then stop the tape between para-

## SOUNDTRACKS: THE RIGHT SIDE OF THE SCRIPT

graphs of narration. But, as is true in most cases, you'll make a mistake when you have music under the voice. If you stop and start the tape, you'll disrupt the music as well as the voice. And the result will be a "glitch" in the soundtrack where the music abruptly stops and starts.

What most producers do is run through the four-track tape once or twice while taking notes on the script. Then they will refer to those notes while actually mixing the track. They may write "Be sure to bring track one up here" or "Track three gets hot here. Drop volume." This annotated script also comes in very handy if you must remix a track several months down the line.

In this final step in soundtrack production, you are simply transferring all the materials that you put onto the multitrack master onto a final tape. It may be the actual tape you will be using to present the program or a tape you will be using to duplicate many copies of the program. In either case, what you will do is run through the program and adjust the sound levels of each track in relation to the other tracks. When you've finished, you will have a tape with music, voice, and sound effects all adjusted correctly in relationship to each other.

The great thing about a multitrack master is that you can make mistakes without messing up the relationship between tracks. You can, for example, accidentally keep the volume of the music too high so that it overpowers the opening words of narration. All you have to do is go back and try it again, with the volume level of the music track lower. You don't have to start from scratch with the original materials. And you can experiment with various starting and stopping points for each channel's information. That's why you typically record music or sound effects so that they start and end a bit before and after you think you will need them. You can always get rid of the excess sound by fading the volume control on that channel of the mixer down to zero. But, if you need to add more music or more sound effects time, you have to go back to the source materials and rerecord that section of the multitrack master.

So it saves you time in the long run to invest time in making the multitrack master. However, if your program is very simple, such as a few seconds of music up and then faded under while a narrator talks for several minutes, then music faded up again at the end of the show, you may want to skip step two. You might be willing to risk wasting a little time trying to get a final mix directly from source materials in order to keep quality high.

### The Importance of Staying Near the Source

It's possible to invest days in the process of creating a solid mix of a complex show. After you've invested that kind of time, it's difficult to be told by your client that he or she doesn't like a certain segment or a certain music score. When that happens, the temptation is simply to use the final mixed version of the program as a source for all the materials that don't need to be changed. For instance, suppose everything is okay except that you are pulling a paragraph of narration out. It is simple to duplicate all the other tracks onto another four-track machine and just fix the narration track. But there is a problem with this method.

The problem is that all media materials lose something in the process of duplication. It's just as true when you make a duplicate of an audiotape as it is when you make a photocopy of a picture. So the best way to keep any media program at a high level of quality is to keep close to the original materials. In audio, this translates to keeping close to the original recordings. Edit the narrator's voice track by physically cutting the original (carefully), then put that edited voice track onto the four-track master. Don't make a duplicate of the narrator's voice, then edit the duplicate. If you do, you're being safe . . . but you may be sorry.

To see why, just begin to count the "generations." The original voice material is the first generation. When you make a duplicate, you are at the second generation. After you put that duplicate onto the four-track interim master, you are at a third generation. When you mix that four-track into a final mix, you are at the fourth generation. And if you use that final mix to make duplicates for presentation, you are at the fifth generation. That's five times removed from the original voice. If a little quality is lost each time the tape is duplicated, you can imagine how much will be lost by the fifth generation.

What happens is that the noise gets a little higher with each generation and the frequencies get a little muddier and the volume gets a little lower. It isn't much for any one generation, but it gets worse with each succeeding generation because the problems compound each other.

Incidentally, that's why it is often smart to make all duplicates of a program from a master tape rather than making a duplicate from a duplicate. When making audiocassettes, for instance, it's often easier just to hook up two cassette recorders or to use a high speed duplicator that makes four or six copies at a time. But it would be better to make each individual cassette by returning to the four-track interim master and remixing the program onto cassette. It all depends upon how important perfect quality is, and upon how many generations of interim materials you already have used in the program.

## CONCLUSION

We've found that the best way to make sure that an audiotrack is done well is to do it last. Make it the final thing you do on a presentation. In that way, you have all the changes made before you begin. Also, you can tell precisely how much music you need as a transition or where it would really aid the program to have a sound effect that fits a specific visual.

We also do the audiotrack last because we are most ego-involved in a project by that time, and feel that the project is important. Therefore, we're willing to spend the time and care it takes to go through all the tedious processes that result in an interesting soundtrack.

# 7

# Visuals: The Left Side of the Script

## STATIC VERSUS DYNAMIC VISUALS

Describing the elements that could be included on the left side of the script, the side containing visuals and visual instructions, is more difficult than describing the right side of the script. That's because there is an enormous variety of visualization possible. Each medium, in fact, requires a different way of thinking about visuals. And each presentation requires a different type of visual support to ensure that the program objectives are met.

Although there are numerous variations within each of these areas, visuals fall into the following general categories:

*Graphics*, including text slides and charts or graphs. These are generally used to provide factual information or to call out key words and phrases from the soundtrack.

*Artwork*, including cartoon-style drawings and concrete or abstract renditions of real subjects. In motion media, you may use a special type of artwork, animation, that involves moving drawings. For most business communications, artwork is used where actual photography can't be used or where there is a need to show something that can't easily be photographed, such as gears housed within a metal covering.

*Photography*, including both location photography and studio photography. Photography makes up the bulk of most business visual communications, although some shows are done using graphics or artwork exclusively. Location photography, as we define it in this book, includes almost any type of image shot outside of the controlled studio environment. Studio photography, therefore, includes images shot within the controlled and artificial environment of a studio. That also covers the photographic process used to convert artwork and other objects into slides or film and videotape through copystand work. You will find, by the way, that we make little distinction between still photography and videography or cinematography. The processes differ, but the creative input is about the same in all these image-making systems.

Finally, there's an area of visualization that is growing more and more important each day. That's *computerized visuals*. Computer-generated graphics have long been a staple of business communications, but we did not have the flexibility available today. Modern systems, such as those used to produce the film *Tron* and many television commercials, allow the computer to create a close approximation of real life. As the technology develops, we can expect to see this technique priced right for the business market. And that will open up an entire range of options not available today. For example, a computer can convert a single still photograph of a person or a product into a three-dimensional image, adding the other sides and the depth to the image through a preprogrammed memory. It can even change the colors and size. Further, a computer can "remember" the basic choreography of a person walking, for example, and recall that movement with many variations. So you can begin to develop a file of figures and motions, then "paint" those figures and motions into many different scenes and sequences. Rather than setting up separate shooting situations for each new production, you can refer to your computerized "stock footage" to produce new programs.

Part of the decision concerning which visuals will be appropriate for any presentation is aided by the very nature of the medium; the type of visuals chosen depends upon the type of visuals best done by the camera and recording system. For instance, a filmstrip, a slide presentation, or visuals used in print pieces all involve "static" shots. The photographer is looking for a specific decisive moment when a still photograph can be captured that will

# VISUALS: THE LEFT SIDE OF THE SCRIPT

tell the story. Film and videotape, on the other hand, are "dynamic" media. The cinematographer or videographer looks for the sequence of moments that tells the story.

For this reason, it's important to have some command of visual media before writing the left side of a script. That doesn't mean that you must become a cinematographer or photographer; it does mean that you must develop some sensitivity to the reaction you and others have to various types of visuals and to various visual media. A still photo can be just as powerful as a motion picture scene, as shown by the work of many news photographers in places like Saigon, Kent State, and Cape Canaveral. And a length of motion picture film can be even more boring than a still photograph of the same subject, as witnessed by many of us who have sat through "talking head" illustrated lectures.

The key is to understand what is possible with various types of visuals and with various budgets. Then to create a script that explores that possibility as far as it will go. Equally important, try to create a script that effectively merges both right and left sides into a meaningful whole.

## HOW TO VISUALIZE A SCRIPT

All of these theories and concepts are things you'll absorb over time. But that doesn't help you much the first time you face the task of filling the left side of a script page with effective visuals. It's the sort of job that's overwhelming until you've done it a few times and understand that it can be accomplished.

The best way to begin visualizing a script is by trying to imagine what the final product would look like if you had neither budget nor time constraints. Part of that could be picturing yourself standing in the back of the room, watching an audience watching your program and "reading their minds" concerning their reaction to your work. What reaction do you want?

Next, look at existing visuals available for this presentation. You want the entire program, or at least entire program segments, to have a similar style, and that style will probably be set by the existing visuals. If the program is part of a series, look at other shows in the series to determine the common stylistic elements.

Now it's time to begin specifying visuals. Typically, visuals are written ALL CAPS and single-spaced. If the program is a slide show or filmstrip, you'll probably include individual visual numbers. If it is a videotape or a film, you may include scene numbers or directions concerning time of day and location.

Here's a sample of a slide presentation's visual column:

1. MAIN TITLE, "HOW TO MAKE TIME" (BLACK BACKGROUND, ORANGE HELVETICA TYPE)
2.-7. MONTAGE OF SLIDES SHOWING VARIOUS WAYS PEOPLE WASTE TIME.
8. LONG SHOT (LS) OF FACTORY FRONT
9. MEDIUM SHOT (MS) OF FACTORY DOOR, JOHN ENTERS. HE IS MID-THIRTIES, BLUE-COLLAR.

What you're doing is creating a shot list, not a full description of each and every shot. This is because, in most cases, the visualization is done in two stages. You'll first suggest a general sequence, such as writing down that you would like the photographer to take several shots that lead a person from his or her car into the factory. You'll take a look at how many paragraphs you have, how much music, how many sound effects, and then perhaps specify that you need three or four shots for this part of the script. Then, when it is time to do a final script, you'll specify precisely which shots will cover this area of the script. At this time, you need put in only enough description so that you can tell if the slide you are looking at during the assembly and programming process is the correct one for that place on the soundtrack.

When you produce a film or videotape, you'll do something similar. Here's an example of a film or video visual script:

ACT TWO, SCENE THREE. INTERIOR, DAY. WE ARE VIEWING JOHN AND MARY SEATED IN AN OFFICE. JOHN IS MID-THIRTIES BLUE-COLLAR WORKER, OBVIOUSLY UNCOMFORTABLE IN MARY'S PRESENCE. HE FIDGETS IN SIDE CHAIR. MARY IS MID-TWENTIES, OBVIOUSLY EXECUTIVE, SEATED BEHIND DESK WITH A YELLOW PAD VISIBLE.

Notice that it isn't necessary to be extremely explicit in regard to camera angles, framing, or other creative elements. Most visual communicators prefer to view the scene before deciding upon a specific framing and angle. For the same reason, you need not

## VISUALS: THE LEFT SIDE OF THE SCRIPT

provide a detailed shot-by-shot list for a film or video script. Instructions such as "INTERIOR" or "DAY" aren't always necessary, nor is it necessary to list all the props found in a normal office. You do, however, want to list those props that are essential to the scene, just as you would list elements of dress or of characterization that are important for the still photograph or motion medium.

The best way to visualize a script, we've found, is to begin by going through the script's words and other sound elements, jotting down ideas for visuals as they occur from the reading. You'll probably find that you can determine at least half the visuals in a typical script through this method. Then go back through the script again, perhaps also asking others to do the same thing, and try to come up with a few more visuals.

Look for key words and phrases, then try to think of a concrete or abstract visual that will say the same thing or will add to what is said. Here's an example:

> You're now on the threshold to the future ... and it's a future that is changing at lightning speed. So now we literally serve our customers at the speed of light, using sophisticated computer and telecommunications systems.

On your first attempt at visualization, you might come up with a shot of a computer terminal and a multiline telephone device, but have trouble coming up with a visual that says "future/threshold" and one that shows "lightning speed/speed of light." You could simply "call out" these key words with text slides, but it is usually better to save these for last-ditch problems; otherwise the program looks like a projected book, not an AV presentation.

So you should now begin to think abstractly, looking for symbols or concepts that might suggest some of the topics you are discussing in the script. Perhaps you can show both the future and the speed of light with a space ship. Or maybe you'll use streaks of light or an astronomical view of a distant galaxy. You might want to emphasize "threshold" by showing a wide-angle shot of a person walking down a long corridor, perhaps in a sterile modern building. Your choice will depend upon your personal vision, what's available, and the shots adjacent to this sequence.

This concept of adjacent visuals goes back to the "third effect" we discussed in the previous chapter. Just as the combination of a certain visual and a certain soundtrack segment can say something different than either element says by itself, so can the combination of several visuals make a statement that is different than the statement made by any single visual. Visual communicators have experimented with this effect for years, using "montage" (for combinations of visuals put together in a sequence of individual images, as on film or videotape) and "collage" (for combinations of still images into a single visual element). You see it all the time in theatrical presentations (and sometimes in documentaries and news, too). For example, the lovers kiss and the image cuts to pounding surf. Or the news story shows a crushed and battered car, then a single child's shoe on the pavement, then a shot of a gravestone or hospital room. By combining images, we help the viewer make connections between several shots so that he or she gets a more powerful message.

You should also make sure that the abstract visuals you choose will be understood by audience members. If the visuals jar the audience, it will disrupt the flow of the program. That's because each of us perceives visuals in a very subjective way, based on past associations as well as on our present reading of the specific shot. So a bright-red abstract visual may be perceived as a "happy" image by some audience members, who recall their red sports car or the red wrapping on a Christmas present. But other audience members may recall blood or fire or some other red visual that is not a happy memory for them.

The one thing you want to avoid at all cost is calling up an incorrect association. And you want the abstraction to be understandable enough so that the audience doesn't have to spend time thinking about what it represents. While they are investing this time, they are not listening to the next part of your message.

After you've developed most of the concrete and abstract visuals possible within a program, you'll probably still be stuck with some open spaces. Now is the time to consider graphics or text slides.

## GRAPHICS, TEXT SLIDES, AND OTHER VISUAL CHOICES

In this age of computerization, it's not surprising that many firms have developed systems to create type slides, charts, and graphs using computers. These systems range from simple display screen hookups that allow you to photograph something you've created on the screen to complex digital systems that actually impress various colors and lines directly onto film.

The advantage of computerization is that the computer remembers. You can teach it a pie chart or graph format, then use that same format time and time again. You can change the values, even the size, and the computer will still give you a recognizable image. The disadvantage of computerization is that very high resolution or very intricate and elaborate drawings can only be done when you're willing to spend a great deal of money on the process.

This means that a line drawing of a person or some similar visual that requires shading and curved lines and some irregularities or shadings may be difficult for a computer to handle. But the standard graphic elements are very easy.

Those standard graphic elements include various chart and graph forms, like pie charts, bar graphs, lines and curves plotting points along an "$x$-$y$" curve, and some adaptations of these elements that involve adding depth or volume. And the biggest mistake most producers make concerning these graphic elements is making them too complex.

If you're trying to explain how an Individual Retirement Account or Annuity (IRA) can earn more money over a period of years than a taxable investment will, you could present a series of calculations showing the amount earned over time for each type of account. Or you could simply imply actual amounts by having one bar graph be bigger than another, or by using one graph with a separate color showing that a certain amount of money at the top of the graph will be earned only by IRA accounts. Unless the facts and figures are vital, or required for legal reasons, you'll make your point better with the abstraction. Then people can visually see that an IRA earns more.

Incidentally, it isn't always necessary to use a chart or a graph. You can use a symbolic representation to accomplish the same things. In the IRA example you could use a studio shot of an apple, and add a "Retirement Contribution" label. The next slide could show that same apple with a bite out of it, and a "Tax Bite" label. The next slide could show four apples labeled "IRA" on one side of the screen, while a grouping of two apples—each with a bite out—could be shown on the other side of the screen, and called "TAXABLE."

One reason to use the apple analogy, or to use some other analogy that involves real things rather than the abstraction of a chart or a graph, is that many people are unable to read charts and unwilling to invest the effort required to learn how to read them. This, of course, depends upon your audience. A group of business people will probably be very accustomed to charts and graphs. They may, in fact, prefer to receive their information in that way rather than through an analogy.

In the same way, you have to consider your audience when using graphics or text created by an artist or graphics designer. It's tempting, for instance, to use cartoon characters to add some humor to a presentation. But those cartoons could easily turn off a portion of the audience. Or you might find that the audience members have a real problem trying to translate a line drawing or a watercolor sketch into "real life." They might prefer seeing actual photographs, even black-and-whites, rather than a full-color drawing.

Incidentally, one time to consider line drawings or other artwork is when you want the audience to step outside reality, to think in abstract terms rather than concrete terms relating to their work. These techniques are also useful when you don't want to "poke a finger" at any individual or group within your firm. For instance, you might want to use line drawings or other artwork to depict employee thieves rather than in any way imply that the models you have chosen are thieves.

If you are primarily interested in text slides rather than graphics, again you have several choices. Computers can give you text slides in almost any combination of colors you might imagine. And it is relatively easy for you to shoot graphic slides yourself, or to have them shot. The process usually involves typesetting the words or doing a very clean carbon-ribbon typing job, then photographing that typesetting onto either color slide film or a special black-and-white film of extreme contrast.

If you photograph onto color slide film, you'll typically use a colored filter, or put the type on a colored background, so that the slide has a colored field and black letters. If you use high contrast black-and-white film, you'll end up with white letters on a black background. These letters can be colored, or the letters can be superimposed, or "burned-in," on another image.

Your choice of method for showing text slides or text scenes for motion pictures and videotapes depends upon the medium. A slide is usually viewed as a static element, so the audience won't mind viewing some words or a specific graphic for a short period of

# VISUALS: THE LEFT SIDE OF THE SCRIPT

time. But motion pictures and videotape are dynamic media. It seems senseless to have a motionless grouping of words or other graphic on the screen for any length of time. What producers usually do is create "builds" or "animation," or make sure that the graphics and text can be superimposed over a live image. This is fairly simple with both media, because computerized character generators for video and photography cameras for film are available in every major production center.

The key idea is to keep the graphics simple, and to make sure that the audience has no problem combining the words they are hearing with the visuals they are seeing. If you want to talk about the rise in the number of Social Security recipients versus the decline in number of those in the work force paying for Social Security, one way to handle it would be to show scenes of crowds of people, with more old people than young people in the crowd. But it wouldn't add to the message to superimpose a graph or chart that adds motion to that shot, such as a graph showing payments out going up while payments in go down. With the motion of the crowd plus the motion of the graph, you're asking a lot of the audience. It would be better, perhaps, to first show the crowd, then go to the graph, then back to the crowd again.

What you are trying to do is add interest and information to a fairly static visualization, yet not make the visuals so complex that they can't be read correctly. And one way to make them more readable is to keep some consistency within each visual and within each group of visuals. You could, for instance, set up a certain color consistency, where every time the audience saw green type, they'd know it meant money. Or you could set up a placement consistency, where the audience would always know that information concerning income would be bottom right while information concerning expenses would be top left. You'd make all these decisions early in the program, as part of the program design.

## PROGRAM DESIGN

A vital element in any presentation is design; the design must be consistent from visual to visual and between visuals and words. The type of design chosen for any program is most often based upon the style determined by the person who does the work of visualization—the visual communicator.

In some cases, the visual communicator is you, the writer and producer. In these cases, the person behind the camera must simply document what you've designed, or you must document it yourself if you have the skill. In other cases, the person behind the camera becomes the designer, interpreting your broad description of a visual as he or she thinks it will work best in the chosen medium. As usual in this business, the key to successfully visualizing a program, especially when using support people like photographers, is communication. If you can't accurately describe in words the visual you want, you'll have to accept the visual you get.

This isn't always bad, by the way, because your idea may not be the best idea, the best way to translate words into pictures. The truth is that there are always many different ways to visualize anything, and the choice is one of personal preference as well as one involving audience demographics, budgets, and other "scientific" elements.

That's not to say that you shouldn't carefully select visuals. You should. But you also shouldn't reject visuals just because they don't precisely match your idea of the image at that point. Again, it's a question of pacing. It's better to have two moderately effective visuals, each up for fifteen or twenty seconds, than it is to leave one stunner on the screen for forty seconds.

That's because people read visuals as impressions, and rapid impressions, rather than as detailed sources of information. So the most crucial thing in selecting or specifying visuals is the visual style demanded by the program.

## VISUAL STYLE

Many photographers and filmmakers are "typed" because of the look they impart to every visual they create. It's not that they can't create a different look. They just prefer a certain style and use it frequently. Other visualizers, especially those who work as business communicators, must try very hard *not* to develop a certain look; instead, they must learn to adapt their visual style to the purpose of the presentation.

## VISUALS: THE LEFT SIDE OF THE SCRIPT

We don't expect, for instance, to see the same visual style in a television documentary that we do in a television situation comedy. In fact, those few times when a dramatic program copied a documentary or news format, beginning with Orson Welles' "War of the Worlds," the audience has been left confused about the difference between fact and fiction. And we don't expect a training presentation to have the same style as a motivational or recognition program. What we do expect, however, is that the style chosen for a program will match the purpose of that presentation. If that match does not occur, the discordance creates a barrier to effective communications.

Suppose, for instance, that you are trying to produce an effective training program to help United Way solicitors within your firm handle the bookkeeping involved in their job. At the same time, suppose that you must also develop a program those solicitors can use to motivate employees to contribute to the United Way. Each program will require a different style.

The solicitor training program is pretty straightforward. Show the forms and procedures, and show the solicitors the best way to use those forms and procedures. It doesn't require motion, so you can use slides, filmstrips, or overhead projection. And it doesn't require elaborate photography or graphics design. So the style you choose for this program will probably be very simple and uncluttered, perhaps involving close-ups of various parts of each form and a flowchart or checklist of the proper procedure.

The employee motivation program, in contrast, must reach employees at an emotional level. In addition, it must touch a broad variety of benefits and motives to contribute; and it must entertain, in the sense that it must maintain interest on the part of viewers. A text slide or overhead projection listing benefits probably won't do the job. Instead, you'll probably choose film, videotape, or still photography shot on location, showing United Way programs helping people. And it will require sensitivity on the part of the visualizer to create images that are neither maudlin nor meaningless.

In the case of the training program, the most important thing to remember about the visualization is clarity. The information contained on each visual must be clear and easily understood. Your job will be one of organization: organizing segments of the forms into component parts that can be easily understood without losing the continuity of the entire form.

The motivation program, in contrast, requires more than understanding. It requires emotion. So you will look for the visual style that will enhance the emotional feeling you want the audience to have. You could approach it from a couple of different standpoints.

You might want to evoke an emotion of deep caring for the poor unfortunates served by the United Way. So maybe you would shoot very realistic and harsh visuals of a poor family in a hovel, showing how they lived before the United Way helped. Or maybe you'd like to show how much good the United Way does, using beautiful, heartwarming shots of people after the United Way has helped them improve their lot in life. In actuality, you'd probably do a bit of both. You might begin with the harsh, realistic approach, then gradually change your visual style to show how the people's lives are being changed with United Way's help.

Your job is to designate the style of the program's visuals based on your understanding of the purpose and objectives you've developed. And it's just like talking about music; it's often very difficult to describe what a group of visuals should look like with words. You're better off looking for similar visuals and using them as a guideline.

The idea behind visualizing most programs is to look at both the forest and the individual trees. If you overfly a forest, you'll get an impression of leaves in a giant blanket . . . sort of a feeling of "green" and "thick." If you walk through the forest, studying each individual tree trunk and leaf structure, you'll get several individual impressions, such as "gnarled," "almond-shaped," "big," "brown," or "mossy and dank." Both the overview and the individual impressions are necessary to get an accurate picture of the forest.

We can extend the analogy further to show the way in which the same subject can evoke a different mood. Walking through a forest in daylight, along a manicured path, is a different experience than fighting through a brambled brushpile and forest in the middle of the night, alone and lost. A visual treatment representing that difference between daylight and darkness might involve different filters, different lenses, and a different approach to every individual shot. You might, for instance, focus on tree leaves framing the sun—or on gnarled branches silhouetted against moon and clouds. You might use a wide-angle shot to show wide-open spaces along a path—or a telephoto shot to compress many groups of leaves and branches into an impenetrable image of density.

You might use the same stylistic approach when working with film and with still images, but you'll have to work a bit differently in each medium to give the same impression. A still photograph of a path doesn't give the same impression as a "walk" down that path via film. And an aerial photograph of a section of forest doesn't give the impression of vastness and depth possible by shooting a few minutes of videotape from a helicopter. You set the style when writing the left side of the script, then the task becomes trying to create visuals that will correctly represent that style.

## VISUAL CLARITY

Most adults over the age of about thirty-five did not grow up in a visual age. Most of the learning we did involved written materials, not AV programs or other visual sources. And most of the entertainment media we used, including early television and motion pictures, was content-oriented rather than visually stimulating. So, from both a producer's and an audience member's standpoint, there's a problem with visual fluency.

The problem is that we are not used to looking at visuals and reading them as fast as we can read words on a page. So visuals have to be exceptionally clear for us to grasp the full meaning of that visual message. By "clear," we don't mean just technical clarity, although that's obviously important. Rather, we also mean clear in content and easy to read.

When creating word slides or other graphics, there's a simple way to tell whether or not the visual will be clear and readable by someone sitting ten or twelve feet back from the screen. Just place the artwork or form on the floor and look at it while standing directly over it. If you can't easily read and understand it from that distance, an audience won't have any better luck when it is projected.

In practice, this means that you can probably put one sentence of information on a slide, but that a full paragraph is too much. You can split an 8½ × 11 form into four or six parts, but a 17 × 22 computer form should be divided into eight or twelve parts.

Incidentally, there's often a temptation on your part, or that of your client, to save money and time by using letters, memos or computer forms as they are. The thinking is that the audience will see "the real thing." In fact, the audience won't see much. Computer forms, especially, are tough to read close up, let alone from a distance. Photographing those forms doesn't improve them because the photographic process tends to reduce contrast, not enhance it.

Contrast is the difference between light and dark; that is, the difference between the background field and the foreground letters on a text slide or other visual. A black cat in a snowfield and a white cat in a coal bin are both high contrast subjects. A gray cat in smog or haze is a low contrast subject. In most cases, higher contrast visuals are easier to read than lower contrast visuals. So a light-gray or light-green computer-paper background with the low density type common to many computer printers becomes a smoggy blob on a projection screen.

Most professional producers start with a high contrast original, such as a photostat or at least black type on white paper. They'll invest the money and time required to convert computer printouts or photocopied forms to simplified materials that can easily be photographed. Then they'll choose a combination of background color and text color that offers a pleasant high contrast visual.

One of the most common combinations is a black background and an orange or amber foreground. This avoids the extreme contrast of white letters on black, yet still offers a sufficiently contrasty visual, especially when viewed in a darkened room. In most cases, the darker background and lighter lettering works better than the reverse, simply because the lettering stands out as light against dark. A poor combination, by the way, would be either a deep-blue foreground against a black background or a yellow background with red letters.

You should also consider advancing versus receding colors. Some colors, like red, jump right out at you. Others, like blue, appear to fade back into the middle distance. In general, you want the text or main information to advance while the background recedes. You wouldn't, for instance, want a red background with blue lettering because the audience's eyes would be drawn past the letters to the background.

The style of lettering is also important. Take a tip from billboard creators, who must make sure that what they produce is easily read. They use standard, simple type styles. And they focus on strong, vivid color combinations.

In terms of "real" visuals, the same things hold true. Readability is best when the visual is simplified as much as possible. If you're producing an audiovisual presentation to show grocery store sales representatives how to stock shelves, you might need one or two long "establishing" shots to set the scene, but you'd do well to concentrate most of your visuals on tight close-ups of individual shelves and shelf sections. You want to aid the viewer in seeing the important elements within a visual, not to force the viewer to search through many unnecessary elements to locate the main point of the visual.

That's why, incidentally, it is sometimes better to abandon the realism of a location shoot for the studio. In a controlled studio environment, it's often easier to "dress" a set so it approximates an actual location but doesn't include the distractions of that location. In a grocery store, for instance, it's rarely possible to shoot a long shot that shows an entire width of shelving along a store aisle. That's because you can't back up enough to encompass the entire aisle without running into the next set of shelves. In a studio, however, you can simply set up one row of shelves.

Of course, studio photography can be tedious and expensive. Instead of shooting ten or twelve separate location shots each hour, you are probably talking about lighting, dressing the set, and shooting just one or two shots each hour in a studio. And some things just don't lend themselves to studio shooting. A lawnmower, for instance, or some other item that is usually used outside is better shot outside. So the decision to shoot in a studio rather than on location is usually made when there is no other way to get the clarity required for a shot.

## SCENES AND SEQUENCES

You also want to think in terms of scenes and sequences, even when dealing with still photographs or slides. In a film or videotape, a scene is typically one setting or one group of visuals that makes a specific point. A sequence might involve two or three scenes; for instance, a sequence might begin with a scene at location A, continue with a scene involving some means of transportation, and end with a scene of the arrival at location B. The sequence involves a passage of time or of distance while the scene isolates a place or a moment.

People producing programs involving still images sometimes treat each individual image separately, forgetting that these images will be viewed as parts of scenes and sequences in the final presentation. Professionals use light tables that allow them to see the entire show at a glance, and to make certain that each visual works well as an individual shot and as seen in relationship to other visuals adjacent to it.

Sometimes the relationship between visuals is very subtle. For instance, a close-up shot of a person glancing to the left can be followed by a long shot where the important information is in the left side of the frame. And color is often used as a transitional element, such as by moving from a golden sunrise to an interior shot of an office with yellow walls or to a close-up of some other "warm-colored" element.

The way to learn about sequences and scenes is to analyze entertainment media and other business communications by paying attention to the visual content rather than the verbal content. Watch for transition points and look for common elements between the shots linked together between those transition points. You'll notice several common transition techniques and ways to link shots together.

One of the most common elements is "screen direction"; the motion or location within the frame of the principal subject in one shot is continued in the next shot. The "bad guys" always travel from right to left, whether we are looking at them in close-up or long shots. And the "good guys" chasing them travel right to left, too, so we understand that they are going in the same direction. If the bad guys and good guys were headed to a confrontation, like a *High Noon* shoot-out, the director would begin the sequence by establishing a distinctive screen direction for each group. The "black hats" will move from right to left while the "white hats" will move in the opposite direction, left to right. Even if we are seeing an individual bad guy or good guy, that same direction will hold true. The bad guy would be framed so he is to the right of the screen while the good guy will be on the left of the screen.

You'll see the same concern for screen direction in industrial films or slide presentations. Suppose two people are seated across a

# VISUALS: THE LEFT SIDE OF THE SCRIPT

desk. One will normally be shown on the left, or at least somewhat to the left of center, while the other will usually be on the right. This provides a sense of shot-to-shot continuity and helps the viewer recall which person is in which role regardless of whether we are seeing the entire office or a close-up of a face. The viewer subconsciously expects to see person A on the left and person B on the right, and will be distracted if screen direction suddenly shifts.

You'll also frequently see scenes put together, or transitions between scenes made, using "like-to-like" as a technique. This has become a cliche, in some cases, as when the scene shifts from a fire burning in a fireplace to an extreme close-up of a lit match. But it's still an effective way to link shots together.

If you observe enough presentations, you'll see many different types of sequences and transitions. Many of these linkages just happen naturally during the course of production. In short, they are lucky accidents. But it's still your job to suggest visuals with enough description to indicate your thinking concerning the screen direction, colors, possible transition elements, and other visual considerations.

## HOW PEOPLE PERCEIVE VISUALS

We could write a book about the variety of visuals you can use to impart a message. In fact, we have, and so have many other people. So we won't discuss photography, filmmaking, or videography in any great depth within this section. Instead, we'll concentrate on what you need to know either to shoot effective visuals yourself or to direct the shooting by other people.

We are not talking about the mechanics of choosing lenses and films, or of how to operate a camera. Instead, we are talking about an intellectual process that must take place each time you become involved in the visualization of a program.

It starts with an understanding of what people are looking at when they look at a visual. It's a flat surface, not a three-dimensional reality, but a two-dimensional approximation of reality. We've all seen—and some of us have shot—pictures that make it look as if a tree is growing out of someone's head. That's because what we saw in real life, in three dimensions, is different from what the film saw when we tried to capture that reality. So you have to immediately realize that you are not dealing with real life. If you want people to accept what you are presenting to them, you have to find a way to approximate real life as well as you can, but without the added dimension of depth.

Ocean views are a prime example of the problem that can occur. In reality, those scenes rely upon several senses to have an impact upon us. We hear the cry of gulls and the surf pounding against the beach; we intellectually absorb all that and are impressed. Film is not impressed. You can't hear the wind or the surf or the gulls. You must, instead, capture those feelings on a flat plane that will appeal to just one sense.

Visual communicators use many different techniques to translate three dimensions into two. We'll discuss a few that are especially pertinent to business communications.

You can lend an impression of depth to a visual in several different ways. One of the most common is to use foreground objects. For example, shoot a picture of a house through the branches of a tree or shoot a long view of an office by framing it through a doorway. Using motion media, you can lend depth to a shot by changing the image, using a "pan" (horizontal motion of the camera around a fixed point) or a "zoom" (motion from a close-up to a long shot from a fixed point). Or you can physically move the camera, using a "dolly" (moving toward or away from the main subject) or a "trucking shot" (moving sideways in relation to the subject).

You can also add depth through perspective cues. The classic example is the way in which railroad tracks seem to come together in the distance. But perspective also works with human subjects. You could, for instance, put a person in the foreground of a shot with several people using products in the background. The viewer will automatically "measure" the distance between people and will get a perception of depth because the foreground person is larger than the background people.

You can also isolate certain elements within a shot through the use of selective focus. This technique takes advantage of the fact that camera lenses have limited "depth of field" at various lens openings. As an example, visualize a chess board as seen in close-up through a camera lens. If the lens is wide open, chances are that just one line of chess pieces will be in focus. Let's say that the lens is focused on the king and queen. The two rows of pawns ahead of that row will be blurred because the lens can't focus in depth. If you closed down the lens, changing the opening from a large hole to a pinhole, the depth of field would be greater. Now you would be able to keep every piece on the board in sharp focus.

This selective focus technique allows you to blur foreground objects. You could shoot a factory through a chain fence, using one link in the fence as a fuzzy frame for the factory. Or you could shoot just one item on an assembly line, yet still give the perception of a massive assembly line through blurred foreground and background objects.

With motion media, you can add an element of extra interest to selective focus with a technique called "follow focus." You might start with a telephone in sharp focus in the foreground. On the soundtrack, we'd hear the phone ring. As it rings, the shot would shift focus to a person in the background who looks up at the sound of the ring. Again, this technique lets you emphasize important elements within the frame while still including other elements to add interest to the shot.

The opposite of selective focus is having everything within a shot in sharp focus. And this is often accomplished with a wide-angle lens. Selective focus, in contrast, is often accomplished with a telephoto lens. Lenses can, in fact, be used to create a wide variety of visual possibilities. For example, a telephoto lens normally compresses things, making them appear closer together than they are. So you could really give the audience a perception of "crowded space" by shooting a room through a telephoto lens. The room would look as if all the peple and furnishings were piled next to each other. You could create the opposite effect, of "wide-open spaces," by using a wide-angle lens that makes things look farther apart than they are. In both cases, you are altering reality to give a specific impression to the audience.

It is this impression of reality that allows you to capture three-dimensional subjects onto two-dimensional materials. Without the ability to create that impression, it's very difficult to create a program that will meet your communications objectives. So it is vital to your success as a communicator that you spend some time looking at visuals with an "eye" toward the way in which they translate reality.

## FLUIDITY

The concept of fluidity is vital to the style and feeling of a program. It's similar to pacing, but it involves the content and continuity of the visuals as well as the speed with which visuals change. Fluidity can make a long program seem shorter, and vice versa.

Film and videotape, as motion media, demand special concern for flow. Abrupt changes between shots and scenes are far more noticeable in films or videotapes than within filmstrips and slide shows. When visualizing a program, it's always important to view the intermediate parts of the program in "real time"; that is, as they will be seen by the audience after they are linked together. It's only in that way that you can check the fluidity of the presentation.

One way to keep a program moving, to give it good pacing and fluidity, is by varying angles and camera positions frequently. One rule fledgling filmmakers learn by rote is to change image size and camera angle after each shot. In other words, move from a long shot with the camera at the height of a standing person to a close-up with the camera near ground level and then to a medium shot with the camera high above the subject. This varies the image being seen by the audience and protects the filmmaker from the "jump cut" problem.

A jump cut occurs when two pieces of film or segments of videotape are spliced together so that the subject appears to instantly move, or jump, to another position or so that some object within the scene appears to jump in or out of position. For example, if you've shot a medium shot of a person working on a piece of machinery with a wrench, and then splice that shot to a shot of the same person without the wrench, viewers will observe the wrench magically disappearing.

There are two ways to avoid jump cuts. One, called "matched action," involves repeating the same action in long shot, medium shot, and close-up, as required by the script. You would ask the person with the wrench to repeat the same action three or four times as you changed camera angles and image size. You can see the problem with this approach, especially when using nonprofessionals. They simply can't repeat the same action in the same way time after time.

The second way to solve this problem of jump cuts is with a "cut-away." As the term implies, this is a shot that cuts away from the main action. For example, you see a close-up of a newsmaker answering a question, then the camera cuts away to a shot of a reporter taking notes. You hear the newsmaker's voice over the reporter shot. In a few seconds, you return to the close-up of the newsmaker. But enough time has passed so you have forgotten precisely what the last close-up looked like.

Cut-aways are especially helpful in compressing time to aid the flow of a presentation. You show the person beginning the process, then cut away to a close-up of the person's face in intense concentration, then go back to a long or medium shot of the process near completion. Although just a few seconds of time has elapsed on film, you have implied the passage of more time and found a way to create a concise, fluid sequence without jarring jump cuts or obvious editing.

Although some of these concepts may seem of importance only to professional filmmakers and videographers, they are actually very similar to the train of thought you must have when producing in any medium using visuals. A slide presentation or filmstrip demands fluidity, too. And some concern about sequencing, and avoiding too obvious jumps in action, is also important. You soon learn to specify various camera angles and image sizes, moving from close-up to long shot, back to medium shot, into a cut-away, just as if you were creating a motion sequence.

You do have more latitude, of course, in some still media. If you are producing a single-projector slide program or a filmstrip, there is a finite but very small length of time in which the first image on the screen is gone and the next one has not yet appeared. And the audience doesn't expect you to fill in all the blanks for them. They will accept the fact that in one shot a person is in an office and in the next he or she is in a car. You needn't necessarily show the intermediate steps between office and car because the viewer will automatically understand that those steps happened during the slide change. However, you can't assume that the viewer will be able to automatically fill in blanks concerning things they know little about. So you wouldn't want to create a sequence of visuals that leapt from a view of the outside of a machine to a close-up of the deepest interior of the machine without showing a slide or two of the steps required to reach that interior.

One special type of program that requires extreme care concerning fluidity is the multi-image show. These programs may involve several slide projectors and perhaps a film projector or large-screen video device. Rarely will only one image be on the screen at a time. Instead, you must not only be concerned with images adjacent in sequence, but also be concerned with images adjacent on the screen.

What can happen is that one image is so prominent it takes over the viewer totally. Other adjacent images are never seen. A classic case is a certain diet soft drink commercial in which the model was so attractive that no one ever saw the can of pop in her hand. This can happen in multi-image, especially when you are combining a colorful and vibrant motion picture with still photographs. What you want to do in these cases is use the same theories regarding eye movement we talked about in the chapter on print.

When you are changing images in a multi-image presentation, you should follow the same thinking process. Our eyes normally will go to the source of motion. But there's usually so much motion in a multi-image show (or there should be), that the eye has trouble following it. We can make it easier by setting up a continuous direction of motion, typically always from left to right. So we would change the slide on the far left first, then move across the screen. Or we would change all the images at the same time, but make certain that the image on the far left "pointed" to the images to the right.

## WHEN TO CHANGE SHOTS

There's an old joke that goes, "How long were Abe Lincoln's legs? Long enough to reach the floor." In a sense, the answer to "How long should a shot stay on the screen?" is the same. "Long enough to impart a message." But there are some guidelines:

First, look at the amount of activity within the shot. If it is a still photograph or slide, is it "busy," with lots of action happening? If so, it can stay on the screen for quite awhile, at least long enough for you to see every element at least twice. And if it is a length of motion picture film, you can stay on the same shot for quite a length of time, as long as things are happening within that shot. For instance, a person with an expressive face who is doing some activity on the screen can hold the viewer's attention almost indefinitely.

The motion happening on the screen means that you don't have to add motion by changing the shot.

The producer's rule of thumb says that a still photograph should be changed every six to ten seconds. Under ideal conditions, that makes a lot of sense. About every two to three sentences on a script, you'd change slides. But, if you take an eighty slide tray as a standard, you will be using six to ten slides each minute, or have a maximum show length of eighty divided by six, or less than fourteen minutes. And if you should happen to need a fast-paced opening and closing, you may end up with a maximum show length of less than that—more like ten minutes. Again, the ideal presentation may actually be this short, but a great many business presentations can't be condensed into ten to fourteen minutes. So you end up with a slower-paced visual flow.

One alternative is to go to 140-slide trays. But many producers avoid these because there is a danger that slides may hang up in the narrower slots of these 140-slide trays. A second alternative is to use a two-projector or multiprojector format.

## ASSEMBLING VISUALS

One of the major pleasures in media production is putting together many dissimilar visual elements into a cohesive and interesting program. The actual process you use depends upon the medium, but the theory behind visual assembly remains the same. It involves two separate decision-making efforts, one for timing and the other for visual sequencing. Both must be done simultaneously for the best effect.

In practice, most decisions are made naturally, based on the way the audiotrack sounds and the visuals look. When you are editing film or videotape, there are certain obvious starting and stopping points. You may, for instance, start a shot as a person walks into the room and end it when that person sits at a desk. When you are compiling a slide program, slide changes will usually be triggered by a change in thought on the audiotrack, a change in the beat of the music, or a cue based on a sound effect. So you have to be sure that you are aware of what constitutes an opportunity to make a change.

A paragraph can't be seen on an audiotape, but you can generally tell when a thought shifts. You should plan on changing slides or making a film/videotape edit when the thought shifts.

The technical processes for assembling videotape, film, and slides or filmstrips are dissimilar. But the creative process is about the same. In videotape or film, you generally first compile shots into scenes and sequences, then begin compiling scenes and sequences until you have a finished product. In slide shows or filmstrips, you might start in much the same way, by grouping together individual visuals. The difference between these still media and motion media is that you will typically work with just the visuals and a script when compiling stills. For motion media, on the other hand, you normally need to have a soundtrack, or at least have very accurate timing of the soundtrack segments. Without that accurate timing, you don't know how long to run each scene or sequence.

The way we generally handle assembling either motion or still media is with some "rough cut" of the soundtrack. It may be just the narrator's voice or the music track and voice mixed together with little regard for volume level. But having the soundtrack available while we assemble visuals makes it far easier to tell when we have too many visuals or too few for a certain segment.

On the other hand, most novice producers should do the exact opposite. They should first assemble the visuals, then create the soundtrack. As we indicated in the previous chapter, this makes it easier to adjust music transitions or the length of other audio segments to fit the visuals available. What you're trying to avoid, of course, is any extreme—either having a visual sit on the screen too long or having visuals flick past so fast that they can't be read.

Also, one of the most difficult things for beginning producer-writers to do is to make certain as they write the script that it can be visualized as written. So it is better to postpone recording the narration and mixing the soundtrack until you're sure you have the visuals you need to cover various soundtrack elements. It doesn't do any good, for instance, to put in a sound effect of the Lithuanian Army Marching Band unless you have some visual of a band marching (or at least some close-ups of Lithuanian band instruments) to support it.

As a final tip in this section, let us stress something that all photographers have engraved in their minds: film and processing are the cheapest parts of any production budget. When you're

# VISUALS: THE LEFT SIDE OF THE SCRIPT

clicking away shot after shot or foot after foot of motion picture film or videotape, it's easy to feel that "you've got it covered" and are just wasting material and time. But the truth of the matter is that we rarely have too many visuals for a program. Sometimes we end up with ten or twelve visuals of a group, for instance, in which not one visual has everyone looking good enough to put on a giant screen. So we budget a lot of material and a lot of time for original photography, videography, and cinematography. And we will frequently shoot things not absolutely required by the script, because that script can change or, in a later script, the visuals we shot can save us time and money.

## PRESENTING VISUAL PROGRAMS

You have to consider the final presentation environment from the beginning of the project. For instance, one of the reasons why videotape has not taken a larger chunk out of film's share of the business communications market is the problem with presenting video to large groups or to groups in different countries. A 16mm. film projector is relatively inexpensive and universal. It will work almost anywhere and can be adapted to any size of audience. But it is just in recent years that large-scale video projection systems have been developed. And, even now, some of the less expensive video units can't compete with film projectors as a presentation tool.

The major presentation considerations involve three elements: lighting conditions, audience size, and portability. If you are producing a training presentation that will require audience members to take notes, you must provide some light in the room. Slides and films look better in total darkness or at least very subdued lighting conditions. Overhead projection transparencies, on the other hand, can be seen in high light levels. And video, as shown on standard television receivers, can also be seen in normal lighting conditions. Some large-screen video systems show best in dark rooms, however.

We've already discussed audience size a bit, but it relates here, too. The rule of thumb concerning any visual presentation is that the last audience member should be no more than eight "screen widths" back from the screen. In other words, a person looking at a screen four feet wide should be no more than thirty-two feet back from that screen to see the image. Also, no viewer should be seated more than three screen widths from the center of the screen. So a viewer should be no more than twelve feet to the left or the right of the centerline of the four-foot screen. Further, no viewer should be closer than two screen widths from the image, or eight feet in our example of a four-foot screen width.

Obviously, you have some limitations when you must show a presentation to a large group—or when you must show a large-image presentation in a small room. A three-image multi-image program, for instance, must be shown on a very horizontal and large screen for a large audience, because each of those separate images must follow the screen-width rule. If you have so many people, for instance, that the last seat in the house is sixty-four feet from the screen, each image must be eight feet wide (because 8 feet × 8 screen widths = 64). If it is a three-image-across multi-image show, the total horizontal width of that screen must be 3 × 8 or 24 feet.

And this brings up the final consideration involving presentation—portability. A twenty-four-foot screen isn't extremely portable, nor is all the media equipment required to show a multi-image program. It can be done—we do it all the time—but it isn't a simple one-person task that can be accomplished by anyone. However, just about anyone can rent a 16mm. film projector anywhere and can find someone to help thread it if that's a problem. So the need for portability should be determined at the very start of a project.

Incidentally, one thing we have been emphasizing in all our recent slide productions is that the visuals should be shot "loose"; that is, there should be a "safe zone" that provides plenty of unimportant space around the central picture area so that those slides can be converted to film or videotape at a later date. Both film and video have a proportion that is somewhat squarer than the typical 3:2 horizontal 35mm. slide. If you try to convert a slide that has important information along the edges into the 4:3 proportion of a video screen, for instance, you either lose some of the edge information or you are forced to leave a blank border on the top and bottom of the video image.

Since video equipment is becoming so increasingly available in hotels, conference centers, and offices, we see more and more cases where our clients want to convert multi-image programs or even simple slide programs into videocassette programs. Then all they have to carry is a cassette.

Because many of our clients—and many of your firms—could conceivably do business in the international market, they should have the option of converting slide programs to film. Although this is an expensive proposition, it is sometimes the only way to show a program in a country with a different television than the United States. A film is always a lot easier to carry, and a lot less prone to electronic or humidity destruction, than a videotape, an audiotape, or other electronic media.

## CONCLUSION

The left side of the script is often the part of a communications program that shows the biggest difference between words on paper and the final product. That's because visuals normally must be experienced rather than explained. Writing out a brief description of a shot and seeing the depth of communication possible with that shot are far different.

But this is what makes visualization so difficult, yet so satisfying. It's hard to come up with just the right shot for a given group of words, yet the effect when that right shot and the right words are combined is always far stronger than either the visual or the words alone.

So we stress once again that it is important to consider all elements of a production at the same time. Don't get so tied up in the process of selecting the perfect visual that you forget to add the power of the soundtrack to that visual. What this means is that sometimes you can't find the perfect visual. But you don't have to, because you can rework the script to communicate a message with the visual you have.

You should also keep in mind that you are rarely working with one visual. Instead, you are working with sequences of several visuals. Although it is great when a single visual says it all, it may be even better when you can combine many visuals, none of which are absolutely stunning, to produce a program that communicates effectively.

# 8

# Interactive and Computer-Aided Programs

## INTRODUCTION

One trend in business communications that is bound to continue is the move toward more audience participation. Just as likely to increase is the use of computers as part of that participation. When these two factors are combined, the result is interactive programming.

At the current time, however, interactive and computer-aided programs are few and far between. Those that do exist are primarily used for sales presentations, for special training applications, or for high-volume "electronic receptionist and information booth" situations. However, there's little doubt that interactive and computer-aided programs will one day be options you should consider when designing business communications programs. So, within this chapter, we'll discuss some of the basics to help you think ahead to the time when a business communications program may benefit from this new technology.

## WHAT MAKES A PROGRAM INTERACTIVE?

Perhaps the best way to begin learning about interactive programs is to design one. You don't necessarily need a computer to do so. In fact, almost any medium can become part of an interactive program if it is correctly designed and used. A "passive" program is one in which the audience members simply passively absorb what's presented, whereas an "active" program is one where the learner is actively involved.

An interactive program is one in which the user may sometimes be actively involved, and may "interact" with the program by one means or another, even if it is only to choose those program segments he or she will passively view. So the crucial part of the design process is promoting that interaction.

One familiar example of an interactive communications program is a troubleshooting chart, such as you might receive with a new television set or automobile. In one column, the writer has listed common troubles. Then, in a second column, he or she will list probable causes. A third column might list some diagnostic procedures you can follow to precisely locate the troublesome component or assembly. And, finally, another column will list some suggested action steps to solve the problem.

Notice that the troubles will usually be listed logically and in some certain priority. And the diagnostic suggestions may include several steps, asking the reader to do something and then return to the troubleshooting chart before doing something else.

You'll also see a flowchart version of this troubleshooting procedure in many cases. For instance, problems will be listed in little boxes from top to bottom on a sheet of paper. As you go through each problem, you'll be asked various questions, such as "Is the light lit or not?" If you answer "yes," you'll follow an arrow to another part of the sheeet called a "branch." If you answer "no," you'll be sent along a different branch.

The same concept works for designing and using interactive business programs. You chart out the most logical paths for people to follow, giving them simple choices at each point within the program so they can easily follow the correct path.

This can be done using media no more complex than a printed handout. The reader would begin by receiving an introduc-

# INTERACTIVE AND COMPUTER-AIDED PROGRAMS

tion to the topic. Let's say it is an instruction sheet that will explain how you can plant a collection of vegetable seeds. The introduction may tell you what seeds you have and what tools you will need to plant them. It could end with a question or two about your latitude and longitude. That would immediately involve you in the program; you have to interact by answering those questions. You might know the latitude and longitude at your location. If so, you could answer the questions immediately. If you didn't, if you didn't even know what latitude and longitude meant, the handout might suggest that you look at an appendix containing North American latitudes and longitudes on a map.

You've just reached a branch in the program. If you can easily answer the question, you can stay on the main program branch. If not, you have to branch off until you get the answer.

Let's say that you know the latitude and longitude of your location. Now the handout may suggest that for various latitudes and longitudes, you should go to different pages within the handout. That's because each location will probably have a different growing season. So the next step would be a branch based on an "If, Then" statement: If you live in the Northeast, Then go to page 6; If you live in the Southwest, Then go to page 8.

After you read the information pertaining to growing seasons, the page might end by sending you back to the main branch. Or it might present you with a number of other choices, such as "What kind of soil do you have?" or "What is the general geographic orientation of your garden?". Again, you would have to interact, either by simply answering the questions—probably from a multiple-choice list—or by actually going out and checking the soil or figuring out which way is south or north.

Somewhere within the program you may be given a "menu" of choices, such as a listing of options concerning things you may need to know to really put together a good garden. The menu would tell you where to go for more information about fertilizer, watering, or other general topics. Within each menu item you may have to follow several branches to get the precise information you need.

Obviously, in an example like this the amount of interaction is fairly limited. But we could expand the example by including a number of videotapes or slide presentations. Now you would get to the question about latitude and longitude and be told to either answer the question or put Videocassette One into the machine and go to counter number 4300 to find a short segment about World Geography. Or you might be told to look at color slides 43 through 50 to determine which soil looked like yours.

From the reader's point of view, this sort of program should be far more helpful than a standard handout. He or she can obtain the information required without plowing through information about other geographic areas or purposes. A reader with a high level of knowledge can speed through the questions and rapidly get the new information he or she needs concerning these plants. And a reader with a low level of knowledge gets a "tutorial" to help learn whatever is required to do the job correctly. In addition, the process of learning may be more enjoyable because the reader gets to be involved in the process. At the very least, frequent questions and page shifts help refocus flagging attention on the program.

Those are the general reasons why interactive programs are worth considering: They allow you to tailor a program for a specific audience member; they get the participant involved in the process; and they can be more interesting than passive programs. However, interactive programs aren't a cure-all, and they certainly aren't the best solution for every communications problem. In fact, sometimes it is good to force an audience member to review all materials concerning a specific topic, rather than allowing him or her to move past the basics.

One great danger with any sort of interactive program is confusion. When you're asking people to skip around in a workbook or select various segments of a videotape, you're also asking them to create their own sense of order concerning the program. In our example, the reader could very easily be distracted by page 6, on soil types, when he or she was supposed to be paging to 7, geographic location. As a result, the information is obtained out of order, and perhaps doesn't easily fit within the mental organization of that person. This is not to say that people are stupid, or that they can't absorb things without a firm plan to follow. It is to say, rather, that one goal of any communications is to make that communications understandable and easy to absorb. So why make the job harder than it has to be?

That's why we sometimes suggest that the best way to start using interactive programs is to start small. Don't leap right into a full-blown interactive videodisc program. Instead, begin designing suitable programs for your audiences with an increasing degree of interaction required by each program. In that way, you're teaching your audiences how to use interactive programs while teaching yourself how to create them. And you're doing it without the massive investment in time and equipment required to get into computer-assisted interactive programs.

## THE WISDOM OF SOCRATES AND THE PATIENCE OF JOB

Although there are many forms of interactive programs similar to the one outlined above, this is usually not what we think about when we think about interactive programs. Instead, we think of the computer. There's no question that many programs can benefit enormously from the power of the computer, but a computer is not a cure-all. Many people still think of the machine as a genius—some sort of electronic Socrates. Actually, the exact opposite is true; the computer's intelligence level is just one or two points higher than that of the silicon used to create the machine's components. A computer does not have the wisdom of Socrates, but it does have the patience of Job.

What a computer can do extraordinarily well is repeat a task it has been given . . . and repeat the task perfectly and patiently many millions of times. That's why computer-assisted programs are ideal for "drill-and-repeat" training, such as foreign language vocabulary-building, and for "information booth" applications, such as providing a directory and a map of locations at amusement parks or similar environments in which a great many people ask the same sorts of questions over and over again.

But computer-assisted programs may not be the best choice for communications programs that involve discrimination or intuition or any of those other intangible elements that require experience, education, and sensitivity. For instance, a computer could certainly be taught to present a sales pitch, listing product benefits, answering standard objections, and closing by asking for the order. But a computer could not "read" a prospect as does a good salesperson, and could not pick up those nonverbal cues or verbal intonations that are so important in most selling situations.

To use computer-assisted programs most effectively, then, look for problems that can be solved by repetitive drills or for applications that require the same standard answers to the same standard questions. Don't expect the computer to take the place of a person—put the computer to use in freeing up people for other tasks.

One way to effectively use the power of the computer is by combining it with other media, such as videotape or slides. A computer is a great "sorter" of information and an excellent "input/output" device. That means that the computer can accept a request or a question from a person and rapidly sort through many possibilities until it finds the right information to give out to the person to answer that question. "Interactive" uses like this, in which the computer helps the audience member have some control over the information received, are a prime application for computer assistance.

You see this application at places such as Disney's Epcot Center, where a computer-controlled videodisc system acts as an information booth for visitors. The visitor simply touches a display screen to request information. A computer then translates that request into data that tells a videodisc to play a certain response, such as a listing and description of all restaurants within the center or a background program about Epcot.

A key consideration when developing any interactive program is the "computer literacy" of the audience. If the audience is extremely familiar with computers, it makes your job far easier in some ways and far tougher in others. It's easier because you don't have to worry about basic problems such as telling the audience members how to use the keyboard or what to expect from the machine. But it's harder because the audience will expect more sophistication from the program you create. One thing you can do to serve both audiences is provide a "shield" program, like an overlay to a transparency, that can be used by people who have low computer fluency. This program would ask them simple questions, then translate their answers into computer actions. Participants familiar with computer operation could, however, "disable" the shield and work the system without it.

Many interactive computer systems make use of a "menu" of options from which the user can choose. One purpose of this menu is to allow users to bypass options or steps that they have no need to do. An experienced user, for instance, might bypass all the introductory and explanatory steps while a new user may repeat these introductory and explanatory steps several times while learning to operate the system.

# INTERACTIVE AND COMPUTER-AIDED PROGRAMS

When designing an interactive program, one of the most crucial aspects of the process is designing software such as menus, commands, and other elements that will help the user make the system work efficiently. It's as important to make the system easy to use and "legible" as it is important to make a soundtrack intelligible or a manual easy to use. And this means that the designer must either totally understand how the specific interactive system works or must consult with someone who does.

In many sophisticated interactive systems, there's a special "consultant" built into the device. It's often called an "author program," because it is the program you will use to author other programs. An author program translates the machine's capabilities into simple questions or procedures that can be understood by almost anyone. And, conversely, the author program will translate the program developer's wishes into language that the machine will understand. Using author programs, or having a resource person who can make these translations, is vital to designing and developing interactive computer programs.

Although these special "authoring" programs are available for interactive programming on some media systems, not all systems have these programs. So you have two choices: become a programmer or hire one. Basically, the choice depends as much on time as it does on money. The cost for a simple interactive program design won't be exorbitant, but the time it would take you to learn how to program a computer might be exorbitant unless you can justify it with several programs. Unless you're prepared to delve deeply into programming, one thing to consider is having a programmer come in to design the first program, then use the "substitution method" for the next few programs you may do. This will allow you to continue producing interactive programs in the same format until you become facile enough with the medium to make changes.

The substitution method involves plugging new terms or words into an existing structure. As an example, let's look at a simple BASIC command we will be discussing in more depth later. It's the "IF, THEN" command that most computer programs translate into "IF this condition exists, THEN take this step." If the program now reads "If A$ = C, Then Goto 200," you can change any of three elements.

Without knowing much more about programming than what we've just discussed, you can probably see how you could substitute other elements within that statement. You need some programming knowledge to make these substitutions, of course, but far less than you would need to design the entire program.

Even if you have no interest in programming, it's still a good idea to have some familiarity with the processes and techniques used by computer-assisted or interactive program systems. Without knowing what the systems can and cannot do, it's fairly tough to design the most effective program for use on those systems. So we'll spend a little time here talking about some basics of interactive and computer-assisted programming.

## HOW A SYSTEM INTERACTS

Most interactive or computer-assisted systems utilize the same basic building block, a binary logic system. In very basic terms, this means that every part of the system is in one of two states: "on" or "off," "yes" or "no," "1" or "0." Depending upon the state, the interactive system will take some action step or display some type of information.

For example, suppose that you were designing a program to train service people about a new car. You could devise a program that included several self-tests, each pertaining to a specific subassembly or assembly of the car. If the trainee answered questions about the pistons and rings correctly, but had trouble with questions that had to do with the engine valves, there'd be no need for the service person to review everything about the engine. Instead, you could use certain statements, called "conditional statements" or "If, Then" statements, to send that person to the review material on valves. In this way, you can tailor the presentation each service person receives to reinforce and review those areas with which that particular person had trouble. For instance, "If" the learner was able to answer general theoretical questions about what valves do, but had problems with a specific type of valve, "Then" the computer could begin displaying data about that specific valve type.

You can use the same sort of theory to develop a program that would provide specific information for a person based on that person's answers to questions. For example, the person could be asked to plug in age, gender, and income level, and then be shown a specific product demonstration designed to appeal to that person and that person's price range.

The conditional statement, "If, Then" is a general form that can be used for many different applications. Its basic advantage is that it allows for choices—choices on the part of the program designer and on the part of the program audience. These choices are called "branches" because they resemble the branch of a tree or a river.

## HOW TO CREATE AN INTERACTIVE PROGRAM

Usually, you begin creating an interactive program "from the top down." In other words, you break the program into a few major subsets and continue breaking each subset into smaller units—working from the top, or highest, level to the lowest, or bottom, level. So you might start by separating a program into an Introduction that provides general information about several related topics, then a Body that provides specific information about each of these topics, and a Close that summarizes the important concepts discussed in the program.

At various points within the program, you'll provide an opportunity for interaction. These are usually test points, involving multiple-choice questions. In many programs, the answer given by the participant will send him or her off on a certain branch.

To see how this works, let's use a sales training example. Suppose you are designing a program that will help sales representatives learn to handle objections better; that is, learn what to say or do when a prospect raises a complaint, problem, or question concerning the product or service being sold. There are several ways to handle this training task, but we'll select a combination of videotaped dramatizations and computer-controlled statements, tests, and answers. We'll also assume that the videotape system can be controlled by the computer, so that the specific element shown to the trainee depends upon where the computer stops the videotape.

To design such a program, your first step would be to outline the objectives and the method you'll use to reach those objectives.

Your objectives might be to teach the trainee four different common objections and one preferred way to handle each objection. So you'd have at least four separate elements within the Body of the program. You'd also probably have a summary Open and a summary Close that talked about objections in general and reinforced the correct way to handle each objection. You can now begin to flowchart this program.

And here's where creativity comes into play. By programming this presentation carefully and well, you can provide a unique learning experience for each audience member. He or she will receive no more, and no less, information than is required to meet program objectives. This reduces boredom as well as reducing the chance that a trainee may go through the program without understanding it.

It's done with conditional statements, of course. Suppose that every trainee must learn what the four objections are and must learn the overall concept behind answering each objection. You could ensure that this takes place by making sure that every trainee had to view the opening segment of the videotape listing why objections are a problem and how they should be handled. After viewing this part of the videotape, the trainee would then see a multiple-choice question or two on the screen. The questions would be designed to determine whether or not the trainee already understood all he or she needed to know about objections. For instance, perhaps question one would involve a videotaped dramatization of a prospect raising the most common objection. The trainee would then be asked to choose from four possible responses to that objection. Question two could deal with the second most common objection while questions three and four dealt with objections in descending order of importance.

As the program developer, you have several choices at this point. You could set very rigid parameters, such as "If the trainee fails to answer questions one and two and three and four correctly, Then he or she must go to the start of the body of the program and go completely through each segment." Or you could define the conditional statement to allow trainees some wrong answers, such as "If the trainee answers question one or two or three or four incorrectly, Then immediately go to the segment dealing with that objection." This statement would, for instance, mean that the trainee who answered question one correctly could avoid looking at the video segment dealing with the first objection. But if that trainee missed question two, he or she would immediately stop being tested and the videotape segment dealing with the second objection would be shown.

You can see how these questions and segments can be used to define very specific problems and provide very specific training programs. You could, for instance, provide three different types of wrong answers for each question, and send people to completely different video segments based upon which of those three wrong answers they selected. Or you could monitor a person's answers to several questions to see if a pattern develops, such as consistently missing questions that deal with converting objections into benefits. You could then send the person to a specific video segment designed to discuss this concept in more depth.

The strength of interactive training programs is the ability you have to totally tailor the experience for each trainee. You can allow trainees to "test out" of segments they understand well, or you can force trainees to gain additional understanding if they are having problems with a certain bit of knowledge. Of course, each additional option you want means more work for you and added complexity for the program, and for the trainees.

If you are designing an orientation program or similar communications that do not require the audience to learn anything, but rather just to be exposed to those things with which they should have some familiarity, the conditional statement approach can be modified to fit that need. You'd probably begin by "polling" the audience member, finding out some demographic data and learning a bit about the person's current state of knowledge about the topic. For instance, you might create a program like this:

1. What is your age?
   A. 18 to 25
   B. 26 to 35
   C. 35 to 45
   D. Over 45
2. What is your gender?
   A. Female
   B. Male
3. What is your education level?
   A. Grade school
   B. High school
   C. Bachelor's degree
   D. Postgraduate degree

You could ask several other questions to accurately define the person's age, gender, educational level, and other pertinent information, and then use several conditional statements to provide that person with appropriate information based on this demographic data. For instance, "If the person answers 1A and 2A and 3A, Then go to section for young female with grade-school education." That segment might show young females as employees and use terms and concepts and words that would be familiar to a person with a grade-school education. If the audience member were an older female with a postgraduate degree, the conditional statement would be "If 1D and 2A and 3D, Then go to section for older female with postgraduate degree." The material presented would show older women in high-level jobs and would use terms and concepts familiar to a person with a high education and experience level.

By defining elements this precisely, it's possible to create programs absolutely tailored for each audience member. An Orientation program, for instance, could be designed so that only female employees of child-bearing age or male employees who stated that their spouses were covered under their insurance would see the section on "Maternity Benefits," while older employees nearing retirement would be the only ones who saw the section on "Retirement-Planning Services." You could have one set of policy guidelines for managers and supervisors, and another for rank-and-file employees. And you could even have special translations for people who speak foreign languages or who need closed-caption or Braille communications vehicles. The possibilities are limited only by your equipment, your budget, and your creativity.

## TYPES OF INTERACTIVE MEDIA

There are actually many types of interactive media; two people talking on the telephone are interacting via a medium, for example. But the term means something specific to most producers of communications programs. It usually means a combination of a computer as a "control mechanism," "text display," and some other medium that is the "presentation medium" controlled by the computer. A common example would be a videocassette recorder controlled by a keypad so that the user can select one of six or seven program segments at the touch of a button. Another example would be an audiovisual programming device that allows someone to randomly access any slide in any of several trays, and then display that slide on a screen. Both these devices use small computers to manage the medium.

Some interactive media use the computer only for the control function; that is, it provides the information required by other media to locate the correct spot on a tape or in an electronic workbook or some similar presentation medium. But the computer can also become an interactive medium in its own right. It all depends upon the application and upon the program objectives.

The major problem with the computer as a communications tool is that it is basically a "print" medium; that is, you type things into the computer and get type out in return. Certainly, many computers are capable of fantastic animation and full-color graphics and some are even capable of a form of synthesized speech, but the basic things input to and output from a computer are words or symbols. For some applications, this is no problem; the computer becomes an interactive textbook. But it has drawbacks.

Some people find it very difficult to look at computer screens for a long period of time, and even more difficult to rapidly read words displayed on a screen. In addition, referencing things stored in a computer is more difficult than flipping through the pages of a book. So the computer has limits when used to replace textbooks.

The computer also can't replace audiotapes or videotapes for those applications that rely upon inflection and intonation. The current state of technology makes inflection and intonation difficult for computer-generated speech circuits. As a result, the computer can't provide the same variety when reading the same sentence as can the human voice. For instance, the same sentence can mean several different things, depending upon where the inflection is placed. A sentence as simple as "Do you like computers?" can be read as "Do YOU like computers?" or "Do you LIKE computers?" or "DO you like computers?" or "Do you like COMPUTERS?"

Other messages really require color and sound and motion. A computer can generate a graphic representation of an aircraft cockpit, for instance, but it can't add the noise of the engine, the buffeting of wind and turbulence, the feel of the air on control surfaces, and the precise color of the air and ground. Yet pilots rely upon all these things and more when flying aircraft.

However, this last example leads us to one thing that computers can do well, and that is to act as simulators for applications that are too dangerous, too remote, or too costly to experience "live." The flight simulator is a common example of this, as are the simulators used by NASA and by various nuclear power companies. But there are many applications that will work for everyday business life, as well.

What about typing training, for example? There are many ways to teach typing without simulation, of course, but one especially effective method with young people is to turn the building skill required for typing into a game. In one game, letters "drop out of the sky" by skittering from the top of a computer display screen toward the bottom. The keyboard operator has to hit the same letter as it is falling or else the "letter bomb" will explode on impact with the bottom of the screen. This simulation turns the drill-and-repeat necessary to learn touch typing into an arcade game. It is especially useful for getting people to pay attention to the screen, not to what their fingers should be doing automatically on the keyboard.

In another application, various circuit board schematics are shown on the display screen. The electronics technician trainee must troubleshoot the board by taking various meter readings or replacing components. A correct "fix" results in a congratulatory message, and an incorrect fix may result in a screen filled with graphics of an explosion or of smoke. Obviously, this is far cheaper and less dangerous to the trainee and to the company's equipment than if he or she made those same mistakes on actual circuit boards.

Note that there's a common denominator in both these applications—they represent two-dimensional objects. A computer has a little trouble creating the feeling of depth, so it is difficult, for instance, to teach a person how to build a shelving unit or to fix a motor through a simulation.

However, the computer can be used for three-dimensional applications by linking it up with other simulators. One well-known example is the computer-controlled "Resusci-Annie" used by the Red Cross to teach CPR. The dummy has sensors built into her body. These sensors transmit messages to a computer. The computer, in turn, transmits a request for certain messages to a videotape or videodisc machine. If the CPR student accidentally presses too hard on Annie's chest, the chest sensor may tell the computer to have the videodisc play the segment on the required pressure and on problems that can occur if the pressure's too high.

## SELECTING SPECIFIC MEDIA FOR
## INTERACTIVE PROGRAMMING

Some of the common media used for interactive programming are videocassettes, videodiscs, sound-slide systems (that use a special device to locate and move each tray slot on the slide tray), and audiocassettes. The choice, as usual, depends upon both application and budget.

An application that requires high speed access, such as "Resusci-Annie," is ideal for the videodisc. In fact, it is only because of the new technology exemplified by the videodisc that interactive programs can be used at speeds approximating noninteractive programs. An interactive communications program implies that the audience member will be able to take part in two-way communications, and to do so in "real time." That means that interactive systems should be designed so that there is very little lag between the moment when the participant requests information or answers a question and the moment when the system responds.

To understand why the videodisc is ideal for this application, contrast it to a different type of video system, the videocassette recorder. If you link together a videocassette recorder and a computer, you are linking together a "random access" device (the computer) and a "serial access" device (the VCR). "Serial access" means that the VCR must take things in order. If you are at inch one on the videotape and want to go to inch one hundred, the VCR must follow a linear path to get to inch one hundred, speeding past inches two through ninety-nine to get there. This takes time.

Videodiscs and computers, in contrast, are "random access" devices. A more familiar form of random access device is a phonograph record; to select any spot on the record all you have to do is pick up the needle and immediately move it to the new spot. You're not forced to move back and forth in a linear fashion, as with videotapes or audiotapes.

Videodiscs can also store a great deal of information, and provide each of those bits of information with a specific "address" so it can be found easily. It's a simple matter for the computer to tell the videodisc to "Move your stylus precisely 12mm. further into the disc and rotate the disc 270 degrees to address location 12,567." This information can be translated into very precise movements of the stylus and the disc, so there is little search time or search error.

You can see that the videodisc offers great potential for those interactive situations requiring fast and accurate access to a large amount of data. However, videodiscs have problems, too. They tend to be rather costly in small quantities, and they are almost impossible to revise. So there's a place for videotape in interactive communications. The challenge for the developer, then, is to carefully select what order he or she will use to put segments on tape, so that search time is minimized.

Other media can also be used for interactive communications programs. Slide projectors capable of random access are available, so a program could link the computer to a slide projector through a cable that would automatically advance the slide projector to a certain tray number, depending upon the audience member's response. And audiotapes can also be used, with the same limitations of videotapes and videocassettes.

## CONCLUSION

With each year that we work within the communications business, we find the computer more a part of our daily life—and less of an oddity. That's probably what's going to happen to interactive programs. They'll become just another medium that can be used to meet specific program objectives.

For now, we strongly advise that anyone who thinks that the power of a computer-aided program will help meet communications objectives should pause for just a moment. Ask two questions: Is the audience ready for this? and, Is this the only medium that will do the job? If the answers to those questions are "yes," you're a candidate for computer-aided programs. If the answer is a strong "maybe," then go slowly and carefully into this new area, and get plenty of help along the way. If the answer is "no," breathe easier, because you have a few more days or weeks or months to accept the inevitable, and to prepare for it by learning more about computer programming and the design of interactive systems.

# PART THREE
# Case Studies and Postproduction Considerations

## SITUATION AND NEEDS ANALYSIS

The common problem we see in most unsuccessful attempts to produce effective business communications is not that people do not have the technical skill to produce a good program. Rather, it's that technically sound programs don't have a sound conceptual basis.

When you distill any communications program down to basic elements, there are just three: An objective, a plan to help people attain that objective, and execution of a program using that plan to reach that objective. If you know anything about probability theory, combinations, and permutations, you can see that there are a number of ways these three elements can be combined that will result in failure. And there's only one way that will result in success.

Success comes when correct objectives are used to draw up an effective plan to execute a communications program. Failure comes if the wrong objectives are identified, or if the right objectives are identified but the wrong plan is used, or if the right objectives are identified and the right plan is used but the program execution is faulty.

Through most of this book, we've been talking about execution. In the next chapter, we'll offer some plans; some case studies of successful programs. In this introduction, therefore, we will once again stress the other major element, identifying correct objectives. From that solid basis, we'll discuss ways to develop an effective plan.

## NEEDS ANALYSIS TO DEFINE AN OBJECTIVE

The reason we produce any program is to meet a need. Effective programs are produced in response to well-identified and well-defined needs. We'll go even one step further—well-developed programs are usually designed to meet one specific need.

The trick is to determine the greatest need. That's not any shocking revelation. In fact, an eighteenth-century philosopher named Pareto codified this idea into a rule. "Eighty percent of the problems are caused by 20 percent of the causes," is a version of Pareto's Rule. The 80-20 rule holds true for a lot of things. You can probably think of many examples yourself. For instance, don't 20 percent (or less) of the words that you use cause 80 percent (or more) of your spelling errors? Doesn't it seem like the same 20 percent of every car rusts out? Isn't it true that there are always a couple of people who stand out—for well or ill—in any group of ten or so?

In business terms, doesn't it seem like many of the same causes result in a number of different business problems? Isn't poor time management often a major cause of low productivity? Doesn't lack of training result in high waste? Can't you tick off, from a list of ten mistakes you make, two that you make over and over again, and that lead to most of your problems at work or at home?

The idea behind a needs analysis is to locate those major problem-causers that can result in the most good when they are eliminated. Needs analysis is a prioritization tool.

For instance, suppose that a briefer tells you that he or she wants a program to improve product knowledge concerning a certain computer-controlled device. Sales reps, the briefer says, just don't know enough about the product to sell it. So the briefer has identified a need for a product knowledge training program about that product.

# CASE STUDIES AND POSTPRODUCTION CONSIDERATIONS

But is that the real need? An analysis might show that 80 percent of this product is just like every other product that the reps have no problem selling. But 20 percent of the product relates to computers. So a more accurate needs analysis would identify that the real need is for a program that will help representatives learn more about computers, and how to sell any product that involves computers.

You can see the side benefit to this more-detailed approach. If you find a root cause for an error or a problem and eliminate it, you don't just eliminate it for that specific product or process. Rather, you eliminate all its "kin" in other areas with which the audience is involved.

## SITUATION ANALYSIS TO DEVELOP A PLAN

After you've identified a need, it's also important to identify the situation that exists around that need. This involves things such as audience demographics, boundaries and limitations, and available resources.

For example, if you have identified a need for more computer training of sales representatives, you next have to understand what the reps already know and how they can supplement that knowledge most effectively. You have to know where they learn best and how they learn best. Further, you have to know if they will learn this information or not. Do they see this need as being high priority?

You also have to know your limitations and boundaries. You may see a strong need within your organization for a full-scale revamping of all new-product brochures or all personnel-policy manuals. But will you have either the money or the clout to get that revision accomplished? Or should you concentrate on revising one piece of material at a time? How far can you go? How much time, money, and power do you have, or how much is the firm willing to invest in meeting this need?

What are your available resources? What people, equipment, and programs can you bring to bear on this problem? How much time and money can you invest in developing further resources?

Based on the answers to these questions, you'll develop a plan to meet the objectives identified by the needs analysis. But don't develop that plan until you consider the last part of the equation.

## EXECUTION ANALYSIS TO ENSURE EFFECTIVENESS

If you know what's needed and know how you're going to go about meeting that need, then all that's left is deciding what outcome you expect. And that's tough, because it implies that you can predict the future.

In some ways, of course, you *can* predict the future with some accuracy. You can look at the past, for instance, and be fairly certain that what didn't work then won't work now. And the more past experience you have, the more certain you can be. If you've had one bad past experience using video as a communications tool, for instance, you probably don't want to infer that all future video experiences will be bad. But if you've had a dozen or a score or a hundred bad experiences using video with your audiences, then you might want to skip video as a possible means of executing this program.

The flip side to this coin is that things and people change. What worked in the past may not work in the present, but may work again in the future. So a part of your execution program might be to look at all the elements involved, from available resources to needs, to see if this program might be a place to make a breakthrough, using a new medium or method, or if this is a place to stick with winning media and methods from the past.

Further, execution analysis involves two stages: your execution of the program and the execution by the audience members of an action based on that program. So you have to analyze what action you would like to occur based on this program. Do you want people to immediately begin arriving at work on time, all the time? Or will you accept a 30 percent decrease in tardiness as a perfect response to the program? Do you have a short-term and a long-term goal, like an immediate decrease of 10 percent in employee theft and a long-range 99 percent decrease in all employee crime? Or do you have an immediate goal with no concern for the long term?

What you're doing, of course, is defining and refining the outcome you want from your communications program. Then you must determine what steps you can take to reach this outcome. Some of those determinations include the message, the medium, the presentation arena, and the process you will follow to persuade and inform and motivate the audience.

Perhaps most important of all, you want to look very carefully and realistically at the expected outcome from your program. Can it be accomplished? Can more be accomplished? Should less be expected? In short, can this program be produced with the quality required, when "quality" is defined as "conformance to requirements and specifications"?

Sometimes this is the most difficult of all analyses to perform. It means you must have a very clear understanding of what the requirements and specifications are and of how the program and the audience's actions will conform to those requirements and specifications. If you don't have that clear understanding, you may find that some of the problems mentioned in the next section come to roost on your doorstep.

## WHY DO GOOD PEOPLE PRODUCE BAD PROGRAMS?

It's hard to believe that anyone would deliberately produce a bad business communications program. Yet it happens all the time. People work as hard as they can, yet end up going way over budget to produce a program or end up with a program that doesn't meet expectations. All it takes is a few mistakes, either not spotted or not corrected fast enough, for good people to produce bad programs.

Within this section, we're going to try to identify the few problem areas that account for most of the major problems in business communications programs. These problems occur again and again. All any of us can do is attempt to recognize them early, limit the damage that can be done by them, and vow to make it less likely they will happen again.

### The Briefer Is Not the Approver

This is a classic communications problem. It occurs time and again in those programs that have a high failure rate. Even with a knowledgeable briefer, willing to spend the amount required to put together a program with an image of quality, it's possible to produce a bad program because the briefer and the briefer's boss or bosses don't agree or won't discuss the program until it is too late to do anything about the disagreements.

It's not unusual in these cases for the approver to kill some program elements or to make some last-minute changes or additions to other program elements. It's about the same thing as deciding to put together a car by running along an assembly line and picking up pieces here and there. Each of the pieces might be very good, but what are the real chances that everything will come together as a car that will run? Instead of a fully engineered, assembled, and tested program, the result will be something scrambled together out of bits and pieces.

### Revisions After Approval

Every program typically goes through several approval processes: Treatment sheet approval, script approval, typesetting approval, and on and on. It's ideal when the program developer can wait for each approval until going on to the next step.

But sometimes there's a deadline constraint that makes it difficult to spend the time it takes to chug through a long approval process. So program producers will go on to the next step before the entire chain of command approves the last step.

In some cases this can backfire. Revisions after approval almost always cost money. In addition, they can result in some loss of message strength. When you produce a program piecemeal, picking up revisions from draft one, adding comments from the briefer and approver into draft two, then allowing the approver to revise further into draft three, you lose fluidity and style. It becomes harder to focus the message, and the message gets diluted.

### Insecure and Uncertain Client

Some people have a tremendous need to gain consensus on every program element from as many people as possible. What makes this so tough is that the last person to whom that individual speaks is the one who has offered the most valuable and correct opinion. So the other people involved in the program feel like popcorn being bounced around inside a popper, first going this way and then that way and then another way entirely on the way to yet another way.

The problem here is twofold: First, you never know if the version of the script you are writing or the visual assembly you are doing is "for real" or for practice; that is, will this plan for production be changed as soon as the approver talks to someone else in the firm?

Second, no program just comes together. Someone pulls it together. That's the job of a program producer, and of the producer's main approver. A big part of that job is image. If you have an image of confidence surrounding a program, other people will develop that same confidence. But if you have an image of insecurity and uncertainty, people will sense that in the program.

### Practicing False Economies

A prime example is the decision one firm made to "save" the cost of a professional narrator by having employees narrate a program. They spent three days of internal time searching for the correct voice. Then they spent two more days of their time and of on-location audio engineering time to do the job. The cost of the audio engineering time alone was $780 . . . and a professional narrator would have cost no more than $360.

### What Is the Common Denominator?

In all these cases, there is a common denominator, isn't there? It's clearly a lack of communications. No big surprise there.

Sometimes people fail to communicate well due to pure ignorance. A person is not aware that he or she must have a certain approver sign off on a project, or isn't aware of a certain policy that prohibits the use of, for instance, the word "certifies" and insists upon the use of the word "acknowledges" instead.

Sometimes it's laziness, as when a briefer (or a producer) postpones writing a script or shooting a videotape until it is too late to go through a number of "rough draft" steps before the final deadline. Or when it's easier to tell a vendor to go ahead from prep work to final production without approving the interim steps.

And sometimes it's arrogance. It's the client deciding that this is "my project" and paying no attention to anyone else's opinions. Or it's a producer ignoring what the client wants and doing it a different way . . . without knowing enough about the client or the client's objectives to present a rational reason for doing it differently.

The result of these communications problems is always the same—good people do a bad job. And the result of that can be extraordinarily costly, both in time and in lost credibility.

# 9

# Case Studies

## INTRODUCTION

In the introduction to this part of the book, we discussed several forms of analyses required to make certain that you were not missing the mark when producing a media presentation. In this chapter, we'll follow that same approach to analyze a number of different media programs.

### A Program Analysis Checklist

For any type of media program, the first step is a needs analysis. In a needs analysis, you should include at least these items:

1. What is the most pressing need?
2. What are the key elements in the current situation?
3. How do you want to change the situation?
4. What medium, message, and plan will effectively change the situation to meet the need?
5. What action or result should be expected on the part of the audience?

### How to Analyze Our Case Studies

It's doubtful that any of the case studies in this chapter will provide you with a specific road map that will lead you directly to your destination for a program you are designing or will design. Instead, they are concept-oriented; that is, it is more important that you understand the underlying concepts behind producing a certain type of program than that you understand precisely why we did a specific program.

## QUALITY IMPROVEMENT MOTIVATION AND TRAINING

### What Is the Most Pressing Need?

A major multinational corporation faced a problem common to firms with an independent dealer network; that is, dealers were associated with the corporation by the public, yet the corporation had no actual way to monitor or control what each dealer did. So a dealer who exhibited poor service or poor product quality was not perceived by the public as simply a poor dealer. Rather, he or she was seen as an example of poor work on the part of the entire corporation. That negative example carried over into the hundreds of other products and services that the public bought from this corporation.

So the corporation needed to improve the quality of their dealer' products and services, yet it could not mandate a training program or a certain level of quality.

At the time of this program, the corporation had about 150 dealers, each with a staff of four to eight people. Some dealerships were "Ma and Pa" operations, while others were moderate-sized corporations in their own right. The service area these dealers offered involved a technical element as well as pure labor. And the typical dealer had little time for formal training, nor was he (99 percent were male) likely to release employees for formal training.

Also, the business itself was labor-intensive, so time was literally money. Many dealers felt that it was better to get a job done fast, then play the law of averages in the hope that most jobs would be done to an acceptable quality level. Finally, most dealers were struggling to survive against intense competition from other dealers who sold the same product and services as they did.

## How Does the Client Want to Change the Situation?

The most obvious way the corporation wanted to change the situation was by improving the quality level of dealers. An easily measured indicator that would tell if that improvement took place was the number of complaint calls from customers. Although dealers were responsible for sales and installations, the corporation handled the day-to-day operation of the service. So irate customers were not calling the dealerships about problems, they were calling the corporation. The corporation, therefore, had to instill a sense of the importance of absolute quality to avoid getting a great many complaints from irate customers.

Of secondary but substantial importance, the corporation wanted to bring more independent dealers into the fold. So any special benefit that this corporation could provide over other corporations offering similar products and services would be an image of difference that might recruit new dealers.

## What Medium and Message Will Work for This Audience and This Need?

Because the dealerships were spread throughout the country and were small operations, there was little hope of conducting on-site training. Also, few dealerships had any kind of media equipment and few would invest the time away from work to allow employees to go to a central location where media equipment was available.

So the key was to reach the dealer and convince him that quality improvement would not cost money—that it would, in fact, pay off in increased sales and decreased costs. And this message had to be given through a medium that could be used at any time by the dealer and in any location.

Further, the corporation already had a successful nationwide quality improvement program in place for all employees. So this new program would be based upon that program. As part of that established program, the corporation used a workbook and various recognition items. Part of our mandate on this program was to use some of those existing materials, because they had already proven successful and because it would reduce the cost.

### What Action Step Was Desired?

The best possible action would be if every dealer adopted the concept and commitment of quality improvement as defined by the corporation. The lowest possible range of acceptable action would be if all dealers at least had some sense that quality improvement was important. (Then future programs could reinforce this and begin to generate interest in training.)

An unacceptable outcome would be if the dealers felt that the corporation was trying to run their businesses for them.

### How the Need Was Met

The need was met using four basic elements:

A brochure that identified the need and the benefits to the dealers.

A training program in workbook form that helped the dealers learn the concepts of quality improvement.

An individual recognition certificate to acknowledge the dealer's achievement in completing the course.

Decals and other promotional materials that could be used by the dealer to identify himself as a member of the corporation's quality improvement team.

The theory behind this grouping of materials was that the brochure would introduce the program—creating awareness. After dealers thought about the benefits, they would literally "sign up" to receive the training program—creating commitment and involvement. The training program would provide the information they needed to implement a quality improvement program—the action step. Finally, the dealers would receive various recognition items, such as decals and a certificate of accomplishment after completing a case study that was the final chapter in the training program.

We used a case study approach throughout the program

design. Whenever possible, we emphasized important ideas by putting them in terms of the dealers' business, using terms the dealers understood. And we made certain to stress the "partnership" idea that quality improvements needed to happen in the corporation as well as in the dealer network.

This case study method works well when there is a lot of dry information and information which does not seem extraordinarily pertinent to a specific individual's case. By showing how that information can be put to practical use, solving practical problems, interest is created and so is an understanding of how the information relates to the individual.

For example, we chose a case study as the "final exam" for this program. The dealer in the case study was created out of a composite of all dealers in the program . . . and the problems he faced were those that these dealers would face every day. The participants were asked to look at the dealer's operation and comment upon what he was doing right and what he was doing wrong.

In addition to adding interest and relevance, there was a specific reason for using this type of final exam. The exam had to be simple to complete and had to tie together the training program.

By insisting that participants finish the case study, we were able to increase the credibility of the program and increase the value of the recognition items they would receive. Also, it gave us a chance to reference various parts of the training program within the critique materials we sent back with the participant's case study and recognition items.

To reduce costs, yet keep an image of high quality, we set up a standard page layout, using a logo, the title of the program, and a pair of lines that defined the text area. We then printed this "program page" in gold, using a buff paper stock.

Because we printed about 10,000 pages in this color, the cost was very small. Then we went back through the press, this time in limited runs of about 250 pages each, and imprinted the text for each page in black ink. The result was a page with a two-color look at just slightly more than the cost of one color.

We also tried to fit our new copy into existing pages of the corporate program wherever possible. Although it took a little longer to write the new copy, because we had to make sure it would fit and because we had to make sure it logically flowed with the copy before and after it, the result was a less costly production. That's because we had existing typesetting and existing page layouts, including some pages that required no changes at all.

We also knew that the only part of this program that might require frequent revision was the final exam. For instance, if the corporation began to identify new problem areas that weren't covered in the exam or if the corporation found that some parts of the final exam bothered participants, there'd be a need for a change. So we produced the final exam differently from the rest of the book.

We final-typed the pages of the final exam with a carbon ribbon typewriter rather than typesetting them. Those pages were printed one-color, using an inexpensive paper stock and printing process. We also made sure that various sections of the final exam case study began at the top of a page and ended at the bottom of a page. So, if the need arose, we could change individual pages to revise the case study quickly and inexpensively.

As an added creative advantage to this approach, the case study did not look expensive . . . it looked like a working document. So the participants would not have much hesitancy about jotting notes directly onto the pages. And we provided extra margin width to encourage that process even more.

### How Did It Work?

The program has proven fairly successful. Everyone involved enjoys the case studies, proving that this was the best way to present material to this audience. Also, we have revised the exam case study, and it was inexpensive to do so. Some of the sales representatives for the corporation have found that this program gives them a better understanding of their dealer-audience, and some dealers have stated that this program shows that the corporation actually does understand the problems they face, and how the problems of a small dealership differ from those of a Fortune 500 corporation. Finally, the client was able to get "value added" out of the program by having sales representatives deliver it to the dealers. This was a trade-off, frankly, because it meant that the dealers would not first get a brochure and then have a while to decide to sign up. But it was felt—and we think correctly—that the corporation could help sales reps gain an image of being concerned about the dealer's overall business, rather than being perceived as "just a sales rep."

# PRODUCTIVITY IMPROVEMENT PROGRAM

## What Is the Most Pressing Need?

A firm involved in manufacturing a specialized line of heavy equipment was losing market share year after year to foreign companies. These foreign competitors had lower labor rates within their own shops, and they paid less for raw materials produced at lower cost in other foreign shops. The firm saw only one way to meet and beat that competition—to increase productivity.

The firm is very labor-intensive, and much of that is union labor involved in semiskilled hard labor. However, the firm also employs a wide variety of technical, clerical, and engineering people. It was felt that productivity should be improved in all areas, not just in the union labor area. In addition, the firm had a history of labor problems and did not want to antagonize union people by making them seem to be the cause of all problems.

The audience for this program ranged from people with no more than a sixth-grade education to those with Ph.D.'s. And it ranged in age from late teens to early sixties. This group was spread throughout the country. For a number of reasons, both logistic and psychological, it was necessary to provide the same training at the same time to all people in all plants.

A series of focus-group interviews revealed that most people in the firm, regardless of their occupation or educational level, knew about Japanese productivity improvement techniques. They were aware, therefore, of the problem, and they had some sense that foreign competition could affect their jobs.

Finally, this program had support clear up to the board of directors, but there was little money available to spend because the firm was already in some degree of financial difficulty. So there was a need for an economical production.

## How Does the Client Want to Change the Situation?

The client wanted to let people at every level in the organization know what productivity improvement methods would be implemented in the firm. Also, the firm wanted the support of all levels, because without that support these productivity efforts would be futile.

In addition, the firm wanted to encourage all employees to think about their jobs; not only so they would do the job more productively, but also so they could suggest ways to improve the job. And the firm wanted to make it very clear that every job, from CEO to clerk, could be improved to increase overall productivity.

Of special importance to us, the firm had very few trainers on the staff. So any program we produced had to be self-directed. The audience members had to get the information without relying upon additional input from an on-site trainer.

### What Medium and Message Will Work for This Audience and This Need?

Because the budget was tight, the firm wanted to use whatever in-house personnel and equipment they could. The firm already had a television production capability, although neither the equipment nor the operator was of professional quality. And each plant within the firm had video playback capability. Further, our client contact within the firm had extensive experience with print production.

So we designed a program that used both videotape and workbooks. In addition, we provided emphasis items—called "environmental conditioners"—that could be used to set the scene within each local plant.

The basic message that would be imparted was that the employees and the firm were partners . . . partners in progress. If they worked together to improve productivity, everyone would progress.

### What Action Step Was Desired?

The firm had no great expectation concerning this program. They knew that productivity improvement was a long-term effort. So they expected that this program would do two things:

First, they wanted to create awareness of the productivity problem and of some potential solutions. Second, they wanted to get all employees committed and involved in the improvement effort.

The goal for this program was not measurable by numbers. Instead, the firm felt they would be satisfied if no union complaints arose because of the programs and if there was a general positive feeling toward productivity improvement.

## How the Need Was Met

The major problem we faced as communicators was that the audience for this program was extraordinarily diverse in occupation, education, and point of view. So we chose to use an analogy approach, discussing major productivity improvement concepts as they related to something that was universally understood by all people.

We also used analogies to explain abstract concepts in concrete terms. For instance, we used videotape footage of an airplane in a spiral to emphasize what would happen to a firm that got into a downward productivity spiral. It illustrated that lower productivity brought lower sales, which brought less money to buy equipment or pay staff, which resulted in even lower productivity. We used the idea that "the sky was the limit" in an upward spiral, but there was a finite and disastrous limit to a downward plunge.

Because the audience was so diverse, we chose three people as narrators and on-camera talent. One was an older male, business executive type. Another was a mid-thirties female who could be taken as an executive or as an executive secretary. A third was a younger male, dressed as a supervisor or union laborer.

Because this program involved seven separate concepts, we used seven separate modules. Each module involved approximately twenty minutes of videotape and a twelve-page workbook. But the budget would not allow us to actually shoot seven modules using video for every minute of time. Instead, we combined some video lead-ins and lead-outs and transition pieces with sound-slide programs transferred to videotape.

This method provided several advantages. First, we could get slides that had been previously shot in every plant, so we could show many different environments and allow many different groups within the corporation to identify themselves or people like themselves. Second, we could write scripts that would be read as voice-overs by the narrators, rather than forcing them to memorize several minutes of copy or read off teleprompters. Third, we could use on-camera video when it would add emphasis to the message or when there was simply no other way to visualize the concept being discussed.

We also used talent on-camera to help make the transitions between the workbooks and the videotapes. This was one of the most difficult aspects of the entire production because we needed to make this program somewhat interactive; that is, the participants would view certain segments of the videotape, then do a series of workbook exercises related to what they had seen, then go back to the videotape for further information. With no on-site trainer, all this had to be handled through notes in the workbook and comments on the videotape.

We were able, as a side benefit to the need for video transitions, to add interest and an image of quality to the production. We did this by investing in an animated video segment that involved line art of a workbook opening and closing. In addition, we created an animation of the program logo and of the program titles for each module. An on-camera narrator would say, for instance, "Now please turn to your workbooks and make a list of your own priority items." Then the viewers would see the animated workbook open, and the tape would go blank. At this point, a person in the room who had been instructed to turn off the tape unit waited until everyone in the room appeared to have completed the workbook lesson. When the tape was turned on again, the viewers saw the workbook close and saw the module title again.

This animation cost just $2,000, but it made the program look far more expensive. It gave the viewers something similar to what they would see on broadcast television . . . at a small fraction of the cost.

## Problems

The major problem within this program involved the workbooks. The client felt that the workbook should contain exercises rather than readings. So, for instance, the participants would first learn about Maslow's Hierarchy of Needs through a videotape analogy, then read a bit about Maslow's Hierarchy, then make lists of their own needs.

Well, can you imagine what happened when a group of fifty young factory workmen viewed an attractive woman on tape telling them to "turn to your workbooks and make a list of your own needs"? Although many of them played it straight and treated the question as meant, a few shouted catcalls and wrote down some interesting needs.

Expecting any group of people who may have been out of a classroom environment for years and years to bear down and do written exercises was optimistic thinking at its best. Some of those with a great deal of education found the material boring because it was simplified. Some of those with very little education just had no built-in "respect" for the exercises. We would have been better off either giving a proctored exam or just providing a brief set of readings that related specifically to what each group of participants did each day.

### How Did It Work?

The program was successful. Most employees got the message. One of our analogies proved especially popular, because we put the young male talent on-camera, near a fireplace, with a young child goo-gooing at him. It was the first video segment people saw, and it set a casual and friendly tone for the entire piece. People who could easily have been turned totally off by a factory environment or an office environment really enjoyed seeing some of the benefits of continued hard work—a nice home, a warm fire, and a loving family.

The client tells us that people really do seem to be more productive at this firm. Union and nonunion workers have raised few objections to certain changes in the work environment, and many employee participation systems have been set up.

## MULTINATIONAL PROMOTION PROGRAM

### What Is the Most Pressing Need?

A firm that manufactures and markets a line of products involved in the recognition and award area had captured about as much of the United States market as possible. And, although it was never stated in words, many of the firm's leaders were shaken by the latest economic depression, when sales in the U.S. fell off sharply. So the firm needed to expand into international markets.

However, chauvinism and national pride on the part of European, South American, Mexican, and Canadian firms and individuals made it imperative that the United States firm link up with firms in each of these areas. In addition, those same factors made it difficult to convince foreign firms that this concept and market area would be just as successful in their countries as it was in the states.

So the firm needed a promotional presentation that would outline the benefits of this market area, make it clear that the concept could work, and show why the foreign firm should link up with the U.S. firm to make it work.

The U.S. firm had spent nearly sixty years building a market and manufacturing base in the United States. Their success was based on a large sales force, with each sales representative operating in a small territory. Supporting that sales effort was a series of regional plants and distribution centers and a national marketing and administrative center. Although early successes involved just one product, recent changes in consumer attitudes had forced the firm to diversify to a broad product line and a number of new ways of selling those products.

Those foreign firms identified by market research as being somewhat compatible and receptive to this type of operation operated in a different sales environment. Most were one-product firms or firms that represented various manufacturers who each manufactured a similar product. Most had a very small market share and did little to increase that share or to expand into new markets. The conventional wisdom was that foreign prospects were different from prospects in the U.S.; that award and recognition items would not sell in those countries.

### How Did the Firm Want to Change the Situation?

First, the U.S. firm needed to expand their market because the domestic market was as big as it was going to get; second, they needed to convince foreign firms that there was, in fact, some similarity between their potential market area and the existing U.S. market area; and, third, the U.S. firm needed to convince foreign firms that it could add something special which would result in greater profit for both partners.

## How Does the Client Want to Change the Situation?

The U.S. firm knew that this would be a long-term effort. They were willing to invest the people and funds required to develop a broad base of support in several different countries. So all they really wanted to do at this stage was to gain some favor among a number of foreign firms and to create some awareness of the potential for profit in a joint venture.

As a secondary purpose, the firm felt that they might be able to export some goods to serve these market areas immediately. So they wanted a strong selling message concerning their firm to be part of their joint-venture promotion presentation.

## What Medium and Message Will Work for This Audience and This Need?

This is the heart of this case study. First, there's the problem of incompatible media formats. Second, there's the problem of incompatible audience perceptions of certain message channels and words. And, third, there's the problem of portability.

The only truly compatible worldwide format is the visual... a drawing or photograph or even some scratching on the desert sand. A representative of this firm could take along a flip chart or a booklet of photographs, then accompany those photographs with words. He or she might need a translator in certain countries, but the visuals would speak for themselves.

However, not every visual means the same thing to every person from every country. Some common gestures or situations might be offensive in one country or ridiculous in another. In the same way, certain idiomatic phrases or individual words might give offense or have no meaning at all in various countries.

One way to solve that problem was to create a program customized for each country, using visuals and words that were appropriate and understandable to that country's people.

Further, it was important that the words be spoken by someone with almost native fluency in the language of that country. In France, for instance, the U.S. firm's European specialist had learned from long, hard experience that French business people did not appreciate his efforts to speak their language. When he butchered phrases, he lost sales.

So the firm decided to create a number of canned media presentations, each presenting the same information but each tailored to a specific market area in a country and narrated by someone fluent in the language, as well as knowledgeable about the mores and customs, of that country.

Because of the problem of incompatible media in various countries, the firm chose sound-slide as the appropriate medium. Using a small, self-contained projector and cassette player that fit under an airliner seat, the U.S. firm's representative could travel all over the world with the message. In most countries, in fact, it was possible to find compatible equipment.

The message presented in this sound-slide program had to involve three elements. The first element was a perspective that showed how the U.S. firm had built a market share in the American market. The second element was a sales message that sold the benefits of working to build a market share in the prospect country, and a message that the U.S. firm thought that market did exist. The third element was a strong benefits message to show the prospective partner why it was to that foreign firm's advantage to work with the U.S. firm.

## What Action Step Was Desired?

There was no question of this media presentation doing anything but creating awareness and a certain amount of receptivity. The long-term objectives of the U.S. firm could be met only by a great number of face-to-face meetings. So the major action step desired was that, after viewing the presentation, the audience members would feel it worthwhile to ask a number of questions and to perhaps think about the possibilities of a joint venture, then schedule further meetings.

## How the Need Was Met

The major problem involved in this program was shaping the message so that it would interest, and not offend, people from foreign countries.

(For instance, we had some past experiences working on programs for foreign audiences that led us to believe a major problem was the politeness of the people. We once did a program for Middle Eastern military officers that was supposed to outline all the benefits of a certain electronics firm's systems. We were assured by the firm that all the audience members spoke English and understood it. Pretests conducted with people from that area of the world who had already spent several months in the U.S. showed that this assurance was not backed up by reality. As in many other areas of the world, the problem of "face" appeared here. The pretest audience people did not want to admit that they didn't understand the message. To do so would have made them impolite to their "host" as well as making them appear to be stupid.)

In the multinational promotion program being described here, we especially needed to avoid making the prospects uncomfortable. But we also needed to make sure that they understood the message. We obviously couldn't "talk down" to these successful business people by producing a program that any fool could understand, yet we couldn't test their understanding of what we presented, either. So we had to take particular care in scripting and visualizing this program.

We followed a three-step approach: First, we wrote a script in "American" that outlined the main points we felt should be covered. Then we asked a marketer with years of experience in European countries to look at the script from the standpoint of conceptual problems. He found a few, such as our emphasis on the display and recognition value of awards. In many European countries, he said, people did not display awards in their offices or homes. They might have them available should anyone want to see them, but they did not blatantly display them. So we had to downplay that idea.

Third, we hired a specialized firm to handle the narration of these programs. This firm provided several benefits. First, they translated our American script into European English and into French. And they did so by translating concepts, not by making a literal translation. Second, they provided a native Frenchman and a native of the United Kingdom to do the actual translation. Third, during the recording of the programs, they provided both a grammar expert and a concept expert to help us make sure the inflection, phrasing, and words were correct.

When we visualized the script, we also paid attention to this firm's advice. In addition, we made sure that the visuals chosen were very readable. In many cases, this meant using a long shot rather than a close-up. For example, if an American sees a close-up of a woman dressed in an abbreviated cowboy outfit with a stick topped with multicolored paper streamers in her hand, the American would know that the woman is probably a Dallas Cowboys' cheerleader. But a European or United Kingdom native may not know that. The foreigner would need some long shot that showed the cheerleader plus the stands plus the teams on the field to read the message.

We also used text slides more frequently than we would normally do so. We had found when doing the Mideast show that many people for whom English was a second language could understand much more if they both read and heard the same information. So we made sure that the same words appeared on the slides that appeared in the script. And we sometimes used superimpositions, we that words were coupled with a visual on the screen.

Technically, we provided far more copies of this program than we would of one being used within the U.S. And we gave the presenter many options. Under normal conditions, he would use an audiocassette that was pulsed with the "de facto" standard for AV shows—a "1,000-Hz inaudible tone on a separate audiotrack." But we also gave him a version of each program that had audible beeps, so he could simply borrow a cassette recorder and a slide projector and show the program by listening for the beep pulse that signaled the need to change slides. Finally, we gave the presenter an unpulsed version along with a script that was clearly marked with the correct place to change slides.

We also made sure that the show ran no more than eighty slides. That's because not all Kodak projectors, nor projectors using Kodak format from other firms, will accept the 140-slide tray. So if the presenter had problems with his take-along unit, he could still probably find a slide projector that would work.

Finally, we provided the presenter with several foil bags to use when transporting the audiocassettes from country to country. These foil bags were to prevent accidental erasure of the audio signals by X-ray machines at airports or by other electromagnetic sources in hotels and office buildings.

In terms of basic message content and creative concept, we emphasized one thing in this program: The potential market for this idea knows no boundaries—no geographic boundaries and no limits to growth. We supported that idea by discussing the history of the U.S. firm and by stressing the universal need for recognition of accomplishments.

Because this message had both an intellectual and an emotional base, we used a strong orchestral score that emphasized strings and flutes. We avoided using any "pop" music that might not appeal to a multinational or mixed-age audience and we avoided using any lyrics that might be misunderstood or unintelligible to a person from a foreign country.

Finally, we concentrated on just two things within this entire program. First, selling benefits that would interest a business person. We emphasized new profit centers, existing manufacturing and marketing support, and low risk to the joint-venturer. Second, we complimented the audience time and again on the fact that they were the necessary ingredient because of their knowledge of their existing markets and their enthusiasm and energy. In both cases, benefits and compliments, we were fairly certain that we could not offend any ethnic group or nation by showing them how they could make money and suggesting that they were valuable allies.

## Problems

There were few problems in this program. One minor problem was in visualization, because we wanted to find visuals with which each country could identify. So we had to avoid some of the common American things like football teams and, instead, seek out soccer shots. And we had to liberally sprinkle shots of people who "looked French" or "looked British" into the show. We also had to keep the show moving rapidly, yet keep it to eighty slides.

To accomplish that last task, we were forced to go to multi-image slides. In this way we could show two, three, or four images on the same piece of film, using just one slide tray slot to make several points. (We rarely go beyond four, by the way, because each individual image gets too small to be read easily.)

We found one problem with this approach. Shots of people are almost always more compelling than shots of things. When you combine a person shot with a thing shot, the person will take precedence. Further, a person in long shot is still recognizably a person while a thing may become a "blob" in long shot although it can be clearly distinguished in close up.

### How Did It Work?

It's too early to tell how successful this program is in meeting the firm's objectives. But we can report several minor successes from review groups who have seen the English version.

Perhaps most important from the conceptual standpoint for your programs is the fact that the firm now wants to revise several of their corporate programs to mimic these programs. In the past, these "corporate capability" or "corporate tour" programs have been little more than laundry lists: "The firm does this, and this, and earned this much money, and has this many sales people." This wasn't important for the foreign market. Rather, they would be interested in how the firm's resources and personnel were used to solve problems and make a profit. So we wrote a program that was almost a case study, or at least a series of anecdotes and examples. We used few facts and figures and a great many analogies to common things.

What the firm is realizing, and what many firms are realizing today, is that the United States market is just as segmented as the multinational market. What works in the South may not work in the West. And each market area seems to change almost weekly. So specific facts and figures don't work as well as concepts and anecdotes. It's better, given segmented markets and continual change, to provide a program that will look at the underlying concepts and ideas that will pertain to any number of markets or facts and figures.

In terms of this specific program, we think it will be successful—and we know that one reason it will be successful is that we invested the time and money in hiring people with expertise about foreign markets. In the program, we imply that a lot of similarities exist between all people in the world. But in our design of the program, we made certain that the differences between people from various countries were considered.

## A SALES TRAINING PROGRAM

### What Is the Most Pressing Need?

One of our clients had an excellent training program for new sales representatives, but had some problems in upgrading sales representatives' skills after they reached the field. This was a vital need, however, because the firm kept adding product lines and identifying new market areas that required more sophisticated or more specialized selling skills.

In addition, many of the firm's sales reps had been with the organization for years. They had solid incomes from many long-time customers and had little interest or enthusiasm for expanding into other areas. They knew how to sell well in their existing markets, but were a bit stale in some of the basics of selling. Yet the firm saw a crucial need to expand into new markets because existing markets were reaching saturation.

So the firm wanted to provide a continuing training effort that could refresh sales representatives' minds about basics as well as giving them information about new markets and techniques. And this continuing effort had to be portable, so it could be delivered by field sales managers with little skill in media—and little room in their automobile luggage compartments or under their airliner seats.

Further, the product lines these reps sold were seasonal. During the selling season, the rep was far too busy to attend any meetings or to devote any time to training. He or she was continually on the road and overloaded with detail work and administrative tasks. So the sales training had to be delivered during the short off-season, not during the peak selling season. As a result, the rep would have a need to know about the material many months after he or she learned about the material. So there was a strong need for a take-along component as a review medium.

Because many of these reps earned substantial incomes, they were a tough audience. Most believed that no one except another successful rep could possibly tell them anything of value in their situation. And few enjoyed plowing through reams of printed material. They were doers, not thinkers, and they were very accustomed to receiving information in AV formats.

Finally, these representatives fell into two general categories: One group was composed of long-time salespeople who were reaping the rewards of seniority. They had developed a customer base years ago and it continued to pay off handsomely. The other group was composed of newcomers, some from fields such as teaching in which their former jobs had dried up. This group was eager to develop that same customer base but was lacking in vast sales experience.

## How Does the Client Want to Change the Situation?

The major change desired was that the sales reps would attempt to open new markets or to bring new products into existing markets. This goal could be measured by increased sales volume, by new accounts developed, and by a number of other easily quantifiable criteria.

Less easily quantified, but just as important, the firm wanted to make sure that all reps were using basic selling techniques effectively. It wasn't possible to convince some of the old-timers that they needed sales skill training, but it was possible to provide that training embedded within other programs.

## What Medium and Message Will Work for This Audience and This Need?

There would be several specific messages within the programs of this series. But the overall series message would be that the basic selling skills that worked in one market and for one customer could be adapted to work in other markets and for other customers. The benefit to the sales rep of doing this adaptation and prospecting for new markets would be increased diversity and increased opportunity for profit.

One important element within this case study is the choice of medium. Although any audiovisual medium could have been used, the client chose filmstrips. Some of you, right now, should be surprised—because filmstrips are seen as an ancient medium that can't compete with videotape or sound-slide. In this case, filmstrips competed very well.

Filmstrips were chosen for several reasons. Because the presenters were unskilled in media, we could not use any complex devices. Sound-slide units fit into that category because they required the presenter to correctly set up a slide tray and a cassette, and then to be able to fix synchronization problems if they developed. The filmstrip projector selected for the program used a cassette that contained both visuals and audio. All the presenter had to do was load the cassette. If during the course of the program the

# CASE STUDIES    *233*

visuals and audio went out of synch, the unit automatically adjusted itself.

But the true beauty of this filmstrip system is its portability. Its projector is smaller than a briefcase, and the cassettes themselves are about the size of a standard audiocassette but about three times as thick. It was no strain to carry the projector and half a dozen filmstrips. But it *would* have been a strain to carry videocassettes and a cassette player or a sound-slide unit and a bunch of slide trays.

The client was a former field manager. He knew well that strain was the last thing these managers wanted to think about. They had become truly sick of lugging sample cases and brochures when they were sales reps. Now that they'd moved up in the firm, they wanted fewer things to carry. The client was certain that if he did not make these programs easy to carry and easy to use, they would not get carried—and therefore would not get used.

We were still faced with the problem of having to present the program before the need for the program's information arose. So we added a reinforcement element, a workbook filled with individual pamphlets that gave a reprise of the information contained in the filmstrips.

In addition, much of the filmstrips' effectiveness depended upon role playing of actual selling situations. So we provided each sales rep with audiocassettes that contained the soundtrack of each filmstrip. In this way, they could refer to the audiocassette just prior to using the techniques in sales presentations.

## What Action Step Was Desired?

The action step was for sales reps to sell more products and to sell in more markets. So there was a strong motivational element required within the program—to get out of a rut and to try some new things.

But the client was a realist. He knew it was unlikely that some of the sales reps would make even one call to a new prospect or mention a new product to existing customers. So he wanted, as a secondary action step, for all representatives to be presented with the basics of selling. Although it couldn't be measured in any simple manner, he felt that this program might help the reps sell better and increase their sales despite themselves.

## How the Need Was Met

We developed a continuing series of programs based on a set of priorities identified by the client. Each program is designed to meet a specific need, but each fits a standard format. That format is a filmstrip of approximately twenty minutes that is presented to a group of reps at a regional or local meeting. After the presentation and some reinforcement by the presenting manager, the reps are given a cassette of the filmstrip soundtrack and a four- or six-page 8½ × 11 printed piece that uses photos from the filmstrip and words that reinforce key concepts from the AV program. Both the cassettes and the print pieces are contained within a three-ring binder.

Although there may be two dozen programs in the series, we are producing them in far smaller quantities. We try, for the sake of cost efficiency, to produce them in sets of two or four, but have produced them one at a time when the need arose.

The reason that sets of two or four are more cost effective is that we can fill two sides of an audiocassette at one time. It also allows us to die-cut an even number of tabs and to produce workbooks in larger quantities.

These programs rely heavily on the involvement of successful sales representatives who help us write the scripts and print material and who appear in the filmstrips. As a result, the programs have a "field" flavor that is well-received by the sales representatives. This points out the importance of peer involvement because the representatives who appear in the program are successful in the same field, with the same kinds of territories and same products, as the audience members. There is no problem of trying to persuade audience members to believe what the "company mouthpiece" has to say.

But this same benefit has a flip side. It's tougher to produce these kinds of programs. That's because we were using untrained people as photographic models and voices during the role plays. In addition, we were often working with the first draft of a script that had little relationship to the final product. That's because not until we actually arrived on location and met with the subject representative did we find out he or she did it differently than the corporate office expected it to be done.

What can, and did, happen was that the sales reps tried, at first, to follow the corporate line when we were recording their presentation. But it soon became obvious from the amount of fluffs and general hesitancy each rep exhibited that this was all new to him or her. So we'd then take a break and discuss how the rep actually made the presentation.

After we learned how the rep actually did the presentation and convinced the rep that the corporation wasn't going to object to that method, we'd go back and shoot the visuals and record the role play as the rep would normally do it. Of course, we'd also cover ourselves by keeping the recordings made according to the company line.

The program design involved the use of a narrator who provided introductory and concluding information plus transitions. The narrator's role was to compress time and to emphasize important points covered in role-play dramatizations of actual selling situations. For instance, the rep might actually spend twenty minutes discussing all the options available concerning a specific product. But the filmstrip soundtrack would simply fade out as the rep began discussing those options, then the narrator would refer the viewers to the printed material that listed all options.

The printed material was done with large type and a great deal of white space. It was meant to be scanned, not necessarily read word-by-word. We also used indented columns and bullets . . .

- Like this . . .

to list key points. We chose representative visuals from the filmstrip to add some visual variety to the print material and also to recall the physical setting of the filmstrip for the audience member.

## Problems

A major problem involved with any program that uses an audio-only component is that the audio must stand alone. So we had to make certain that the information contained within the visual portion of the program was either repeated in the text or repeated on the videotape. And we had to make sure that the audio could be understood without reference to the visuals.

A second problem involved the client's need to use a sound-slide version of this program for large audiences, such as the new-hire sales training program. The particular filmstrip system we chose involved the use of an inexpensive projection and audio playback system. In addition, all filmstrips are duplicates, not original camera shots. For large groups, the client wanted the quality of a sound-slide program.

But the format of a filmstrip is different in proportion from the format of a slide. So we had to make sure that the images we shot for the show could be used for both formats. In general, this meant we had to shoot "squarer" images than we normally would for a slide program and we had to keep important information away from the edges of the frame. As a result, the slides used in the large-audience presentation looked a little strange—as if the composition was off a bit.

Finally, we never knew exactly what we would include in the print material until after we had completed all the scripting, recording, editing, and compilation of the slide programs. So we were faced with two choices. We could either shoot a great number of black-and-white negatives at the same time we shot color slides, or we could simply determine before the shooting session what black-and-white shots we would use in the final print material. The first choice would have broken our budget, while the second limited our options. So we chose a third course.

We had black-and-white prints made from color slides. This system works okay, but there is a quality loss. Basically, it's a photographic process in which the color slide is shot with black-and-white film and then a print is made from that "conversion neg."

If cost is no object, you can experiment with each slide to make sure it translates well to black-and-white, then you can spend a bit more money making sure that the screen print or halftone (the picture with all the dots on it, necessary to reproduce continuous-tone material) was also of top quality. Finally, you could make sure the paper, ink, and printing process were all designed to deliver top quality, very sharp reproductions.

Cost *was* an object, so some of our photos didn't translate well. They needed color to work effectively, and in some cases the conversion process resulted in a slightly fuzzy print or one in which the tones were compressed so that there was no black or white, just middle grays.

What we did reaffirm for ourselves, however, was that a good printer is especially important when you are providing marginally bad material.

### How Did It Work?

This has been an extremely successful program. The sales reps feel that they are listening to and learning from one of their own. The managers don't mind lugging the gear around or setting it up. And the corporation is finding that reps are trying new markets.

Of most importance to us, this program is proving that it might be possible in the future to eliminate some of the travel done by these area managers and others who deliver training to the field. The managers report that their role is minimal in these presentations, that the AV does most of the work. Because this corporation, like many others, is facing both an economic problem and an employee-morale problem relating to extensive travel, the firm is looking closely at delivering more training by this method.

Perhaps the best indicator that these programs work is that we are not hearing negative comments about them from some of the "old salts." They may not be using the programs, but they are at least not standing around with us at various convention receptions and telling us how useless the programs are for any representative.

## A THEFT-REDUCTION PROGRAM

### What Is the Most Pressing Need?

This retail firm was experiencing high theft rates, both from shoplifters and from internal thieves. It also had high turnover and a relatively young average personnel age.

The firm was losing millions of dollars each year, yet it could not afford the psychological or actual costs of clamping strong security measures onto employees and customers. It was felt that both customers and employees would abandon their relationships with the retail store rather than submit to stronger security measures such as electronic scanners or tighter supervision.

### How Did the Firm Want to Change the Situation?

The firm wanted to reduce both forms of theft. They believed this could be accomplished by motivating and training employees to recognize that theft was not only morally wrong, it was also a poor financial "bargain." By convincing some employees that theft was bad for many reasons, the firm wanted to increase peer pressure by these people on other employees and increase awareness of the problem.

### What Is the Best Medium and Message for This Need?

The firm wanted a program that could be used for large groups and for individual employees. Also, the firm had many stores within a relatively small geographic area. So they wanted equipment that could be transported easily from place to place and set up rapidly and easily by untrained personnel.

We chose a sound-slide program produced specifically for use on one of the self-contained devices that includes an audio-cassette player, a slide projector, and a small screen. Many of these units have the capability of projecting images either onto the built-in screen or onto a large screen. They may have some limitations, such as a small audio amplifier or few lens choices, but they have the advantages of simplicity and flexibility.

The message was fairly clear—stealing may get an employee goods for free, but there are costs. Some of those costs involve legal action and the possibility of jail or a fine, but other costs are involved, too. The loss of a job and having "thief" on your employment record is incredibly costly. And so is the intangible cost of lost funds available to the company for employee benefits or other things of value to the employee. Finally, there's the psychological cost of working for a store that is experiencing thievery—everyone's a suspect.

### What Action Steps Are Expected?

The action steps expected were obvious—reduced theft. From the client's standpoint, any theft-reduction that saved them more than the cost of the program made the program a "freebie." They wanted a reduction of 2 or 3 percent, and an indication of the size of this problem was that this percentage would result in a savings of almost a million dollars in just one year. We didn't charge that much for the program.

## How the Need Was Met

The major problem in programs such as this is making a point without pointing a finger at thieves. It also allowed us to call for visuals without regard to whether they could be easily photographed or not.

Because of this and several other reasons, we chose an opening for the presentation that involved "great thieves of the past," such as the pirate Blackbeard and Jesse James. The idea was to show that these people often were idolized, but not by the people they victimized. We especially wanted to emphasize the fact that many people who participated in thefts, such as the bank employees who gave Jesse James inside information, ended up getting nothing for their trouble but more trouble.

We also accentuated the positive throughout this program. This goes back to the "Big Carrot, Big Stick" theory of motivation; you can motivate someone to do something either by threats or by rewards. In this program, it made more sense to talk about the positive benefits of reduced theft; for one thing, more money would be available for employee salaries or for fringe benefits. Because the majority of employees were honest, there was no sense in threatening them or insulting them. That could cause more damage than that already being done by thieves. Instead, we assumed that people were honest and we expected them to be honest because people prefer to meet expectations rather than to fall short.

We also chose to begin with an overview of the scope of the problem, and then rapidly to talk about specifics for this retail chain. When someone talks about billions of dollars in theft, to most people the problem appears to be astronomical and unsolvable. It also can appear as if the problem is so enormous that one person can't make a difference. However, when the immediate follow-up describes how one specific theft affects an individual employee and the firm, the problem is seen in human terms. For instance, we described how stealing one $35 camera from the dozen cameras in stock can have several costs, including the lost profit on that camera plus the cost in bookkeeping to try to locate the camera and the cost if that camera is sold to someone (because it is thought to still be in stock) yet can't be delivered. As a result of this and similar thefts, we suggested, the camera operation within that store might not show a profit or customers might get the idea that the store can't deliver merchandise. This meant that a clerk interested in working with cameras might be out of luck if the store closes the department.

We continued with similar specific examples throughout the program, always bringing the general statement into specific focus. Then we completed the program by returning to the general situation, talking about what could happen if everyone worked to reduce thefts.

The visuals chosen for the program were very realistic looking four-color pastel drawings. We could have chosen cartoon-style art or simple line drawings, but we wanted to lend credibility to the program through the quality and complexity of the visuals. One important element in the visualization, by the way, was that we had the same artist who created the drawings create needed word slides in the same pastel form. In this way, we kept the same style rather than forcing the viewer to leap between artwork and hard-edged type slides.

We also kept the presentation format in mind when specifying artwork and soundtrack. Because these images would frequently be viewed close up, we made sure that the visuals included necessary details that would be seen under close scrutiny. Because this program would be shown to large audiences, we made sure that many visuals were close-ups that could be read easily from a distance. And we made sure that the soundtrack was not so overpowering that it would bother a person hearing it through headphones or through a speaker placed directly in front of the audience member.

## Problems

There were very few problems with this program. We found that some of the artwork did not translate well from pastel art to slides, because part of the effectiveness of the original art depended upon the texture and subtle coloring of the work and those effects didn't transfer to slide film. And we found that one or two of the character voices didn't quite make it.

But the only major problem was that the script was written with too many sound effects and some of those effects were impossible to duplicate inexpensively. For instance, we called for the effect of gold coins clinking on a wooden deck when Blackbeard paid off his crew. We ended up changing the script words because that effect proved impossible to "read" correctly when heard on audiotape.

### How Successful Was the Program?

This program was totally successful from our standpoint and from the client's. Thievery costs were reduced. Even more important, the client reported to us that after seeing the program, many people said, "I never thought about that." Now they do, and it seems to be helping the firm reduce thefts.

## A TELEVISED PANEL DISCUSSION

### What Is the Most Pressing Need?

This financial institution was under continuous attack by special-interest groups and under continuous scrutiny by the press because it was frequently forced to foreclose on farms. The institution needed to explain that these foreclosures were not the activities of a group of sadistic and greedy villains, but a necessary step if the financial health of other farmers and similar bank depositors was to be maintained.

In this era of activism, however, gatherings of farmers protesting in front of a bank made great news, as did the sad, but high-impact, visual of a family moving off the farm they had worked for generations. A lot of press was being given to the "other side" of this issue, and the financial institution needed to tell its side of the story better to offset the press coverage.

Also, each new protest disrupted the operation of the financial institution at the branch under siege. The institution wanted to help branch personnel deal efficiently with the press, with protestors, and with their own feelings about being forced to foreclose on people.

### How Does the Client Want to Change the Situation?

The client wanted to provide training to help branch officers deal with protestors and the press. The firm wanted to get their side of the story told, and to begin educating both the press and the general public about the facts surrounding foreclosure. It was hoped that this education would lead to fewer protests as more people understood that many foreclosures were last-ditch responses to years of poor payment on the part of farmers and that foreclosure was the only way to protect the money of other bank customers.

## What Medium and Message Will Work for This Audience and This Need?

The institution had a fledgling video capability that they wished to expand. They felt this program would be a good test of how effective video could be in imparting training. The institution also employed several experts in various aspects of farm banking and wanted the branch officers to know about these experts as resource people for the future.

One of the clients had seen an effective network television program using a large panel of experts who discussed a problem in depth. So this format was chosen.

The message was complex, involving options for dealing with the press plus legal and ethical restrictions involving foreclosure. But the overall feeling that the institution wanted to impart was that foreclosure was a necessary part of banking, yet one that was only used in rare instances. Therefore, bankers should not hesitate to make their side of the story known and should not feel like villains when this step was taken.

## What Action Step Was Expected?

The institution wanted bankers in branch offices to feel more comfortable when dealing with the press. They expected audience members to develop a plan of action for dealing with foreclosure and to call upon the institution for more resources and information.

## How the Need Was Met

The client hired a public relations consultant and spokesperson to work with internal PR people to develop a "scenario" for the panel discussion. Ten people would respond to questions posed by the spokesperson concerning how they would react in a foreclosure protest and similar proceedings.

The program was shot using three cameras in a meeting room within the institution's main office. It was done in a three-hour session, using the firm's equipment plus some that we brought in to allow ten people to have microphones at one time.

The program was then reviewed and "paper-edited" by the internal and external PR people. We then made the actual edits on the tape and added music and graphics. It would be duplicated and made available to branch offices on a demand basis.

There was no script, although the spokesperson did provide some guidance during the taping. We shot the program as it happened, making switches or dissolves between cameras when appropriate.

## Problems

We ended up with a program that had been edited so many times that it ceased to have the quality required for reproduction. Also, we ended up far beyond the initial budget. This problem resulted from two factors. First, the principal in-house producer of this program had never worked with video before but had a great deal of experience with print media. As a result, he edited the program by first transferring the audio portion of the tape to paper, then editing the words into whatever order he wanted without reference to the visual on the screen at that time. It became an extraordinarily complex editing job, involving putting together phrases and sentences that were far apart in the original program. Second, after we had spent all the time and money to create this complex edited version, the approvers of the program began to make changes and, in fact, to shift the entire focus of the program. Yet they still wanted to keep the budget very low. So we could not go back to the original tapes to make changes. Instead, we made changes to the edited version, losing a generation of quality in the process of duplication and editing.

One problem worth further discussion is the problem of dealing with this many people at one time. Out of any ten people, one will probably be coughing or rustling papers at each instant of recording. So it's difficult to get a "clean" audiotrack. One way to do it is to give each person a microphone and run each person's microphone through a separate volume control; when that person is not talking, the microphone is turned off. But this firm's budget did not cover the cost of all those separate sound channels. In addition, this program was not scripted, so it was impossible for the director to know who would speak next. As a result, we had to keep all the microphones at a speaking level at all times . . . and the tape sounds like it, with coughs and hiss from air conditioning and all sorts of other noises.

On multiple-camera shoots such as this one, we used a "switcher" that allowed us to go from one shot to another without stopping the cameras. So we'd first "take" the long shot of the panel, then switch to take the close-up. We did this in real time.

What this means is that we had to make instant decisions during multiple-camera shoots. And an unscripted multiple-camera shoot doesn't make those decisions any easier. So often we could take the next shot a little too late or a little too early. A person would begin talking while we were still on a shot of someone else who had just finished talking. Or we would take a shot of the person we thought would talk next, but he or she didn't.

When it comes time to edit program segments, all of these mistakes add up. We wanted to edit from the end of one statement to the start of another statement that happened several minutes later in the tape. But the second statement began on audio a few seconds before the director and camera operator focused on the speaker's face for the visual. This left a shot of some person totally unrelated to either the first statement or the second at the front end of the second statement.

The final edit would show the person making the first statement, then a brief glimpse of this unrelated person as the second audio statement began, then the second person's face. It's disconcerting. So we looked for "cut-aways" to help make the transition smoother. A cut-away is a visual that can be put into a film or a videotape to help the viewer "forget" the shot he or she just saw or to cover a problem area, as when the camera operator has a focus problem or a fly lands on the nose of the subject. It's typically a visual without sound, inserted over existing sound. For instance, the shot of the unrelated person could be replaced with a shot of someone nodding his head or someone writing on her notepad while we still listen to the beginning of the second statement.

Well, we didn't have enough cut-aways. We couldn't get the people to stay seated long enough to shoot cut-aways, and we didn't have any obvious cut-aways in the show because somebody was always talking. And we couldn't show a person talking without also letting people hear what that person had to say, so a cut-away doesn't work well unless the person or thing shown in it isn't making any noise.

One way out of this problem is with very tight editing. When most people stop talking, or before they start talking, there's a second or two of silence. When we listen to someone, we don't notice it because the silence is so short. So we took advantage of this short pause by keeping the visual of the person who had just completed a statement while taking the audio-only of the person who was beginning the second statement. In many cases, that gave us just enough covering shot to avoid the need to use cut-aways.

Unfortunately, we expect to hear that pause. If you eliminate it, it sounds as if everyone is interrupting everyone else and as if everyone is talking at top speed and as if there is a sentence on top of another sentence without any breathing space as in this sentence.

So, if you are shooting video or if you are the client of someone shooting video, shoot cut-aways. Shoot shots of pens writing on paper, of people listening and nodding their heads, and of people during the production. You won't regret it during post-production.

### How Successful Was the Program?

The program, despite the cost and creative problems, was successful. Some outstanding comments were gleaned from the panel members. Although a scripted presentation may have been better, in terms of cost and time, we would have lost the realism that came from the words and ideas of these people who had already been through protests and foreclosures.

## CONCLUSION

One of the most difficult tasks facing a business communicator is justifying the effectiveness of business communications as a business tool. In contrast, a person who manufactures something tangible can simply tote up the number of units manufactured to show productivity, and a person who sells something can simply tote up the number of sales to show sales success. However, part of the manufacturing and sales process involves knowledge and communication. So the work of the business communicator may contribute to the success of other business endeavors, yet be so embedded in the business process that it can't be separately measured.

That's why it is important that one part of the situation analysis for any program should be to determine the action step required. Then one part of the post-program analysis should be to determine if that action step is being taken by the audience. In that way, it is possible to get some sense of whether or not the programs you are designing are doing their jobs.

# 10

# Producing Specific Types of Programs

## BE A SUCCESSFUL IMITATOR

There are times when it pays to be different, when it's worth the time and effort to develop a business communications program that is unique and unexpected. But there are many more times when it pays to follow the established patterns of successful programs. So, in this chapter, we will outline several successful program designs that have stood the test of time.

It's interesting that many of these programs created without regard for imitation still imitate successful programs designed by experts. That's because so much expertise is just common sense coupled with time and focus. Most successful programs are so sophisticated they are simple—because after the experts have tried several unique and unexpected ways of solving a problem, they go back to the basics when the basics will work best.

## PUBLIC AND PRESS RELATIONS

### The Need

It may not be true, as someone once said, that all of us will be famous for fifteen minutes in our lifetimes. But it probably is true that all of us will "make the news" in one way or another. That's especially certain now that there are so many different outlets for news, including specialized newsletters and publications as well as many hours of broadcast and print journalism available each day.

It's not surprising that many firms and organizations have designated a staff person as their public relations person. What is surprising is that not *every* firm or organization has done so. Whether in a desirable press coverage, like news of a major breakthrough in chemical technology, or in an undesirable coverage, such as a discrimination suit or plant disaster, every organization should be prepared for the probability that it will find itself famous—or infamous—for fifteen minutes or more. The way to make the most of that fame, or the least of it, is through public and press relations.

## The Necessary Elements

Journalists do not put on magic shoes when they get their press cards. They are subject to the same failings as the rest of us. Most of the work you will put into public relations is designed to minimize those failings, which fall into three categories: memory failure, misunderstanding, and deliberate misrepresentation.

The basic tool any public relations person should create is a "press kit"—a compilation of material that can be taken back to the newsroom by journalists or can be mailed by the PR person to interested media. A press kit provides reference material that can avoid the problems of memory failure or misunderstanding. Nothing can help you avoid misrepresentation, but providing good background materials and developing a solid working relationship with the press can help you counterattack through more responsible media.

Press kits typically include far more material than any journalist wants or needs to cover a single story regarding your organization. But that's okay; it's better to provide too much information than to neglect to provide the one bit of information the journalist needs to write an accurate story.

You should include the following materials in a comprehensive press kit:

A *background and position paper* that outlines how the firm was developed, what products and services it manufactures and sells, and any other overall information that helps position this firm in relationship to other firms.

*News releases or specification sheets* that describe and explain things of interest to the general public and to the specific audiences of interest to this firm or organization. Each of these specific items should be slanted so it explains the topic in terms of benefits and advantages to the audience for which it is written.

*Photographs or illustrations* that show the product or service in action. You can also include product shots, such as those showing a widget against a plain background or being held in the hand of a model. Look at the photographs or illustrations that run in most media; they rarely are product shots, but frequently are shots of people using products.

A *contact name and telephone number* so that media people can follow up by asking more questions or by clarifying their understanding of some topic. If the specific situation is one where a fast-breaking news event could occur, you might want to include an after-hours number. Avoid having the press say, "Company spokespeople could not be reached for comment," because some of us associate "no comment" with having something to hide.

*Copies of previous press coverage,* such as magazine and newspaper articles or transcripts of radio or television stories. Include any and all coverage that might help the press understand your organization better, including those stories that may not be entirely positive. (Journalists can always gain access to other stories, so you may as well provide the stories. In the case of negative stories, include a response from your firm so that the press gets your version too.)

If your organization has produced *magazine articles* (even for company publications) or has created audiovisual shows or films, include copies of the articles and scripts.

You will probably put these items into a folder or notebook, but don't expect the journalist to put that folder in a prominent place on his or her shelf. Most of what you put into the press kit will immediately hit the wastebasket as soon as the journalist returns to the office and scans it. Be content if the material is viewed and if a few items are stored in a file. So spend the money on substance, not packaging.

The two elements that probably will be filed are fact sheets about the firm and photos. These will be important resources for most journalists, providing some good details and pictures for a story. So spend some time putting these together, and prioritize them so that the first thing the journalist sees is the most important.

Include some facts that support your point of view on issues. For instance, an airport operator might want to discuss the issue of aviation safety as well as the issue of airport noise. So the airport's press kit should outline the field's excellent safety record, and include some overall information about the safety record of aviation. Any facts concerning how much revenue the airport brings into the area or what things are being done to reduce noise should also be included.

Photographs are usually in short supply in most press rooms. You can increase your chances of having a story about your firm or organization run if you can provide decent photographs. Provide both black-and-white and color, even if the medium to which you are sending the press kit uses just black-and-white. Many of these media use color for magazine covers, or for special emphasis. During a television news report, for example, color slides concerning various topics are shown over the anchorperson's shoulder.

Be sure to include a photo caption with each photo. This is often done by typing up the caption on a piece of 8½ × 11 paper, beginning halfway down on the sheet. Then the paper is taped to the back of the photograph so that the caption typing hangs down below the photo and can be folded over as a protection for the front of the photo. On that caption, if you wish, state that you will allow the media to use this photo if "appropriate credit is given to [your firm]." In this way, a photo can turn up two or three months, or even years, later and still get you free publicity.

### Editorial Mention

Free publicity is what a lot of this is all about. You can always buy advertising space, but editorial mention usually can't be purchased. And editorial mention is worth its weight in gold because it is not a paid ad; it is the words of the objective (sometimes) press, not of a company with something to sell.

You can get editorial mention—good editorial mention—in several ways. One is through a press event of some kind, like a ground-breaking ceremony or formal presentation of the firm's latest product. Another is to send out releases and invite the press to call or simply write a story based on the release. A third is to write an article or produce a film or videotape and give it to the media.

This last option is especially effective if you want to reach audiences in smaller towns and communities. It's rare for a big-city newspaper or broadcasting station to use something that comes in "over the transom," but these pieces are welcomed by small-town editors who are doing triple duty as reporters, editors, and sometimes as printers or television directors.

You can often write and produce these programs yourself, or you can hire the work out, just as you'd hire any other type of business communications.

## Press Releases

The heart of any public relations effort is the press release. It's included in press kits, handed out at press conferences, sent to a mailing list of interested media people, and given whatever other distribution that seems appropriate to the topic.

As magazine editors and contributing writers, we see a lot of press releases—and see a lot of them being dumped into wastebaskets. Once in a while we come across a jewel that really helps us do our job better.

In most cases, the ones that get dumped are "blanket" releases, where the same copy is sent to all media. It might be a "mug shot" of the person who was just promoted to sales vice-president plus a brief biography.

The ones that get used, and the ones that will help you the most, focus on a specific benefit or topic of special interest to the people who use that particular media vehicle. If you manufacture a product that can be used in several different ways, try to feature a specific use of interest to the people who make up the audience of each publication or electronic medium to which you send the release.

For instance, suppose your firm produces an energy-saving device that can be installed on existing home furnaces. If you send a release to a do-it-yourselfer magazine, you might want to emphasize the fast payback period and ease of installation. If you send a release to an industry magazine for furnace companies, you would probably emphasize profit margin, giving the customer something extra, and marketing support available to furnace firms. For a general-interest audience, such as that for radio and television, you might incorporate many other energy-saving tips, like cleaning the chimney and adjusting pilot lights or burners, with your product shown prominently on every furnace, by every burner.

## What About Bad Press Coverage?

There's a joke about knowing it is a bad day when you walk in the office and a "60 Minutes" crew is waiting for you. But that's not so funny if you do become the subject of a press investigation. What you want to do in these cases is to minimize the effect of the investigation.

If you don't talk, however, don't expect that the media will leave the story alone. In fact, "no comment" is often the worst thing you can say, because it isn't accepted as "I don't want to talk about it now" or "I don't have anything to say about it." Instead, it's taken to mean, "I'm afraid to comment on the grounds it may incriminate me."

The best way to approach these problems is with preplanning. Have a press kit ready and think about what you would say if the awful thing you fear ever happened. It's obviously pretty hard to put some disastrous event into a positive light. But you can show that the events surrounding the disaster were unusual. And you can certainly point out the rarity of the event, showing that this was a freak problem, not part of a trend.

If the media will use quotes, either on-camera or as information in a print piece, make sure the spokesperson states everything in a positive manner and avoids using negative/positive statements like, "This was an awful accident, but it's the first accident in twenty years." You can see how easy it would be to take this quote out of context: "This was an awful accident." It would be better to phrase that statement as, "This was the only accident we've had in twenty years." (Notice "only" instead of "first," and no mention of "awful.")

Finally, don't be afraid to follow up with more information to the media or with a call that asks how the media person is doing on a story. In the hot-and-heavy world of breaking stories, a journalist will often be sitting at a typewriter trying to decipher scribbled notes or trying to hear a badly taped interview. If you can clear up some of the confusion, through press kits, press releases, or in-person contact, you'll be helping yourself as well as helping the journalist and the journalist's audience.

# ADVERTISING AND SALES PROMOTION

## The Need

In many cases, public relations can't do the entire job. That's when it does pay to advertise. Although advertising and sales promotion can become expensive, there's little doubt that they do help organizations generate interest and increase sales. There is some doubt, however, about the best ways to go about accomplishing these tasks, and that's why advertising and sales promotion specialists exist.

For a small firm, or one with limited advertising and sales promotion needs, it may not be cost-effective to hire specialists. In part, that's because specialists are not specialists in the businesses they advertise or promote. Instead, they are specialists in communicating advertising and promotion messages. So they have to spend some time, and charge some money, to be able to learn enough about the firm to promote it effectively. If you're talking about a $2,000 brochure or a $200 radio ad, you might also be talking about $3,000 or more in research costs.

We're not discounting the importance of these specialists, by the way. After all, they make up a large portion of our client base. But we are suggesting that certain advertising and sales promotion vehicles are so cut-and-dried that they can be done in-house. Those are the kind we'll discuss in this section, not the expensive and/or extensive programs done by advertising and sales promotion specialists.

## The "FAB" Approach

Most effective sales promotion and advertising campaigns concentrate on FABs—features, advantages, and benefits. A feature is something associated with the product, like a special locking system for a home door. The advantage of this feature is that it makes the home door lock impossible to open with a small crowbar or a credit card. The benefit is increased protection for the homeowner.

Most good advertisements and sales promotion pieces lead off with the benefit. That's just common sense; people want to know why they should bother to read on or to listen further, so you give them a reason to do so . . . a WIIFM (what's in it for me?). Then you will normally discuss some features, show some advantages, and return to the benefits at the end of the piece.

This holds just as true for a television commercial as it does for a major sales brochure. And it holds just as true regardless of the product or service you are selling. Of course, if your product has no special FABs, you have to take a different approach, perhaps selling the FAB of your company's long history and excellent reputation. In general, the FAB approach works best for most applications.

### Standard Sales Promotion Media

Sales promotion typically involves either a "point-of-purchase" (P-O-P) application or a "take-along" application. You might, for instance, have a countertop filmstrip or videodisc presentation explaining the FABs of your product and place brochures near the AV device so people can review the product's FABs at their leisure.

P-O-P programs, including those used at conventions or for other display-related applications, should be short and repetitive. Make sure that people who may view the program for only twenty or thirty seconds, and who may start or stop viewing at a random point within the program, still get the necessary selling pitch. The program should be attention getting, with catchy music and lively visuals, to help draw people into the viewing experience.

P-O-P is also an ideal place for an interactive program. This need not be an elaborate computer-controlled videodisc program, although these systems are used for P-O-P frequently. You could, for instance, provide separate filmstrips on each topic area or separate slide-sound sets. Or you could use a "random-access" system that allows you to punch in a location from a keyboard and automatically move the media material to that location.

The advantage of interactive P-O-P is that when people become involved in something, they are more likely to pay attention to the topic and to spend time on the topic. The disadvantage is that you must either set up several systems or accept the fact that people may walk away if the unit happens to be busy and the topic on the unit is not one which interests them.

Take-along material comes in several forms, ranging from simple handouts to lengthy brochures and pamphlets. One key to success with take-alongs is to make the cover as compelling as possible. If you're going to use color at all, use it on the cover.

In a standard take-along brochure, you'll probably simply highlight main points. The action step you want is for the person reading the brochure to request more information. A sales promotion brochure might be the information you send, so it should be more detailed and more in keeping with the image you want for your product or service.

We find that it is usually better to write as few words as possible for sales promotion pieces. You want people to "sell themselves," and they can't do that if they must read reams of material.

One special form of sales copy is the sales letter, either a direct mail piece or one enclosed with a brochure. Here, too, you can make the words stand out by using as few words as possible to state your message. For example, you could perhaps write a two-page letter concerning your product or service, filling every line to narrow margins. But chances are that the only people who will read that entire overstuffed letter are those who are already sold on your product or service. They either want more information or want reassurance that they made the right choice. To generate interest on the part of most readers, you'd be better off using fewer words, and maybe highlighting the most important benefits of your product or service by making that particular paragraph smaller or by underlining and double-spacing the words.

### Internal Sales Promotion

One form of sales promotion common to most businesses is communication with sales representatives. This is often done with a special form of letter, a sales bulletin. One of the things we have noticed in years of writing these bulletins is that very few of the large corporations that use them actually put their internal resources to work to make the bulletins effective.

As an example of a better way to handle sales bulletins, why not use the computer power available in most firms? Most companies realize that a personalized form letter works a bit better than a nonpersonalized form letter, so why not follow that same idea with letters to sales reps?

For instance, why can't the sales vice-president or some other sales executive "personally" congratulate sales rep A for his sales of

$2,800 last month and, with a simple sorting program, use the same general sales bulletin to congratulate sales rep B on her sales of $3,300 last month. The same personalized bulletin could also list A or B's sales for the same period last year and for the year to date, and provide other information.

Of course, part of the bulletin should still put the sales rep's sales in perspective with those of other reps and should provide the standard congratulations to the top sellers. That's an important aspect of the sales bulletin because it adds the element of competition.

### Less Formalization, More Personalization

As a general statement concerning sales promotion materials, in fact, the idea of less elaborate formats and more personalization holds true. We rarely do large-volume four-color print jobs any more. Instead, we do a lot of simpler brochures or pamphlets that contain information for segmented markets. It could be that this means many firms are seeing that the modern, sophisticated consumer is more interested in information than in slick brochures. (On the other hand, a recent Pontiac sales brochure is a stunner; maybe it just depends upon who the audience is and how much the product costs.)

### Print Advertising

In most advertising, but especially in print, the old realtor's list of the three most important things to consider—location, location, location—holds true. You'll pay a premium price for premium locations, like covers or on inside pages next to lead stories. But you sometimes can't guarantee readership even with a prime location.

Most of the "little" ads you're apt to write as a business communicator get their impact from the words you use. So look for a key phrase that says it all, and then run that key phrase big in the ad. That's because many surveys show that once a person has spent a few seconds reading the head of an ad, he or she will spend a few more seconds reading the rest of the copy.

It also helps to tie the headline to some visual, either a graphic or a photograph. For example, we advertised some generic AV programs that could be used for sales meeting support with a headline that read: DESIGNER PROGRAMS AT PLAIN POCKETS PRICES.

We put this headline and the accompanying copy in reverse over a drawing of a blue-jeans pocket. The drawing was not done as a total reverse, as a solid black, because we wanted the copy to be readable. Instead, we simply screened the blue-jeans drawing so it was slightly grayer than the surrounding magazine page. This separated the ad from the rest of the ads on the page, yet didn't force the reader to try to shift the normal reading process from black on white to white on black.

## Trade Ads

One type of ad commonly written by in-house communicators is the trade publication ad, used in industry magazines or newspapers. This is one of the places where you can write more copy than in a standard ad because most of the audience members have a need to know about the information. But you should still emphasize a solid headline and you should accompany that head with a series of subheads that list the main benefits described within a certain section of the ad.

One question we are frequently asked is whether it is better to run one full-page ad or several part-page ads. Our thinking is that repetition pays. An ad works best when it strikes the prospect at a time he or she has a need for the product or service advertised. So a full-page ad run at the wrong time of the year won't necessarily be memorable enough for that prospect to recall when he or she has a need to know. Of course, size and position always help, but if the trade-off must be made, run more small ads.

Another consideration is getting people to respond in some way to the ad, even if they do not have a current need for your product or service. We've seen several examples where advertisers offer a free pamphlet or some handy small item, like a calendar, just to get people to write to the firm. Along with the item, they get a sales brochure. This is especially helpful for two reasons; it helps the firm develop a qualified mailing list and it helps the firm give prospects something they might keep on their desk or in their file until they actually have a need for the product or service the firm offers. (That's why the entire field of specialty advertising developed—everyone needs a pen or a coffee cup or a calendar.)

## Broadcast Advertising

With the high cost of television and radio ads, it almost always pays to hire professional help in creating these ads. We can, however, discuss some things to watch when producing these ads or having them produced.

First, don't forget how people will view or hear your ad. If you want them to take a certain action step or to recall a certain fact, repeat it or make it so memorable that it doesn't require repetition. If you want them to call a number, either make the number so memorable they can't forget it or link the number to something they already know.

In some cases, as in retail store operations, the most important thing is to give the location, and then to give people a reason to go to that location. That's why so many retail store commercials highlight a specific product and price.

In both television and radio ads, the spokesperson can make a lot of difference. As the advertiser, you have quite a bit of clout, if you care to use it. You can, for instance, specify that your commercial will be read by the disc jockey of your choice or will be presented by the television station's favorite host.

Finally, don't neglect the effectiveness of other forms of advertising. Direct mail, of course, can be used to reach specific audience members who have a need for your product and service. You can also advertise through signage on your vehicles, through posters and fliers placed in locations frequented by audience members, and by displays at conferences or in high-traffic areas.

# 11

# Packaging, Storage, Distribution, and Presentation

## FROM THE ABSTRACT TO THE CONCRETE

One of the pleasures of producing business communications programs is that you can watch your work take form, going from an abstract idea to a concrete audiovisual presentation or print piece that meets the objectives set for it. Frankly, it's one of the things that makes all the work worthwhile.

Perhaps that's why we frequently use the analogies of architecture and construction when discussing business communications programs. As in these fields, business communications programs begin with an idea, continue through designs and plans, and culminate in the framing and finishing of a presentation that will stand as a useful and effective product. And, as with dwellings, the most important considerations are the finishing touches—the packaging and presentation of the program or print piece.

## PACKAGING

There are several things you must think about when deciding how to package a business communications program. You must couple decisions involving the look of the program with decisions involving durability and ease of use. Further, you should start thinking about these things from the very start of program design, not as an afterthought. That's because many of the little touches you can add to make a program package more effective take time and thought.

## Protection

The first packaging consideration should be keeping the materials in the package free from harm. For a book, this is accomplished by a cover. It might be a hard cover, offering maximum durability at a relatively high cost, or it might be a soft cover, lower in cost and in durability. The choice depends upon how long you want the printed material to last and how frequently the material will be used. Obviously, a reference book used daily by mechanics should be bound in a durable, grease-resistant material, while a brochure that is read once and then stored or tossed need not have such a durable cover.

For photographic media, like slide programs or films, the major concern is physical damage. You don't want the film material to become wet or brittle, and you want to keep it from physical harm. If films or slide programs are to be transported or mailed, you'll probably choose a plastic case with a watertight seal. If they are to be used within your office area, you may save money by using a hardboard case instead.

For electronic media, like videotapes and audiocassettes, you must consider the additional possibility of electronic harm. These products can be hurt by stray electrical or magnetic signals, as well as by water, fire, or other natural disasters. So you want a package that will identify the material as electronic media—perhaps with a warning of the possibility of electromagnetic damage—and that will somewhat insulate the material from stray electrical fields. This is usually accomplished by the factory case provided with the material, but it is not provided by the housing of the material. So it is important to keep these electronic media in their cases. An audiocassette housing, for instance, still will allow liquids or dust to enter the interior of the cassette. In addition, most audiocassette housings are made of thin plastic, with the actual tape in direct contact with the plastic. So the factory container within which the audiocassette is sold will inhibit both physical and electronic harm.

All media can be damaged by crushing or dropping the material, so you usually want a durable container and one that holds the media materials in place within a cushion of air or of padding. Especially with slide programs, you'll want a package that will help keep the slides in their slots in case the ring comes loose in the packing box.

Many companies manufacture packages that meet these criteria quite well. Most use plastic, although some film reel containers are metal. These packages may seem like an unnecessary expense—after all, most material does come from the factory with some kind of package—but the expense is worth it the first time you dump a cup of coffee over your desk and watch the liquid pool up around a slide-tray container.

Don't be fooled, however, into thinking that all plastic containers are equally effective. Look for a tight mechanical seal, perhaps even a special watertight gasket, to make certain that the container will actually protect the contents from harm. And, especially if you are shipping materials during the winter months or the "rainy season," add a bit of protection by sealing the container with water-resistant tape.

### Ease of Access and Use

One reason packages don't get used correctly is the same reason people with headaches want to throw those "child-proof" aspirin containers through medicine-chest mirrors. The package is too difficult to use. That's why the plastic wrapping around a video-cassette box gets tossed and why certain intricate and bulky audio-cassette boxes stack up, empty, on shelves.

Boxes should offer protection, but not so much that they can only be opened with a screwdriver or magic words. Boxes should fit on standard shelves and have square edges so they won't roll all over the shelf. Finally, boxes shouldn't require some secret method of repacking material to fit everything in. They should be easy to use, and easy to understand.

Many packages can be used incorrectly just as easily as they can be used correctly. A slide tray box, for instance, will stand up on a shelf along any of its dimensions. If there is a special need for material to be stored in a certain manner, clearly label the box to show the correct orientation.

## Some Examples of Good Packaging

Several firms manufacture an "AV Tray" that can be used to store an audiocassette and a standard Kodak slide tray. Usually of high-impact plastic, these packages can be imprinted through an embossing process so that the imprint remains on the box even if the paint or ink wears off. They are especially useful for situations requiring mailing of both a slide tray and a pulsed audiocassette. It's too easy, otherwise, to lose the cassette or to jam the cassette into the center of the slide tray box and then be unable to close the box completely.

You can also buy three-ring binders or vinyl folders that allow you to include several audiocassettes or filmstrips along with workbook pages. In addition, you can buy cassette page inserts for three-ring binders that provide a plastic housing for several cassettes. One caution, however, is that most of these inserts require you to remove the audiocassette from its box. These page inserts are really little more than a sheet of plastic with indentations shaped like a cassette that hold the cassette in place, with no covering plastic. If the binder happens to be open to the cassette insert when you spill coffee, you have no protection for the cassettes.

One advantage of these cassette inserts is that they can be sandwiched into the middle of a workbook, protecting the audio material by the bulk of paper on either side. It doesn't take much distance, maybe no more than six inches, to totally insulate audio materials from the possibility of erasure by a stray magnetic field. If you have the cassettes in the middle of paper, you have even more insulation.

For videotapes, the cases provided by the manufacturer are excellent. But you can still personalize these by having custom labels created. This is an especially good idea if you fear that someone may steal your copyrighted material. If you emblazon your firm's name and the copyright paragraph onto a bright label, it may deter a potential thief from stealing a dupe. And it will certainly alert any professional duplication house that there could be a problem in honoring a thief's request for dupes.

For print materials, such as pamphlets or thin workbooks, three-ring binders are also effective. So are the binders used to store copies of magazines. One advantage of these magazine binders is that they do not require three-hole punching. Instead, you run a metal rod through the center of a booklet. For this reason, print material of several sizes can be easily kept in the same binder and there's no need to ruin pages by punching holes in them.

Finally, consider the packaging of the package. If you ship materials, such as individual three-ring binders or filmstrip cartridges, you'll probably have to box them within a cardboard container. That means you will be trusting your media materials to someone with a knife or razor blade at the other end of the shipment. In the case of three-ring binders or books, it's easier to pack and seal a carton that is front-opening, but it's also easier to slice through the cardboard into the vinyl. So it pays to spend a bit more packing time by using end-opening cartons.

## Personalization

All media materials can be personalized. You can imprint them with your firm name and/or with the title of the program, using an embossing process, a stamping process, or just a marking pen.

This personalization has several advantages. First, it shows that this program's producer has taken professional concern, even with the finishing touches. Second, an imprinted package or one marked with indelible marking pen is less likely to be lost forever in the mail. Third, developing a consistent packaging and personalization plan for your programs means that everyone who views the programs knows these presentations are part of a continuous, well-planned effort, not something haphazardly thrown together.

By the way, you should consider including identification and personalization within the media material itself. Make sure your identification, such as a logo and an address, is included on the film reels, the audiocassette labels, or the slide tray. And, if space and budget permit, put a slide, film scene, or video scene in at the start and end of the show that includes your logo and address. In this way, even if the packaging is lost, someone can still find out to whom the program belongs. These ideas hold just as true for internal communications within medium-sized companies and large corporations. You might not have the volume of work to make special packaging worthwhile, but you certainly still have the need to identify and personalize packages so they don't get lost within the organization.

## STORAGE

Good packaging is just part of the finishing touch required to make sure your program materials stay intact. Storage is the other part. And storage includes some organized method of keeping track of what you have stored and where. We'll discuss organization later. For now, keep in mind that there's a lot less danger of damage to the materials you're shoving around in your search for the correct program.

### Storage and Retrieval Devices

The best organization and categorization system is useless unless there's some way to protect media materials from harm and to access the materials easily. Dumping all the prints from a certain brochure into one envelope is easy, but it's also a good way to scratch or bend the photographs. And this is especially true if you must sort through every photo within the envelope to find the one you want at a specific time. A good way to store prints is within standard files, sorted by subject area. An even better way is to purchase a special file cabinet with shallow drawers. In this way, there's less danger of crushing or bending photographs by stacking them too high.

Photographs can also be stored in special slide sleeves, as can slides. But some of these sleeves are made of chemicals that can conceivably cause long-term problems with the media materials due to chemical breakdown. With prints this is not a serious problem because prints are made from negatives; that is, they are not an original material, but are a final product created from a master material. Slides, however, *are* an original material. If something causes the color of the transparency to fade or creates surface damage to the slide, the image is often ruined.

For this reason, many professional producers keep their slide masters in small file boxes, like miniature card files, and make sure the storage room is climate-controlled. Or they spend a few extra dollars to make sure that the slide storage sleeves they buy are composed of "inert" materials that won't cause a chemical reaction.

The choice between these two methods of slide storage illustrates a larger choice you must make when selecting storage devices for any medium. In the card-file type of slide storage, you

## PACKAGING, STORAGE, DISTRIBUTION, AND PRESENTATION

can place hundreds of slides in a small space, but you must sort through many slides each time you want to select a specific image. For example, you might have an index tab that says "456.100" for "scenics, water." Within that area, you may have fifty slides. To find the precise slide you want, you have to pull out all fifty and look at each one. Each time you pull out the slides, you risk the possibility of damage and you most certainly will increase the dust and fingerprints on the slides.

One of the specialized slide storage and sorting devices, in contrast, puts each slide in a plastic sleeve and then puts all the sleeves into a turntable device like so many pages in a book. You can flip through hundreds of slides quite easily, yet never touch the slides until you find the one you want. This makes it far easier to sort slides, and lets you look at a lot of slides that may just trigger a visual idea or two for a show. But these devices are costly and take up a lot of space; in addition, you must load all your slides into the sleeves.

If you expect to be the only person who uses your slide storage system, the card-file method will work fine. You'll be careful of your own slides and you'll pretty well know what sort of images are in each section. But if many people will be using the same slide storage system, or if it is a system that includes many slides you have not personally shot and stored, the sleeve-turntable system might be better. You'll get a continual update on which slides are available each time you flip through the slides.

If you extend this idea out to all media, you can see that the primary concept is the difference between ease of access and inexpensive/compact storage. Further, it's the difference between being able to sort rapidly through many different materials or knowing the contents of a file well enough to skip through most options to locate the one you want.

Obviously, we can't list all the options available to you. But we can offer some suggestions. First, make sure that whatever system you buy is an add-on system, so you can increase storage capacity easily. Second, pay particular attention to protection of the media. It's worth spending a few extra moments sorting when that time is compared to the time it took to create the media material in the first place. Third, consider a cross-reference system. For example, we keep a file of "contact prints," which are sheets of photographic paper that contain a number of small, same-size prints of negatives, as well as a file of individual, enlarged photographs. In that way, we can rapidly scan thirty-six shots on a contact sheet to see if we may have anything in the photo file that relates to our specific requirement.

### Climate Control

As a general rule, most media materials like the same climate as we do—moderate-to-low humidity and a temperature around 70 degrees Fahrenheit. If the humidity is too low, materials become brittle. If the humidity is too high, materials become water-logged and can grow fungus. If the temperature hits either extreme, materials can shrink, expand, or otherwise become damaged.

That's why it isn't a good idea to store any material in a storage area where the temperature is allowed to soar or to drop. And it is especially dangerous to store master materials in these places. Instead, it's a good idea to store master materials in vaults; this service is offered free or at low cost by many production houses and laboratories. Take advantage of it, even if it means that you have to make a special trip to the film lab to pick up materials if you choose to use a different lab to redo a program.

Although humidity is the major moisture problem facing media materials, water comes in many other forms—like flooding into a basement. It helps to keep materials wrapped in sealable plastic. But be sure you include a desiccant—a product that absorbs moisture. Otherwise, moisture from condensation can build up inside the sealed plastic and create problems.

Surprisingly, not all materials will be totally destroyed by moisture. We've more than once spilled coffee or a soft drink on slides and found that we could rapidly clean off the excess and save the image. But you have to be very careful, and very quick. If something's been soaking in water awhile, you're better off calling for professional help.

### Electromagnetic Hazards

We've mentioned that stray electric or magnetic fields can destroy electronic media. But that doesn't mean much unless you know what devices generate electromagnetic fields and know where they are in relation to your media materials. With the increasing number of computers found throughout business offices, it's hard to say what sort of stray signals are pouring through walls near your storage area. Every computer puts out some signals, as does every telephone, television set, radio, and electric motor. So do the magnets used to clip notes to filing units!

So the best way to protect electronic media is to create an air buffer around the storage area. If you're storing all media in a small room, for instance, store slides and films along the walls. Store video and audio tapes on central shelving units with a corridor around them. And keep them on open shelves, so that people can easily see what type of media is stored on the shelves. Also, you might want to post signs that caution people against using any electromagnetic devices near the storage area. And you may want to make sure that the people in your firm responsible for space allocation and layout are aware of the potential problem.

## Physical Orientation

Most material has a correct orientation and several incorrect orientations. Stacking books one on top of the other would make it difficult to pull out any one book. So the correct orientation for a book is with the spine out, standing upright on a shelf. In the same way, videotapes, audiocassettes, slide trays and similar media materials all have correct orientations. The way to determine which orientation is correct is by looking at where the manufacturer puts the label on the outside of the container. That manufacturer wants the label to read correctly when the material is stored in correct orientation. So a slide tray label reads right when it is flat, with the box lid on top and horizontal. A videocassette label reads right when the cassette is stored like a book.

## Refreshing the Material

When programs are infrequently used, you should make an effort to refresh them by running them occasionally between uses. You should run audiocassettes and videocassettes forward and back, either run a slide show or blow the dust off the individual slides, or do both, and riffle through the pages of print material. If you don't do this, the materials can become useless because mechanical parts cease to function or because moisture and dust combine into a glue that makes the materials stick together.

Some audio engineers, incidentally, store all tape "tails out"; that is, they run the program through but do not rewind it before storage. That forces people to rewind the tape before playing, giving the tape a chance to breathe a bit.

In addition, most good producers will make certain that all media material has a buffer zone around it, like a leader on film or tape. This buffer provides some unessential material that can be chewed up by a faulty projector or recorder without destroying the main program material.

### Store Directions and Scripts with Materials

Finally, don't trust your memory. The program that seems so much a part of you that you could never forget where each slide pulse goes will soon fade away. Sometimes that's a blessing. If you remembered all the pain you went through to precisely program a show you might never do it again. So keep scripts, and especially keep the annotated copies of scripts that have sound cues and sync-pulse locations on them. Store at least one copy with the media materials, and store another copy in a central file.

## FILING: FINDING WHAT YOU'VE STORED

### Spend Time Now to Save It Later

Everyone knows that it pays to do things right the first time, that good logical organization of media materials starts as soon as the material is created. When you get a box of slides back from the processor, choose the slides you need for the current show, then carefully label and store the rest of the slides. When you send a print job off to the audience, immediately wrap up all the interim materials, mark them clearly, then store them. Making that happen is difficult, because it requires both time and a variety of organizational techniques.

### Adapt the Dewey Decimal System

One organization and storage system is the Dewey Decimal System used by libraries. This can be adapted to most media. For instance, you could create a slide library that uses a specific code number for each type of visual, such as "300" as the code for "computer operators." Then you could segment 300 into, for instance, "300.100" for "young male computer operators" and "300.101" for "young male computer operators of Hispanic descent."

It may seem that this system is "shotgunning a mosquito" for an organization's slide library. But it makes more and more sense as the organization needs to store more and more slides. At first it might be very simple to recall exactly where every shot of a young male Hispanic computer operator is, but it may not always be that simple. There may come a time, in fact, when it's necessary to add another decimal level, like "300.101.100" for "young male Hispanic computer operators using the Model 1297." The advantage of this decimal system is that you can subdivide to whatever level you would like, both when storing slides and when trying to retrieve them.

### Computerized Filing Systems

One of the advantages of a "hierarchal" system like Dewey is that you can easily sort through a section by adding segment addresses. For instance, you can begin by looking at all the subcategories under category 200, then look at just one of those subcategories, or even a subcategory of a subcategory. This is especially easy to do with a computer, because you can treat the subcategories as just another grouping of numbers.

For example, you could make a file listing of all pamphlet titles within your company library using a three-level decimal system. Perhaps the first level might be "100 to 400," with each broad topic area having a three-digit number. Let's say that "330" is the heading for the topic area "Management Forms." You could now break it down even further, into "330.220.110" for "Management Forms Dealing with EEO for Nonexempt Employees."

The advantage of this system is obvious to a person who uses computers. First, there's a lot of space within each of those headings to list more materials. For instance, you might begin by separating filed materials by 100s until you've used all the available 100s. Then you could start using 10s, until you've used all the available 10s. Then you could go to 1s. Between 100 and 200, therefore, you have 100 filing spots.

In addition, although the computer can be programmed to respond to words, it's much easier to find existing programs or to create new programs that allow the computer to sort and search by number. So it's easier to say "Computer, go to 200 and list out all the 200.190.000 to 200.190.300" than it is to say "Computer, I want you to go to the listing under Pollution Control and print out a listing for all pollution control devices used in water environments."

So the real advantage of a computer is that it can store and sort and retrieve listings of what information is available, and even cross-reference information in many different ways. It can't do the filing or storage for you, and you still have to find the time to plug new data into the computer, but it can make the listing and retrieval far easier.

## DISTRIBUTION

### Getting the Message Out Intact

Business moves more rapidly every day, so it's no wonder that many private distribution systems have been developed to compete with the old standbys like the United States Postal Service. But all these options mean that you have many more factors to consider when choosing the best way to distribute programs which will not be hand-carried for presentation.

### Mailing

Trusting a media program to the mail is not as dangerous now as it once was. But we still recommend taking some special precautions, if only because the enormous amount of mail moved each day means that your program will be treated very democratically, even though you want it to be treated as one of the elite items in the system that day.

Don't trust an outside mailbox, especially in inclement weather. Instead, take the package to the post office and see that it is correctly weighed, stamped, and placed in an outgoing container. If you're lucky enough to have letter carriers coming to your office who will pick up as well as deliver, you may want to give *them* the package. But we'd still advise taking master materials directly to the post office, reducing the chance for error or unforeseen hazard (except on the truck or the aircraft; you can't anticipate all eventualities).

If you do mail packages, make sure that you address everything, and return-address everything, too. Put this information on the outside of the package in at least two places and on the inside as well.

You can also pay a bit more than first class postage and get several special services from the U.S. Postal Service. Express Mail, for instance, can get the package to its destination faster as well as perhaps getting it somewhat better treatment. And there are other services, like Priority Mail or Registered Mail, that also separate your package from the bulk mail and advertisements.

Insure your package, regardless of what distribution method you use. Some transporters will allow you to insure the package only for the value of the material itself. But most will allow you to insure for replacement value—that is, what it would cost to duplicate the program. It's a cheap safety factor that's worth the price.

### Private Package Delivery Firms

Although most of what we've said concerning the post office holds true for air and ground private delivery firms, there are a few other things to consider. First, you should realize that many air freight firms operate under a central hub concept. Even if your package is going from Minneapolis to Duluth, for instance, it may go to Memphis first. Although the leaders among these firms are extremely efficient, you may find that it is faster, and not much more expensive, to send the package by bus to Duluth, because the bus can make the 155-mile trip in 3 hours at 55 mph. Even though the air express plane travels faster, it travels farther, and your package must be transferred between planes somewhere at the hub.

Second, look for carriers that have offices in the town to which you will be shipping the package. If you're shipping to a major city, most carriers will have an office. But that's not true in smaller communities. You may find, for instance, that a package you entrust to a major air freight firm actually travels the last few miles by bus or van, and it may not make that trip until many hours after it arrives at the nearest destination airport. So make sure that there's a "branch office," not just a "licensed agent" in the destination town.

Third, if you're with a large corporation, consider hand delivery of materials. One firm found that it could save several thousand dollars each month just by keeping track of where employees were traveling and linking up the travelers to people within the firm who wanted packages or Special Delivery mail sent to the same location. Yes, it was a pain in the neck . . . and no one asked the CEO to lug a few packages along on *his* trips. But the majority of the people involved as travelers were also shippers, so they knew that the favor would be reciprocated.

Finally, make sure that whatever delivery system you use provides door-to-door delivery, not just delivery to a central sorting location. Further, check the "add-ons" and "fine print." We've found that, all too often, cheapest isn't necessarily cheapest when everything is considered. For example, one air express firm provides us with cartons and labels. It seems like no big deal until you price a cardboard box.

### Electronic Distribution Channels

With the continued emphasis on microwave transmission of telephone and television signals, and with the growing number of satellites in orbit, it's not too farfetched to predict a time when you'll be able to transmit many media materials electronically.

For instance, the national newspaper *USA Today* is transmitted via satellite and microwave to many locations throughout the country where it is typeset, printed, and distributed. And most broadcast and cable networks use separate "feeds" to transmit information and news stories in the time during commercials and station breaks when entertainment programming is not on-line.

At our current level of technology, however, there is some quality loss involved in these transmission methods, just as there is some loss involved in the reception of certain television or radio signals under specific weather or terrain conditions. So this alternative is something to consider for the future, not the present.

# PRESENTATION

### Make a Good Impression

If you look at a great photograph that has been crumpled and soiled and then stuck up on a wall with pins, and you look at a mediocre photograph that is well-mounted and hung on a gallery wall, you may have trouble distinguishing the great from the mediocre at first glance. The presentation counts.

That's not to say that substance doesn't count. It does. But it's hard to overcome a bad first impression. So save a few budget dollars to make sure that your media materials get presented well.

For print material, this means good binding and some care that pages are not left uncut or even left out of the book. It also means good design, layout, and packaging, so that the words and illustrations are framed well on the pages.

For audiovisual media, more-technical considerations are important during presentation. And each set of media, photographic and electronic, has its own set of technical requirements.

### Photographic Media

Perhaps the single most important thing you can do to enhance photographic media is turn out the lights. Slides that look awful in room light look wonderful, sometimes, in subdued light. And there's something about viewing a program in a darkened room, isolated and focused on the screen, that makes the experience more powerful for most people.

But of almost equal importance are sightlines and image size. We've discussed the "screen width rule" before, but it's worth recapping here. No viewer should sit farther than eight screen widths from the screen or closer than two screen widths. And no viewer should sit farther than three screen widths on either side of the screen center. It's almost as bad to be too close as it is to be too far away, because both extremes make it difficult to view the material easily and comfortably.

If the photographic medium involves sound, it's a nice touch to have the sound come from the same spot in the room as the visual. So you might want to use an auxiliary speaker to bring the sound signals up to the screen area. Be careful, though, not to make the sound so loud that it overwhelms people in the front of the room while forcing those in the back of the room to strain to hear the information.

The type of screen you use can also make a difference in the way your images look. A simple "matte" screen, one that has a soft white finish, is the basic screen version. It's fine if your slides or film are bright and sharp. But it will add nothing extra to help you.

This "extra" is called "gain," and it's found in several more expensive screen systems. A beaded screen, for instance, is made up of many thousands of bead-like lenses that focus the light onto the screen surface. The result is a brighter image than with a matte screen—a "gain," even though the screen is not actually amplifying anything as in a standard gain-creating device, such as an audio amplifier.

But the problem with some of these high-gain screens is that they have a narrow viewing angle. A person sitting to the far left or far right of the audience area will not see a crisp, consistent image across the entire screen area. And this is especially true in those high-gain screens used for video projectors.

### Videotape Projection and Playback

Although videotape is not a photographic medium, the problems of videotape projection are similar to the problems of photographic projection. Let's begin by setting up a continuum of available videotape projectors.

At the low end of the range, you can purchase a lens system that attaches to your television receiver. It operates like any other lens, by enhancing the light waves that pass through it. But the problems with this system are many, beginning with the fact that the lens system must be precisely adjusted and ending with the fact that so much light is lost through this system that the image must be viewed in a totally darkened room.

For this reason, most business applications of videotape projection would be impossible with this simple lens system. You need a projection system, not just a lens.

Several firms manufacture a self-contained projection system that includes a screen and videotape projection tubes, called "guns," that will project an image onto the screen. Most of these self-contained units provide an image about six feet in diagonal measurement but that has the problem we noted earlier about viewing angle. Because of this, they are useful for small groups, but should be thought of as the videotape equivalent of those tripod-based slide projection screens.

For quite a bit more money, you can buy a videotape projector unit which will project to almost any screen size. These units require some technical expertise for set-up and alignment, but they can fill a screen that's large enough for an audience of several hundred people. The only limitation you have is that the light output from the projector determines exactly how bright the image will be on the screen, so long "throw distances"—the distance between projector and screen—will result in quite a bit of light loss on the screen. Some of the more expensive projectors allow amplification of the light so it can provide a bright image in, for instance, a football dome or hockey arena. But most of the business-budget projectors are only useful to a throw distance of a hundred feet or less.

Videotape projection systems help eliminate one of the problems that has kept videotape from totally taking over from film as a medium of choice for business communications. But some cautions are in order. We find, for instance, that even the best videotape projectors available for business (in the $12,000 range) can't yet provide an image that is as sharp or as bright as an equivalent film projector. This is a technical problem inherent in the television medium, not a quality problem on the part of the videotape projector. Briefly, television works because a great number of lines of information are sent across the screen in a very short time. It's like painting a picture by starting in the top left and working across the screen, left-to-right, top-to-bottom, in small paint strokes. Because it happens so fast, our eyes see a single image rather than a number of individual dots of data.

On a 25-inch television set, these little dots of data seem to flow together into a single image. That's because there are 525 lines jammed into that 25-inch screen area. But when you blow up the image to ten feet or more, as with a videotape projector, those same 525 lines each take up a lot of space and the image looks a bit fuzzy.

The alternative to videotape projection is setting up a number of videotape monitors. A "monitor" looks like a television set, or "receiver," but there are some significant differences. In a standard television receiver, signals are received through an antenna input—whether those signals come from a broadcast transmitter or from a nearby videotape recorder. If you're using a videotape recorder with a receiver, the recorder's output is sent through a device that converts the signal into a simulated broadcast transmission, then that signal is sent into the receiver through the antenna input, and reconverted back into a video signal. The result is a series of electronic steps, and each step can become a stumbling block to clear, crisp reception.

In a monitor, by contrast, the output from a videotape recorder is sent directly into the audio and video system of the television monitor. This means fewer steps and less potential for problems than with a receiver.

A monitor offers special advantages when you want to use more than one television set in a room. By "looping through" with cables, you can run the same output from a videocassette recorder, for instance, through many monitors—it's just like connecting up a number of garden hose sections end-to-end. Each monitor will show the same program at the same time.

There are advantages and disadvantages to using a number of looped monitors rather than one large videotape projector. Each of the smaller monitor images will probably be better than the single large-projector image. But the audience will not be focusing upon one central location. Instead, each audience group will be looking in a different direction. (This is no problem if all information is being imparted through videotape, but it can be a problem if you want the audience to shift attention from videotape to a live presentation.) Also, the space taken up by individual monitors will usually be greater than the space taken up by one projection system. You have to provide an island of clear space around each monitor, so that the people very close to the monitor won't be craning their necks to see the screen. In addition, you have to make a decision concerning the sound: Do you want all the sound to be heard from a central source, such as a room-front speaker, or do you want each individual monitor to also carry sound? Since people like to hear sound from the same place they are seeing visuals, the individual monitor system works better, but that means that people will hear sounds from the other monitors spread throughout the room, too, and this can be distracting.

In general terms, we use monitors for small-audience presentations, perhaps using one monitor for each 20 people. When audience size reaches 120 or so, we shift to projectors. We also use projectors, even for small audiences, when it's important that the audience focus on the same point in the room, as when the videotape is being presented as a portion of a training program.

In the future, the videotape projector versus monitor decision will be easier to make. Many firms are now working on projectors that are bright, easy to use, compact, and inexpensive. Wall-size TV has been predicted for years, and soon it will be widespread.

### Rear-Screen Versus Front-Screen

For any projection system, you have two choices concerning screen orientation. If you put the projector out in the audience and project onto a screen at the front of the room, you're doing "front-screen projection." This is the most common system. But you can also rear-project, by putting the projector behind the screen and projecting through the screen.

The advantage of rear projection is that all the equipment is out of sight, behind the screen. So the audience doesn't hear the whir of projectors or clatter of slides. The audience doesn't see projectionists and equipment out in the main viewing area. Some rear-projection systems allow you to keep room lights up a bit, as long as no light falls directly onto the screen.

We use front projection for things like single-projector slide shows or motion pictures, especially when we can put the equipment into a projection booth to reduce noise. We use rear projection for videotape, for multi-image programs that involve a number of projectors, and for presentations to very large audiences, where the throw distance for front projection would be quite long.

### Print Presentation

One of the keys to effectively presenting any materials, but especially materials such as print that are audience-paced, is "previewing" the materials so the audience knows what to expect and why they should care. In audiovisual work, this is often done either in a live introduction or in the early stages of the presentation. That works fine for AV because you have a "captive audience." But, for print, you should consider some other ideas.

First, consider the cover of the presentation. The title and any artwork on the cover should do two things: add interest and set the tone for the message. No one, for instance, picks up a copy of the magazine *Skiing* without knowing it will contain articles about skiing. The cover always uses a photograph of something having to do with skiing. But, in addition, most magazines, including *Skiing*, use "cover blurbs" that highlight articles within the magazine. The same thing holds true for books, but it is even more important because a book doesn't usually have the wide publicity and built-in audience of a national magazine.

You'll see a wide variety of cover treatments done for books. Some use very traditional graphics, relying upon the book's title to carry the message and add interest. (This is especially true for "how-to" books. If the book-buyer wants to know "how to fix my car," a book with that title will sell regardless of the cover graphics.) Others use strong images, as in the romance novel or adventure novel genre. And still others emphasize the author's name even more than the title.

For business communications, it's not likely that you'll do a cover illustration involving the beautiful heroine and the handsome hero near a fog-covered coastline. But you can adapt some of the same principles to these printed materials.

For example, you can use a drawing or photograph of a person at work on a certain machine or system as part of the cover. This visually describes what the material is about and who the audience is for that material. You can also use heads and subheads along with the title, such as "Contact! A How-To Manual for Supervisory Communications. Learn How to Make Contact with Your Workers Through This Self-Directed Training Program." You could place each of these sentences at a different place on the cover, perhaps putting the title in the center and the additional information diagonally across the page at the top left or bottom right.

You can also provide an inside cover blurb or a back cover blurb that excerpts or enhances material within the program. It's not at all unusual for someone to buy a book based on two or three paragraphs of information within the inside cover. That's why book editors look carefully for the best excerpt they can find to place in the front of the book.

You can do the same thing by listing the main benefits of the print program inside the front cover. Now, this may seem unnecessary because it is a business program and the audience member must have some interest in the piece or otherwise he or she would not pick it up. However, having an interest in something and actually reading for comprehension are two different things.

The way to aid comprehension, and increase interest, is to provide some preview material up front. For example, you may use the standard method used by teachers and list objectives, such as "Within this volume, you'll learn the six ways to improve your telephone techniques. Pay particular attention to . . ."

The advantage of this preview technique is that you identify for the reader what you think is the important material within the printed material. It acts as a subliminal "trigger" so that the person will pay particular attention when reaching the section of the material you highlighted in the introduction.

You can also organize print material at the same time you preview important elements. One way to do this is with tabbed sections or with introductory pages at the start of each new topic area.

A tabbed section with a concise and effective title actually provides a visual outline for the reader. He or she can simply look at the tabs to see what areas will be covered within the material. A contents page operates in much the same way, especially if it contains more than just a title for each chapter or segment.

The idea behind all these concepts is the same—you want the reader to understand, before he or she actually begins reading, what the major message will be. It's a way to reinforce the overall message while also adding interest.

## ENVIRONMENTAL CONDITIONERS

### Those Essential Extras

We live in an age of information overload. In fact, we get so much information that what we've just written is a cliché—you've heard it a thousand times. But it is precisely because so many people get so much information tossed at them every day that you must toss even more information their way.

The real challenge facing most business communicators today is making certain that their communications shout above the crowd noise so they can be heard, understood, and remembered. One way to meet that challenge is by adding some other elements to communications programs that reinforce the importance of the message, and that will aid in recall and retention of that message. That's what we mean by "environmental conditioners"—things to condition the environment for communications understanding and retention.

## Collateral Material

Elements that support a communications program are sometimes called "collateral material"; that is, material that is "accompanying, attendant, or auxiliary" to the main program material. A brochure that describes a film or videotape is a collateral material, as is a film that is used as a lead-in to a series of workbooks. Collateral is the extra added attraction that helps define and promote a communications program.

Collateral materials are used for two major purposes. First, we use them at the "awareness" stage in the process of persuasion, as an aid in explaining why a program is important and what's in it for the audience. Second, we use collateral materials as "take-along" materials for audiovisual presentations or films. For instance, we coupled an audiovisual program on individual retirement accounts and annuities with a take-along brochure that reiterated the main points. In this way, the viewer of the AV program could refresh his or her memory of the benefits of an IRA as well as use the brochure to explain those benefits to other family members involved in the IRA decision who did not see the AV program.

One problem to avoid with collateral materials is making them too good or too bad. It's possible, for instance, to spend more money on a take-along brochure than on the film or AV program it reinforces. It's also possible to make a film or AV kick-off program so poorly and cheaply that the audience won't bother to use the excellent training program workbooks you've devised. There must be a happy medium. We work, just as a rule of thumb, on the 80-20 rule: We spend 80 percent of the available time and money on the main program and 20 percent on the collateral; but we *do* spend the time and money on the collateral, because it is also important.

Collateral material is important because it helps define and refine the message. Further, some people may have trouble understanding and retaining a message presented through just one medium, but will be able to understand the message clearly if they get a slight bit of help from collateral material that presents the message in a slightly different way.

## Specialty Avertising and Emphasis Items

One area of collateral material that is becoming more and more popular in business communications is a merchandise item tied, even if loosely, to the program theme. It's not the traditional imprinted-pen type of advertising specialty item, although many firms that sell those message-carriers also carry the new form of "emphasis item." Rather, it's some product that becomes part of the message of the communications program.

As an example, suppose you are developing a program to persuade people to listen to a specific radio station. Let's assume that the audience you want is 26 to 50 years of age and composed of office workers in a metropolitan area where most people commute by car. You could pass out pencils or pens with the radio station name and call letters on them and give a brief message asking the audience members to listen. But they won't normally be drinking coffee or using pens and pencils while driving their cars. So a better emphasis item might be a key ring, because it will be a visible reminder that will be noticed when the audience member is in an environment receptive to your message.

You can extend this idea into any business communications program. You might, for instance, give every supervisor who attends a training program on human relations a coffee cup with the program slogan on it; perhaps seeing "Put yourself in their shoes" and a cartoon of a person trying to force a big foot into a small shoe will help the supervisor recall the major points of the program. Or perhaps you'll reinforce a "Put It in Writing" program for your staff by giving staff members personalized note pads with that slogan printed at the top of the page.

The idea is to provide an item that will emphasize and reinforce the message at the time that a person needs to recall the message. And the ways you can do that are limited only by your imagination—and your budget.

If your budget is pretty substantial, in fact, you may want to think about putting together many elements to condition the environment. For example, perhaps you're developing a film presentation to introduce a new employee assistance program for the firm. You might begin by creating a series of posters or tent cards that can be placed in the cafeteria or lounge areas. These posters might discuss several different aspects of employee assistance, using a short, punchy billboard technique. Then you might invite all the firm's opinion leaders to a "premiere," perhaps sending them an engraved invitation as well as a brochure outlining why the program is essential to the company's future. At the premiere, you might have some wall banners that state the film's title or the program theme, and you might provide people with refreshments using cups and napkins emblazoned with the same theme.

The purpose behind all these environmental conditioning elements and collateral materials is the same as the purpose of a creative concept or slogan in an audiovisual program. Even if people totally ignore the "meat" of your message, they'll at least recall the "sizzle" because of these emphasis items.

In addition, you might also consider some of the tried-and-true methods of generating interest, like buttons saying "Ask Me About . . ." It's surprising how motivating curiosity can be.

All of this may seem relatively unimportant until you stop and think about what makes you more receptive to certain things. For instance, doesn't a good movie review make you want to see a certain movie . . . especially when it's reinforced by attractive posters and ads, and by word-of-mouth praise from people you respect? And doesn't it help to have some idea of what to expect when you go into an unfamiliar environment or when you are trying to learn something in which you have little background? Further, don't certain songs or certain phrases trigger a certain feeling or set of memories in your mind?

That's really what all these environmental conditioners are all about—making the audience receptive to your message and helping you impart your message clearly and with maximum retention to that audience.

## CONCLUSION

One of the extra added benefits of all these finishing touches and special packaging methods is that they lend an air of importance to the business communications program. If the audience sees that you care enough to be concerned about permanence and the details involved in program distribution, packaging, and presentation, perhaps they will reward that extra effort with greater attention. And that, in turn, will help you meet the objective of any business communications program . . . to create meaningful and memorable messages.

# Index

## A

Advertising. *See* Public relations.
Analogies, 69
   use of, 221
Approval, 210
   points, 34
Artwork, 161. *See also* Visuals.
Attitudes, 13, 25-26
Audience, 5, 24-26, 33, 207
   demographics, 23, 32
   positioning, 30
   print material, 56
Audio. *See also* Audiotape, Soundtracks.
   definition of, 52
   equipment, 139, 140, 142
   uses, 53
Audiotape, 47. *See also* Soundtracks.
Audiovisual equipment, 44, 183, 186, 273-277
Audiovisual media. *See also* Audiotapes, Film, Sound-slide programs, Videotapes.
   creative effect, 40
   definition of, 40
   environment, 44, 46
   selection chart, 60
   types of, 47
   writing for. *See* Business writing.

## B

Behavior change
   action, 18
   awareness, 15
   commitment, 17
   involvement, 16
Beliefs, 14, 25-26
Books, 58
   electronic books, 58
Briefer, 23, 25-26, 210
Briefings, 22-23
Brochures, 57
   use of, 216
Budget, 23-24
   bottom-line, 35
   line-item, 35
   treatment sheet, 35-36
Bulletins, 57
Business writing
   analogies, use of, 69
   audiovisual media, 72-73, 75-76
   basic concepts, 65-66
   definition of, 64
   editing, 69

grabbers, 72
organization of, 67
parodies, 71
print media, 74-76
readability, 68
sentence structure, 65
style, 67
voice, 65

## C

Case studies, use of, 216-217, 218, 225
Charts. *See* Graphics.
Client, 210-211
Closing, 12
Collateral material, 280-282
Color, 43. *See also* Printing.
Communicator, 5, 11
Computerized visuals, 162, 166-167
Computers. *See also* Interactive programs.
  advantages of, 202
  business communication uses, 76
  discs, 82-83
  electronic books, 58, 59
  filing systems, 269-270
  keyboards, 81
  limitations of, 201
  printers, 83-85
  programs, 80-81
  screens, 81
  speed, 81-82
  storage, 82
  systems, 85
  word processors, 77-81
Conclusion, 11
  treatment sheet, 36
Content experts, 25
Cost, 41-42. *See also* Budget.
Creative approach, 22, 33-34
Creative concept, 23, 29, 33

## D

Design. *See also* Layout, Program design.
  elements, 99-102
Distribution, 270-272
  electronic, 272

hand delivery, 272
mailing, 270-271
private delivery firms, 271-272
special services, 271

## E

Effectiveness, 208-209
Environment
  collateral material, 280-282
  presentation, 279
Equipment. *See also* Audiovisual equipment.
  compatibility, 44, 51
Execution analysis, 208-209

## F

Favorable attention, 7
Feedback, 4, 11
  print material, 57
Filing
  computerized systems, 269-270
  Dewey Decimal System, 269
  stored materials, 268-270
Film, 49
  creative effect, 41
  equipment, 45, 51
Filmstrip
  equipment, 45
  use of, 232-233, 235-236
Focus group, 25
Format, treatment sheet, 33
Front-end analysis, 21-22

## G

Graphics, 100, 112-113, 161, 167-169. *See also* Computerized visuals, Visuals.
  screening for print, 114-115
  sizing, 111-112
Graphs. *See* Graphics.

## I

Illustrations. *See* Graphics.
Information, 10
Ink, 101
Interactive programs
  active, 190

audiotapes, 204
benefits, 192
computer assisted, 193-196, 200-202, 203
definition of, 190, 196-197
designing, 190-193, 195, 197-200
flowchart, 190
objectives, 197-198
passive, 190
point-of-purchase applications, 254
problems of, 192
programming, 195-196, 198
selection of media, 203, 204
slide projectors, 204
sound-slide, 203-204
troubleshooting chart, 190
types of, 200-202
videocassette, 203-204
videodisc, 203-204
Interviews, 22-25

## L

Layout, 94, 95
balance, 97
color, 115-116, 119
folding, 117-118
graphics, 100, 111-112
grids, 96
pagination, 117
paper, 101, 120-121
placement, 101
rough draft, 102
size, 121
type, 99, 103, 105-106, 107-109, 110
use of, 217, 235
Learning curve, 13-14
Letters, 56-57

## M

Manuals. See Books.
Medium, 4-6, 22, 33, 40
conversion, 52, 186-187
environment, 33
equipment, 45
selection chart, 60
Message, 4-5, 7, 12, 29, 40
Modules, use of, 221

Motion, 43
Motivation, 8
soundtracks, 136
Multimedia programs, 49
fluidity, 181-182
Music. See also Soundtracks.
use of, 229

## N

Narration. See Soundtracks.
Narrators. See also Soundtracks.
use of, 221, 227
Needs analysis, 206-207
checklist, 213

## O

Objectives, 13, 15, 18, 22, 28, 205
covert, 27-28
defining, 22-23, 27
overt, 27-28
treatment sheet, 32
Opinions, 13, 25-26
Overview, 9

## P

Pacing, 125
Packaging, 259
access, 261
binders, 262-263
books, 260, 262
electronic media, 260, 262
personalization, 263
photographic media, 260, 262
protection, 260-262
shipment, 263
Pamphlets. See Brochures.
Paper, 101
Parodies, 71
Perception, audience, 43, 51, 56
Persuasion, 14
Photographs. See Graphics.
Photography, 162. See also Visuals.
Plan, 205, 207
Positioning, 30-31
Presentation, 272-279
photographic media, 273-274
print, 277-279

screens, 273-274, 277
videotape, 274-277
Press kit, 248. *See also* Public relations,
    contents, 248-249
Press releases. *See* Public relations.
Print media, 122-124. *See also* Books,
    Brochures, Bulletins, Letters,
    Three-Ring Binders.
    audience, 56
    content, 55
    costs, 54
    guide to, 56
    purpose, 55
    revision, 54
    selection chart, 60
    types, 53
    uses, 53
    writing for. *See* Business writing.
Printing
    color, 115
    folding, 117
    offset, 113
    pagination, 117
    photocopies, 113
    screening graphics, 114
Program, 4
    analysis, 213
    elements, 205
    problems, 209-212
    results, 209
Program design, 169-170
    print, 94
Production
    components, 88
    evolution, 89
Producer, role of, 89-91
Progression, 14
Proposal, 31
    conclusion, 36
Public relations, 248
    advertising, 253-254, 256-257, 258
    bad press coverage, 252
    brochures, 255
    direct mail, 255
    editorial mention, 250
    FABs, 253-254
    internal, 255-256
    point-of-purchase application, 254
    press kit, 248-249

    press releases, 251-252
    sales bulletins, 255-256
    sales promotion, 254-256
    trade ads, 257
Purpose, statement of, 22, 24, 28

### Q

Quality, 22

### R

Receiver, 4-6
Research, 22, 26-27
Revisions, 42, 210
    costs, 42
    ease of, 42

### S

Schedule, 23
    treatment sheet, 34
Script
    multinational, 226-227
    visualization, 162, 164-166
Selling, 6, 10-12
Sender, 4, 6
Situation analysis, 207-208
Sound effects. *See* Soundtracks.
Sound-slide programs, 48
    equipment, 45
    use of, 226
Soundtracks, 48
    audio equipment, 139-140, 142, 149,
        151, 155, 156
    components, 130
    decibels, 140-141
    directions, 129
    effects, 134-136
    format, 128-129
    frequency, 138-139
    frequency response, 142-143
    generations, 158
    impressions, 127
    intelligibility, 138
    length, 126
    master, 151-153, 157
    mixing, 155-156
    motivation, 136-137
    multitrack recording, 149-150,
        152-154, 157

# INDEX

music, 132-134
music libraries, 132-133
narration, 130
narrators, 130-131
noise, 144
openings, 145-146
options, 127
overdubbing, 150
pacing, 125
production of, 151-157
presence, 144-145
rough cut, 184
segue, 129
signal-to-noise ratio, 143-144
source materials, 151, 158
sound levels, 147
transitions, 147-148
use of, 240
volume, 138-141
Specialty advertising, 281-282
Storage, 264-268
   climate, 266
   cross-reference, 265
   electromagnetic hazards, 266-267
   electronic media, 266-267
   increase, 265
   photographs, 264, 267
   print material, 267
   slides, 264-265, 267

## T

Text slides, 168-169
Third effect, 126, 165
Three-ring binders, 58
Treatment sheet, 23, 31-32
   approval points, 34
   audience demographics, 32
   budget, 35
   conclusion, 36
   creative approach, 33
   format, 33
   introduction, 32
   objectives, 32
   schedule, 34
Type, 99, 103
   families, 110
   sizing, 107-109

styles, 110
Typesetting, 104-106
   word processors, 78

## V

Videodisc. *See* Videotape.
Videotape, 47
   creative effect, 41
   equipment, 45, 51
   use of, 222, 242-245
Videotext, 58, 59
Visual clarity, 171, 173-175
Visual style, 170-173
Visualization. *See* Script.
Visuals, 161-162, 170. *See also* Artwork, Graphics, Photography.
   abstract, 166
   assembling, 183-185
   changing shots, 182-183
   cut-away, 180-181
   depth of field, 178
   dolly, 178
   fluidity, 180-182
   follow focus, 179
   jump-cut, 180
   lenses, 179
   matched action, 180
   multinational, 228, 229
   pacing, 180
   pan, 178
   perception of, 177-179
   presentation of, 185-187
   scenes and sequences, 175-177
   screen direction, 176-177
   selection of, 162
   selective focus, 179
   specifying, 164-165
   trucking shot, 178
   use of, 236, 240, 244-245
   zoom, 178
Voice-over, 130

## W

WIIFM, 8, 10
Workbooks, use of, 217, 222-223, 233
Word processors. *See* Computers.
Writing. *See* Business writing.

HF 5718 .S58

SEP 1 4 1992
JAN 1 7 1992

DEC 0 1 2001